Ilex Foundation Series 22

MUSLIMS AND METHODISTS

Also in the Ilex Foundation Series

Dreaming across Boundaries: The Interpretation of Dreams in Islamic Lands
edited by Louise Marlow

Strī: Women in Epic Mahābhārata
by Kevin McGRATH

Persian Literature and Judeo-Persian Culture: Collected Writings of Sorour S. Soroudi
edited by H. E. Chehabi

The Rhetoric of Biography: Narrating Lives in Persianate Societies
edited by L. Marlow

Jaya: Performance in Epic Mahābhārata
by Kevin McGRATH

The History *of Beyhaqi (The History of Sultan Masʿud
of Ghazna, 1030-1041) by Abuʾl-Fażl Beyhaqi*
translated and with commentaries by Clifford Edmund Bosworth
fully revised and with further commentary by Mohsen Ashtiany

The Last of the Rephaim: Conquest and Cataclysm in the Heroic Ages of Ancient Israel
by Brian R. Doak

Ruse and Wit: The Humorous in Arabic, Turkish, and Persian Narrative
edited by Dominic Parvis Brookshaw

Kṛṣṇa: Friendship in Epic Mahābhārata
by Kevin McGRATH

On the Wonders of Land and Sea: Persianate Travel Writing
edited by Roberta Micallef and Sunil Sharma

Poet and Hero in the Persian Book of Kings
third edition
by Olga M. Davidson

Comparative Literature and Classical Persian Poetics
second edition
by Olga M. Davidson

Ferdowsi's Shāhnāma: *Millennial Perspectives*
edited by Olga M. Davidson and Marianna Shreve Simpson

Mirror of Dew: The Poetry of Ālam-tāj Zhāle Qāʾem-Maqāmi
translated with an introduction by Asghar Seyed-Gohrab

Global Medieval: Mirrors for Princes Reconsidered
edited by Regula Forster and Neguin Yavari

Erin and Iran: Cultural Encounters between the Irish and the Iranians
edited by H. E. Chehabi and Grace Neville

METHODISTS AND MUSLIMS

MY LIFE AS AN ORIENTALIST

by
Richard W. Bulliet

Ilex Foundation
Boston, Massachusetts

Distributed by Harvard University Press
Cambridge, Massachusetts and London, England

Muslims and Methodists: My Life As an Orientalist
by Richard W. Bulliet

Copyright © 2020 Ilex Foundation
All Rights Reserved

Published by Ilex Foundation, Boston, Massachusetts

Distributed by Harvard University Press, Cambridge, Massachusetts and London, England

Production editor: Christopher Dadian
Cover design: Joni Godlove
Printed in the United States of America

Cover image: drawing by the author.

Library of Congress Cataloging-in-Publication Data

Names: Bulliet, Richard W., author. | Ilex Foundation, issuing body.
Title: Methodists and Muslims : my life as an Orientalist / by Richard W.
    Bulliet.
Description: Boston, Massachusetts : Ilex Foundation, [2020] | Series: Ilex
    Foundation series ; 22 | Includes bibliographical references. | Summary:
    "In Methodists and Muslims, Bulliet has fashioned a critique of both
    Orientalism and Middle East Studies. His memoir also recounts how a
    young Methodist from Illinois made his way into the then-arcane field of
    Islamic Studies, became involved in shaping Middle East Studies, and
    developed relations with the Islamic Republic of Iran, culminating in
    the controversial visit to New York City by President Ahmadinejad of
    Iran"-- Provided by publisher.
Identifiers: LCCN 2020017114 | ISBN 9780674244672 (paperback)
Subjects: LCSH: Bulliet, Richard W. | Middle East specialists--United
    States--Biography. | Historians--United States--Biography. |
    Islam--Study and teaching (Higher)--United States. | Orientalism--United
    States. | Islam--Relations--Christianity. | Christianity and other
    religions--Islam. | Middle East--Study and teaching (Higher)--United
    States.
Classification: LCC DS61.7.B79 A3 2020 | DDC 956.0072/02 [B]--dc23
LC record available at https://lccn.loc.gov/2020017114

Contents

Introduction: Methodists and Muslims   1

Part One: Before Arabic

Before Arabic   15

My Father's Dream   16

Bulliet Is a Peculiar Name   22

Creativity   30

Part Two: Ways Forward

Ways Forward   36

My Grandfather's Library   38

A Harvard Education   43

Art and Romance   51

Going There   53

I Write a Novel   67

Part Three: Things Happen

Things Happen   71

Changing Sides of the Desk at Harvard   72

Coming to Columbia   76

The Middle East Studies Association   91

A Columbia Education   101

Iran 1: *The Tomb of the Twelfth Imam*   104

Iran 2: Islam in Ashkelon   108

Iran 3: Islam in Honolulu   111

The Gulf Scenario   114

Bernard Lewis and Television   120

CBS and Censorship   124

Part Four: Moving On

Moving On   128

Comic Books   131

Computers and Encyclopedias   138

Iran 4: Khatami's Dialogue of Civilizations   147

From Orientalist to Historian   153

Y2K: The Old Millennium Ends   158

9/11: The New Millennium Begins   162

Iran 5: Ahmadinejad at Columbia   165

Part Five: Conclusions

Conclusions   171

Methodism and Islam   173

American Orientalism after 9/11   182

INTRODUCTION:

Methodists and Muslims

OUR HISTORY DEPARTMENT AT COLUMBIA UNIVERSITY used to coerce first-year graduate students in non-Western history – East Asian, Indian, Middle Eastern, African – to take a "Transcultural Historiography" colloquium. Whenever I taught the course, I started things off by asking for a three-page history of a year I would choose from five years or so in the past. I would stress that their histories had to be assembled from their own memories and those of people they spoke with, the way a chronicler of the pre-print era might have operated: no books, no newspapers, no journals.

"What should the three pages cover?" someone would ask. "Personal lives? National politics? World events?" That was their prerogative as historians, I would answer.

The following week I would have them read their pages aloud. The readings introduced them to one another. What they had chosen to include and whose memories they had relied on raised issues of historical method.

One would write about competing in a high school violin competition. Another would recall national headlines. A third would focus on a world crisis. Asked to write about 1978, two Iranian students detailed their country's revolution, even though both had spent the year in the United States. But two Americans, who had actually been living in Iran, wrote only about the United States. Another time, two Chinese students wrote almost identical political narratives – one added an upset soccer victory – and explained that they were remembering what had been drilled into them in school, not actual events that they remembered or that took place during the particular year I had assigned.

One year the class marveled at the memory a woman who wrote about urban renewal in the Connecticut, where she had spent a summer working for a redevelopment board trying to reverse the decline of downtown. She told us how, in July, Banana Republic had moved into the empty J. C. Penney store at Main Street and 4th Avenue, how three weeks later a Wachovia branch bank had opened two blocks farther down Main, and how in early August construction of a mini-mall had begun on the parking lot just off Main at 7th Street.

After she had garnered the praise of her classmates for her contribution, I asked whether her history was true. "No," she said, "I invented the dates and addresses to make it more vivid." The class was stunned. Could a historian do that? Just invent stuff that wasn't true because it sounded like the truth? Could dates and numbers just be thrown in?

I assured them that before print editions, which made possible footnotes that cited precise page numbers, invention for the sake of verisimilitude was neither uncommon nor easily detectable. Numbers in particular raise suspicions in early sources, as do direct quotations from historical figures.

How, then, should the historian in training approach a source that might not be truthful? First, I advised, figure out why the source in question survived the vagaries of time that destroy almost all vestiges of the human past. Second, explore, if possible, the life and outlook of the author and his or her technique of assembling and selecting data. And third, look for corroboration or refutation from other sources, giving precedence to those closest in time to the events being related.

By the end of the term, every student knew how to scrutinize the personal lives, biases, and access to sources of published historians. So in the final meeting I invited them to go around the table and offer some thoughts on how their own biases and personal lives might shape their future work as historians. With few exceptions – one Korean student avowed a commitment to celebrating his nation's glory – they maintained that they themselves had no biases.

I pressed them to think harder. After all, if they could guess at the personality and outlook underlying the work of the noted historians they had read in class, how could they possibly believe that future readers would see their own books as faceless, neutral, truth-telling narratives?

Fortunately, no one ever asked me about my own life and biases. I don't know what I would have replied. Now that I have had several decades to consider the question, however, I at least know that the answer is complicated.

I finished writing *The Patricians of Nishapur*, my first book, in 1970. I was 30 years old and had lived in only two places: Rockford, Illinois, then the state's second largest city with a population around 90,000, and Harvard University. Yet I felt confident conjuring up the lives of the educated religious elite of an eleventh- century Iranian city using the skimpiest of Arabic sources. It never occurred to me to question my hubris.

Two decades later it struck me that maybe I had subconsciously populated Nishapur with versions of the educated, middle-class, Protestant families I had known growing up in Rockford. I toyed with this idea from time to time over the years, but at age seventy-five two things prompted me to think about the matter more deeply.

First, marriage to my second wife, Greta Berman, an art historian who grew up in a far left secular Jewish family in Greenwich Village, sensitized me to a very different life trajectory from my own. I knew thousands of people, of course, who came from diverse backgrounds, but starting out on a new life after forty-eight years with Lucy, my beloved deceased wife, made me think more intensely than ever about what makes people different. Unlike Greta's kinfolk, the Methodists I grew up around despised socialism and gave little thought to understanding, much less sympathizing with, people of color, the poor, or folks with non-European cultural backgrounds.

Second, I had acquired over the years a warm feeling for many aspects of traditional Muslim society even though childhood churchgoing and choir singing at Court Street Methodist Church had never managed to stir any actual interest in God, or to convince me that God existed.

My reflections persuaded me that Midwest Methodism did, to some extent, inform my imagining of eleventh-century Nishapur. Did this mean I had written my several books with the pernicious mindset ascribed to Orientalists in Edward Said's famous book on the subject? This memoir explores that possibility.

Let me start with an age-old question: What is the good life? For Greta, whose grandparents emigrated from Belarus, and who delights in telling about a plane ride during which she conversed at length with Rev. Martin Luther King, Jr., the good life incorporates deep concerns for oppressed minorities, a compulsion to take part in social and political activism to correct injustices, and a lively suspicion of entrenched political and economic elites and the overt and covert power they wield.

The Rockford of my childhood, a staunchly Republican industrial city near the Wisconsin border, knew little of these sentiments. To the best of my recollection, no one in my extended family expressed sympathy with either minorities or the poor – one aunt and uncle supported Governor George Wallace for president – and no one questioned the virtues of a capitalist economy. As a child, I gained the impression that the sign reading "CIO" (Congress of Industrial Organizations) on a nondescript downtown office building signified something deeply sinister, though I had no inkling of what nefarious activities the labor unions incorporated under that label got up to.

Instead, my parents and relatives were mostly concerned with family circumstances, particularly regarding higher education. They had grown up under the strictures of traditional Methodist discipline: no alcohol, no smoking, no dancing, no card playing, no gambling, no lewdness, no blasphemy, and regular attendance at church. These rigidities gradually fell away during my childhood, but they had shaped the lives of my parents' generation, and hence my life as well. To this day I do not smoke, seldom drink, eschew any sort of gambling, wear no jewelry, and feel uncomfortable in bars. (Blaspheming is another matter. Plenty of that.)

Yet an influential counter-discourse that very gradually nosed its way into my life both rejected and disparaged the Puritanism of the Methodist social and moral order, though without adopting Greta's alternative of social engagement. I remember Clarence Joseph ("C. J.") Bulliet, my father's father, only as a portly old man I saw during visits to Chicago. For thirty years he lived there alone, away from his wife and son in southern Indiana, while he gained substantial renown as a newspaper art critic, championing modernism and attacking the academic painting and genteel Impressionist landscapes applauded by Chicago's social elite. In local art circles he earned a reputation for mildly louche and suspiciously French bohemianism, but he continued to describe himself to down-home acquaintances as "a country jake from Corydon," the southern Indiana town where he grew up.

As I grew older, however, and read both the books he wrote and the unpublished manuscripts he left behind, C. J.'s contrarian views on American society overwhelmed me. His continent-wide travels as a theatrical press agent for nine years before his move to Chicago yielded these notes:

Rochester – The colossal ignorance and stupidity of Puritanism ... has made the United States the champion hypocrite of the ages among nations.

Toledo – As a nation we are hopelessly mediocre. That probably is the inevitable fate of republics. Now comes the test for admission to colleges – physical and psychological. Under its rules, Alexander Pope, Sir Walter Scott and Balzac would be banned. Napoleon could not have joined our army.... Columbus could not enter the port of N.Y. under our immigration laws. As a nation we are hopelessly mediocre – God! how hopelessly and helplessly mediocre!

Washington, D.C. – The seller has been held in contempt – not the buyer. That explains why the Jew is the scorn of the world – why the prostitute and not the libertine is the scorn of society. Or, is this putting the cart before the horse? May not the Jew and the prostitute be responsible for the contempt in which trade has been held?

[n.p.] – The danger of national prohibition does not lie in the suppression of liquor – that is a minor detail – but in the robbing of men of another of their liberties. Modern fool legislation, under the direction of cowardly and hypocritical politicians afraid to jeopardize their standing in a community, is becoming more and more intolerable. The bill of rights is becoming more and more a scrap of paper. If prohibition goes through, what is to prevent a suppression of tobacco.... There has already been dangerous fool legislation with regards to cigarettes. Why is it impossible to the restless reformers after liquor is gone to suppress tobacco. Then the prize ring – all but wiped out because of fool legislation, until the army restored it. Then the suppression of the segregated districts [i.e. red light districts].... Sex seems a sin to the twisted-minded reformers, just as do liquor and tobacco, and dancing and boxing and card playing and a thousand and one other amusements with enough tang in them to make life worth living.

Over time his prose became less torrid, but his intellectual idiosyncrasies did not diminish. His 1928 book *Venus Castina: Famous Female Impersonators Celestial and Human* was a lively and pioneering compilation of lore about cross-dressers, castrati, Shakespearean boy actors playing female roles, and the vaudeville star Julian Eltinge, whose drag persona mocked the pretensions and manners of society women. The introductory chapter sets the book's tone:

> Here is the procession through the ages of votaries of the Venus Castina – that goddess supposed to respond with sympathy and understanding to the yearnings of feminine souls locked up in male bodies.
>
> It is a curious throng, motley and miscellaneous.... Some of us fold tight our togas about us as they pass, fearing contamination. Many of us look on with lively curiosity. A few sit dazed and enraptured beside the shrine of Castina, and seek to understand.
>
> It is to the curious onlookers that the author belongs – a curiosity stirred first by observing – not the finest stage impersonator of female types of our time – but the effect his impersonations seemed to exert on the women and girls of his audience. Men chuckled at the satirical flings of Julian Eltinge at the foibles of fair feminine creatures ... but women were stirred more deeply.

C. J.'s precocious discourse on what we now term gender issues contained few anecdotes that could plausibly be attributed to "feminine souls locked up in male bodies." Indeed, at a personal level – he was not gay or a cross-dresser – he was more engaged with what he saw as gender role inversion in the post-World War I generation.

The World War has intervened ... with our policy – growing out of the fetid, miasmatic Ohio swamp of reform – of protecting the morals of our lusty young soldiers in camp. Prostitutes were barred from administering sexual comfort, and the young men were left to work out their own salvation.

There is nothing in the known mental accomplishments of those responsible for the drastic moral and hygienic measures to indicate their ideas were scientifically any further advanced than Ohio psalm-singing or Tennessee fundamentalism – but there are indications that they may have got results comparable with those arrived at by the Greeks of the classic period....

Taking advantage of the moral cowardice of "statesmen" in times of war, the reformers, too, closed tight the public houses of prostitution even to civilians – a move that, like prohibition, had already gained considerable headway and needed only a moment when [Protestant] fanaticism was rampant and experienced reason dormant to be made complete.

With females as difficult to obtain as bootleg liquor – fanaticism has not let go its grip in either domain – dormant tendencies have developed in young male America with the same scandalous rapidity they have long enjoyed in English boys' schools and in colleges of Continental Europe where dormitory rules are rigidly enforced.... The boys and girls are becoming boon drinking companions – the girls rising to male heights of aggressiveness, the boys descending to female....

Venus Castina was illustrated by Alexander King, a young artist who in old age enjoyed brief notoriety as a television raconteur. His drawings were tasteless, but far from obscene. Nevertheless, C. J.'s wife, my strait-laced grandmother Katharine Adams, had her personal copy of the book bound without illustrations. C. J.'s personal copy, on the other hand, included a decidedly homosexual watercolor sketch by King. My father's copy? C. J. didn't present one to his college-student son until five years after its publication, by which time my father had married his high school sweetheart and, within a few weeks, lost her to illness.

My father Leander Jackson ("Jack") Bulliet, who designed electrical controls for a machine tool company, often expressed the conviction that his dad disrespected him because his natural bent was toward science and technology – as he put it, "being a blacksmith with dirty fingernails" – instead of the arts. Possibly that was so, but I believe C. J. may also have harbored a low opinion of his son, whom he lived with only during non-touring summer seasons for most of his childhood, for a different reason. I suspect he saw him as exactly the sort of mother-dominated, woman-fearing, puritanical, timid, neurotic, unmanly Methodist male – I am projecting here my guess as to C. J.'s hypothetical appraisal – that he imagined to be the product of post-war national degeneration. (He might well have thought the same of me if he hadn't died when I was only twelve.)

Yet despite feeling that his father did not esteem him, Jack and the rest of the family always spoke of C. J. with reverence and deference since he was much in the public eye and so highly regarded as an art expert. Jack's frequently expressed view was that his own greatest achievement – various inventions and patents notwithstanding – was passing on the DNA that made me, in his opinion, C. J.'s intellectual and authorial reincarnation.

So what did my being steeped in Midwest Methodist lifestyles, and then gradually becoming aware of my honored grandfather's vehement rejection of those same lifestyles, have to do with Muslims?

In the process of turning my sketchy doctoral dissertation into *The Patricians of Nishapur*, I had to put flesh on the arduously reassembled genealogical bones of the leading *ulama* (scholarly religious) families of Nishapur. I borrowed the term "patrician" from John Mundy's work on the medieval French city of Toulouse, *Liberty and Political Power in Toulouse, 1050–1230*. But the following qualities, with which I endowed my patrician families, were my own deductions from texts:

1 Nishapur's elite religious families shared extensive educational grounding in the details of the Prophet Muhammad's life as preserved in tens of thousands of traditions (*hadith*) orally conveyed by learned shaykhs.

2 The models of behavior (*sunna*) that they derived from those traditions shaped their lives.

3 Their livelihoods were based on agriculture and industry, primarily textile production, and had little intersection with the fluctuating political order fought over by assorted amirs and sultans.

4 They honored the personal virtues of generosity, knowledge, patience, loyalty, reticence, and modesty.

5 They had a low regard for common folk who did not share their educational background or who seemed religiously deviant, either in doctrine or in flouting the behavioral norms of the *sunna*.

6 The issues that exercised them derived from differences of opinion regarding matters of religious law and those aspects of daily life and religious practice that proceeded therefrom.

7 They looked with a suspicious eye on the religious activities of mountebank mystics, but could be impressed by more sober expressions of devotional discipline, whether mystic or ascetic.

8 They took pride in their genealogies and descent from notable ancestors.

9 They did not ordinarily fill, or seek to fill, government administrative positions. Nor did they serve in the military.

10 They revered family life and thought that the greatest legacy they could leave to their offspring was a family reputation for piety.

These qualities now strike me as parallel to what I had absorbed about the nature of a good life while growing up in Rockford. Here's the comparison:

1 Educational excellence commanded more respect in my family circle than any other accomplishment. No one in the family was rich. Nobody owned or operated a store or business. No one had professional training in medicine, law, dentistry, etc. No one served in the military or sought political office. No one excelled in the arts. But everyone was encouraged to go as far as possible in education. Two of my three male first cousins earned PhDs, as did I. (My sister earned an MBA and my mother a PhD in physics, but generally girls were expected to marry and have children.)

To be sure, Rockford's public school curricula differed greatly from the lore the scions of Nishapur's religious scholars imbibed at the feet of venerable *hadith* transmitters. But learning things of little relevance to the real world took priority over today's encouragement of critical thinking, classroom engagement, and intellectual questioning. When I was thirteen, for example, I took the typesetting course required of all boys, presumably to confer upon us a useful skill ... albeit one that had been obsolete for decades in the real economy. I did set type once in the years following, but I doubt any of my classmates ever did.

2 The code of living (*sunna*) I absorbed was that of the Methodist church. John Wesley, the founder of Methodism within the Church of England, had urged his flock proactively to choose the salvation that God held out to every soul (as opposed to John Calvin's narrower belief in predestination for the sainted few). However, the tumultuous response that made Wesley's followers the most numerous of all American Protestant denominations had just as much to

do with shunning the evils that Wesley saw sapping the energies and depleting the paychecks of England's working class: drink, gambling, prostitution, raucous entertainment, smoking, and lewdness. During family trips we would never stop at a restaurant with a beer sign in the window. After all, good Methodists should not just live a pure life; they should also avoid being seen in places where their presence might be interpreted by others as tolerance of sin. I once heard my father wonder what an adult bookstore was like, but he didn't dare being seen stepping inside.

3 Though we were taught the basics of government in school, it remained a topic of remote interest. Rockford's economy rested on factories established and owned by local families. Unions were virtually unheard of, as were Democrats. In high school I was invited, along with two friends, to evening tutorials on the principles of libertarianism given by an ideologue on the payroll of a local industrialist. I dropped out after he explained that people who wanted roads to their homes should pay privately for building them and not depend on public expenditures.

4 The list of Methodist virtues and those of Nishapur's *ulama* was pretty much the same. Not surprisingly, my favorite Muslim saying became: *Inna Allah ma'a al-sabirin* (Verily, God is with those who have patience).

5 Social differences seldom arose for discussion, but young people in my part of town noticed among their elders a pattern of avoidance toward Italians, other Catholics, and Blacks. Targets of milder negativity included Swedes, because they were so numerous on the rival east side of town, and Jews, who were too few to attract much notice. Years later, as the city sank into post-industrial decline, the Rockford school system was placed under federal court supervision because of engrained racial discrimination. Student violence that took root after my own graduation caused my high school to be closed in 1989.

6 While racial and ethnic divisions festered well below the surface, people I knew openly debated matters such as whether Senator Joseph McCarthy was doing a good job rooting out commies, whether "liberal" Dwight D. Eisenhower or "conservative" Robert A. Taft, Jr. was the truer Republican, and whether Unitarians were truly Christian.

7 Camp meetings, a staple of Midwest Protestantism that featured
   impassioned pleas to take Jesus into one's life (see Herbert Asbury's
   lively book *Up from Methodism* [1926]), were not on the event horizon
   of my youth. I gathered that Rockford's ministers frowned on stir-
   ring passions in this fashion. Singing in church was another matter.
   I was a choir member for at least eight years. On Easter our church
   would resound with six choirs backed by organ and trumpets. It
   later struck me that congregational singing was the Protestant analogue of a Sufi *dhikr* (collective oral remembrance of God).

8 Tracing family roots and listening to family stories filled hours of
   conversation with relatives. Stories from "the old country" never
   came up, however, because everyone had been so long in the United
   States. The older generation looked for ancestors who had fought
   in the Revolutionary War so they could apply for membership in
   the DAR (Daughters of the American Revolution), or they imagined
   genealogies that would connect them with European aristocracy.
   Great-Aunt Frances, grandmother Katherine's sister, carried on
   endlessly about belonging to a (remote) branch of the presidential
   Adams family as well as to the DAR, not to mention – this was really
   a stretch – descending from Charlemagne. Her father, my great-
   grandfather Leander Clay Adams, seems in reality to have been
   a respected, though not very prosperous, farmer and sometime
   schoolteacher and postmaster in rural southern Indiana.

9 Though Great-Aunt Frances married a Republican politician and
   lawyer who ultimately was elected to Indiana's Supreme Court, Indiana was not Illinois. Illinois politics revolved around Chicago, with
   its blacks and immigrant factions, a long ninety miles, and maybe a
   hundred years, from Rockford.
       I spoke to only one relative who fought in World War II. Another
   peeled potatoes during World War I. In the Civil War, according to
   a nonagenarian Indiana cousin: "We didn't much care for Negroes.
   But we didn't like the Confederacy. So we took the horses and headed for the hills."

10 Part of a family's reputation for piety derived from its men of the
   cloth. We had a few, but the only one I remember spent most of his
   adulthood with his wife as a missionary in Nigeria. Otherwise, good
   behavior, attendance at church, and avoidance of forbidden things
   substituted for overt piety or prayer. When I became involved in
   studying Arabic, our family minister told my parents that he worried that I would become a Muslim.

Everything that Rockford had taught me about how to lead a good life came under challenge from day one at Harvard College. The people I enjoyed associating with seemed like members of a colorful exotic tribe that I was studying through participant observation: the Mozart-admiring roommate whose father commanded the Brooklyn Naval Yard; the eccentric, guitar-playing son of a Harvard biologist waiting for his Nobel Prize; the Jewish biker, who had attended high school in Madras and could curse in Tamil; the cowboy wannabe from Oklahoma, who claimed he came to Harvard because he was rejected by Oklahoma State; the velvet-voiced, folk-singing scion of a black insurance company CEO; the super-macho, half-Indian poet from west Texas; the list goes on. If I had wanted to associate with people like myself, I could have. But with one or two exceptions, I didn't want to. I wanted more than anything to leave Rockford and its pieties behind.

Only in my senior year did I begin to value my Midwestern roots. That revaluing was still under way four years later when I began to imagine the patrician families of eleventh-century Nishapur. After marrying Lucianne Cherry, my first wife, right after graduation, I began to think that maybe Rockford and the Court Street Methodist Church weren't so bad after all. Though Lucy, whom I had dated and fallen in love with while she visited a college roommate for a week in Rockford, was a ferocious and blaspheming atheist, she came from a social background much like my own in San Diego, but with socialist parents born in Tennessee rather than Illinois and Indiana Republicans.

What struck me most strongly about Nishapur was its cohesiveness and identity as an urban society largely unconnected with any broader political or geographical entities. Like the Rockfordians I grew up among, the Nishapuris seemed to live normal and sedate lives, draw their sustenance and their feelings of worth from their local community, strive as best they could to keep their distance from the warlords that vied to add Nishapur to their domains, and quarreled among themselves over matters that were rooted in their learning and their religious views rather than imperial or ethnic contention.

Was I wrongheaded in unconsciously assimilating the Nishapur I imagined to the Rockford that I grew up in? Of course I was. How could I *not* be? I hadn't been alive in the eleventh century. I wasn't Iranian. I wasn't Muslim. The mosques, madrasas, and marketplaces of that once-great city had long disappeared, their collapsed rooftops and walls buried some twenty feet deep in a vast field of ruins. All I had to go on was my imagination, my own life experience, and an array of textual sources that had almost nothing explicit to say about the areas of social history that interested me most.

Was this Orientalism? Of course it was. At least of a sort. I was a young

American scholar moderately proficient in medieval Arabic cobbling together a version of a medieval Iranian community that I had no connection with. But was my Orientalism devoted, as Edward Said would maintain a decade later, to denigrating non-Europeans as "others," justifying imperialism, and wallowing in exoticism? I don't believe so. It was simply a projection of what I knew upon a medieval historical society that I wished to know better.

Consequently, while I recognize that some individuals certainly did pursue Said's model of Orientalism in their careers, I refuse to cede to him the narrative of my own life as an Orientalist. Americans of my generation who wandered into the study of societies and cultures other than their own have their own life stories to tell.

My story will be divided into five parts: Before Arabic, Ways Forward, Things Happen, Moving On, and Conclusions. "Before Arabic" will sketch what I see as the life-shaping aspects of a family, social, and regional background innocent of any connection to Islam or the Middle East. Since the latter do not figure in this part of the book, a reader interested solely in Muslim or Middle Eastern affairs might be inclined to skip directly to Part Two. But doing so would eviscerate the argument I wish to make about Orientalism.

When I wrote *Conversion to Islam in the Medieval Period* in the late 1970s, I took it as axiomatic that every convert's hopes and expectations of his or her new religion bear a close relationship to their hopes and expectations of the religion they leave behind. Some converts seek a fuller or more satisfying version of the spiritual practices they are familiar with. Some look for a faith that will change patterns of social life that have worked against them. Some want to continue following the leadership of admired spiritual or family members who have already converted. Some feel that a literate faith is more sophisticated, and therefore better, than one based on oral traditions. Some hope to gain employment or some other tangible benefit from conversion, or possibly release from slavery or some other debility. Some want to become part of a ruling class.

In other words, who a convert is before he or she adopts a new faith is important. Indeed, it is often more important than what that convert may subsequently achieve in, or derive from, the new faith. For the historian considering the conversion of a particular individual, tracing that individual's pre-conversion social status and religious outlook offers a glimpse into his or her frame of mind that may be more revealing than what the individual may report about his or her life after conversion, when self-aggrandizement, or at least making the best of the decision to convert, is likely to slant any narration.

This axiom also applies to people who choose, for whatever proclaimed reasons, to step outside the social, religious, and cultural matrix they have grown up in. To be more explicit, a decision made by a non-Muslim American to study or work within a tradition that is remote from his or her family background, or the established career streams of Euro-American cultural activity, is better examined by finding out where that American is coming from than by tracing his or her career achievements in later years. After all, the influential political and cultural roles played by the French and British Orientalists studied by Edward Said were not yet on their career horizons when they made the fateful decision to walk into their first Arabic, Persian, or Turkish class. Once they committed to serious study of the Orient, however serendipitous opportunity – a major force in my life – shaped their futures more than the working out of a preconceived career plan or unconscious cultural bias.

Nevertheless, examining the "pre-conversion" status, if I may call it that, of an Orientalist is not always easy, since the Orientalist may not fully understand his or her decision to delve into the cultural unknown, or be willing to speak candidly about it. I hope that the discussion of the wellsprings of my own path in life before I took my first Arabic class will be understood as an effort to supply the candor that is so often lost to memory.

The second part, "Ways Forward," will trace the filaments that intertwined in determining what I did with my life. Some pathways map jobs or projects that directly involved me with the Middle East or Islam. Others touch on parts of my life that are not so clearly related, such as painting and writing fiction. Yet when I drew pictures while listening to speeches at academic conferences in Saudi Arabia, Tehran, or Cairo, were not the images I created relevant to where I was and what I was doing? Or if I set a novel somewhere in the Muslim world, were the characters and situations I invented not a part of my involvement with that world?

"Things Happen," the third part, will detail some specific stories that reveal the serendipitously wide diversity of my early career experiences. Again, some will be only tangentially, if at all, related to Islam or the Middle East. But one may question whether any serious undertaking by someone who once changed the course of his life by walking into his first classes on Arabic and the Middle East can have remained unaffected by that commitment to a culture not his own.

The fourth part, "Moving On," deals with the period from 1990 onward, when my academic orientation became diffuse and then evolved from Middle Eastern history to several types of world history. Yet at the same time, after two decades as a medievalist, I was becoming more and more involved in what was happening, or seemed likely to happen, in the contemporary Middle East.

"Conclusions," the fifth part, deals with how I look upon my life and career in retirement. What, at the end, do I think about Islam? About Orientalism? About Methodism?

PART ONE

Before Arabic

IT IS SOMETIMES EASIER to report a memory than to explain why it seems relevant.

Sometime in my twenties I was sitting in a barber's chair near my home in Rockford when a pudgy youth in another chair exclaimed: "Aren't you Dick Bulliet?" I acknowledged that I was, and he said that I had been his squad leader in high school ROTC. He remembered me sitting at the head of my squad's row of desks.

I modestly refrained from revealing my pleasure at being remembered by this younger man as a military role model.

"I remember you," he continued, "because you kept banging your head on the wall."

Unfair ... but not untrue. Sometimes, instead, I dealt with schoolroom boredom by picking the paint from the wall with my fingernails. I didn't mind being in the Reserve Officer Training Corps for three years, however. Wearing a military uniform three days a week absolved me of keeping up with high school styles, and polishing brass and shining shoes to march in weekly inspection took the place of gym, which was salvation from hell for someone as inept at sports as I was. Besides, I enjoyed learning to field strip an M1 rifle, even though being right-handed but left-eyed stood in the way of my ever hitting a target on the rifle range.

My Father's Dream

I CAME TO NEW YORK in 1976 as professor of Middle Eastern history at Columbia University. Years later, my father told me of a dream that came to him again and again well before I even suspected that a job might open up at Columbia:

> In my dream I was old and living alone in a residential hotel in lower Manhattan. Every day I would go out and sit on a park bench. Perhaps the park in front of City Hall. Then, one day, I was found dead on the park bench. The police went through my pockets looking for identification. They discovered that my son was a professor at Columbia University.

Jack, my father, died in 1997 at age eighty-eight. When I asked him about his oddly prophetic dream a few months before his death, he only vaguely recalled it. He had never been of a mind to interpret it. Yet three aspects of it speak to his and my sense of identity.

First, New York:

Except for a brief period early in the Great Depression, Jack never lived in New York. He was born in Indianapolis and spent his early childhood in Corydon Junction, a itty-bitty hamlet in southern Indiana situated where the track of the eight-mile "Dinky," a spur line grandiosely named the Louisville, New Albany, and Corydon Railway, branched off from the Southern Railway to go to the town of Corydon, Indiana's first capital. Later he moved with his mother to the nearby city of New Albany on the Ohio River for his schooling. His New York life extended from his graduation from Indiana University in 1931 until his return there for graduate study two years later.

This year-and-a-half sojourn in New York loomed large in Jack's memory, and apparently in his dream life. (My own dreams frequently feature bizarre versions of the Harvard campus, where I was extraordinarily happy until I was dismissed from the faculty, but never of Berkeley, where for two years my wife and I enjoyed a lovely apartment in the hills overlooking the Golden Gate Bridge.) It was there he set up housekeeping with his first wife, his high school sweetheart Mary Royse. Alas, they only had three months together before she died of cirrhosis of the liver, possibly caused by a tonic her mother gave her for menstrual cramps. He lived on alone there after her death. At one point he went to a doctor for his nerves. The doctor told him

16

there were many widows and divorcees in New York; he should find himself one. As a good Methodist, he took up smoking a pipe instead.

Soon thereafter he quit his job with the New York City Bell Telephone Company, telling his disappointed father that he was just anticipating an inevitable layoff in the worsening Great Depression. Escaping New York, he returned to the familiar halls of Indiana University with an assistantship in physics. While he worked on his Masters degree, he met an older doctoral student named Mildred Williams. In 1935 they married and moved to Rockford, Illinois, where they lived for the next 52 years. I was born in Rockford in 1940.

The tragic circumstances of Mary's death are certainly sufficient to explain the centrality of New York City in Jack's memory. As he put it: "The courtship and brief marriage with Mary always remains as a poignant and bittersweet region in my unerasable memory." But she was absent from his storytelling. Not only were Mary's weeks there after an aborted honeymoon on Martha's Vineyard few and pain-ridden, but Mildred would brook no mention of her predecessor. My older sister Nina found out about Mary Royse at age eleven by coming across a marriage certificate when Jack's home in New Albany was being dismantled after Grandmother Katherine's death. I, however, remained unaware of her existence for another six or seven years, until I stumbled across an old insurance policy in her name and innocently asked who Mary Royse Bulliet was. Thus even though the loss of his wife may have etched Jack's New York days into his memory, the etching is eerily empty, consisting primarily of apartments in Brooklyn and Chelsea, lectures at Cooper Union, theaters in Times Square, and long subway rides to explore the city's neighborhoods. Jack seldom mentioned specific people and never visited Columbia University.

Second, the residential hotel:

Though Jack occasionally expressed a liking for the idea of solitary life in a residential hotel – an apartment building with bellboy and maid service – the closest he ever came to living that way was in the assisted living apartment in Quincy, Massachusetts, where he passed his final two years, two decades after his prophetic dream. In New York, before and after Mary, he lived in a rooming house, as he did at Indiana University.

However, Jack's father, C. J., lived for almost three decades in residential hotels in the Chicago Loop: the Briggs, the Bismarck, and the Majestic. During those years, he was a widely-read newspaper arts critic known for his fearless championing of modernism in the land of the philistines.

From my childhood I remember the Majestic Hotel as a somewhat seedy establishment with silent, carpeted corridors catering to people in the arts.

C. J.'s apartment was small and dark. I remember mainly a narrow living room crammed with his collections of books, artwork, and curios: a large portrait of a nude black woman (perhaps by his artist mistress Macena Barton), a small dark picture of a woman on a ring-shaped trapeze, a carved bear, a cane topped with a bulldog head whose spring-operated jaw could be opened by pulling a lever. The breakfast table had a toaster that opened at the sides, instead of the pop-up variety we had at home. I don't recall, as my sister Nina did, the large gruesome painting of a tray carrying the severed head of John the Baptist hanging directly above the toaster. My only memories of the bedroom are of a loud clock ticking and streetcars sparking and clanging in the warm night air.

Third, Columbia University:

Though my mother taught physics for many years at Rockford College, a small women's college – later coeducational – in my hometown, neither Jack nor C. J. had any professional connection with a university, much less with Columbia. As for me, I spent a total of fourteen years at Harvard as student and junior faculty and may still have been there when Jack's dreams of Columbia began. I do not recall ever discussing with him, or even thinking about, the possibility of someday teaching at Columbia. Like most young people drawn into Harvard's gravitational field, I could think of no place that was more desirable than Cambridge and Boston.

Given these three circumstances, one could reasonably surmise that the New York of Jack's dream is simply a substitute for Chicago, and possibly Columbia for the University of Chicago, which Jack had considered attending until C. J. obliquely made it clear that he did not want his son living in the same city where his years away from his wife in New Albany were brightened by various amours. But why in his dream is Jack living in old age as his father lived? And why does the dream climax with the revelation of his son teaching at Columbia, with the implication that his son is in some way aloof or estranged from his aged dad?

I am interested in these questions because my own life has been powerfully molded by the life experience and personal library of my grandfather, a man I barely knew, and, just as powerfully, by my father's ambivalent relationship with C. J. This ambivalence surfaced both in a memoir Jack composed about his own early life, and in the circumstances of its composition. My niece Katie asked Jack one day how he happened to become an engineer when his father had been an art critic. An innocent enough question, but Jack bristled at what he took to be its suggestion that he had wasted his life and failed his paternal model. He thereupon decided to compile on his computer a narrative of his life in the world of technology, or, as he liked to put it, the story of how "a blacksmith with dirty fingernails got sandwiched between two great men of letters."

My father lived most of his life under the burden of conflicting emotional feelings about C. J. From the time Jack was five years old in 1913, C. J.'s work as advance man for a touring theater company, and from 1922 in Chicago as publisher/editor of an art magazine, and later as a newspaper arts reviewer, caused him to live nine moths of each year apart from his wife and only child. Yet rather than C. J. being criticized for leading a separate life, Jack's mother, Katherine, and her sisters, Frances and Grace – the dominating and domineering women in Jack's upbringing – lionized him as an intellectual giant and a luminary in the world of arts and letters.

During C. J.'s touring years, Jack was proud to have a father who worked for an organization that had its head office in New York. Yet he also admitted to growing up with a feeling of abandonment. As a four-year-old in a period when hands-on fathering was not yet stylish, Jack had only a weak grasp of his father as a person. In old age he several times related a story about this that he heard his mother tell. Katherine had schooled him to reply to queries about the whereabouts of his father by saying that he was a traveling man. One day the two of them were on a train, probably a local from Corydon Junction to New Albany. Jack overheard one man telling another that he was a traveling man. He promptly went over to his mother and asked whether the traveling man was his father. Katherine obviously found the story amusing. But Jack didn't.

To add to this burden, Jack's natural fascination with how things worked, evidenced from early childhood, evoked little interest or support from C .J. Jack learned about farm machinery, railroads, telephone circuits, stage lighting, and radio and became a thirteen-year-old family driver as soon as his parents bought an automobile. Convinced he was destined to be an inventor, he sent away for information on how to get a patent. Yet his opportunities were limited. When his quack doctor/chiropractor uncle took to using a fraudulent ERA (Electronic Reactions of [Albert] Abrams) Machine to diagnose illness by electrically "analyzing" dried blood samples mailed in by patients, Jack snooped inside the machine's wooden housing.

> I could see the mechanism.... There were two electric coils and some levers attached to a pendulum through the cabinet cover.... It most resembled an oversized doorbell mechanism. Aside from that, there was absolutely nothing in the cabinet; even the wires to the patient were connected to *nothing.*

Though C. J. had parlayed an Indiana University minor in astronomy – his professor credited him with seeing a previously unnoted canal on Mars – into a journalistic assignment to accompany a university expedition to Spain to observe an eclipse of the sun, his taste as a reporter quickly turned to crime and then to theater reviewing. Thus Jack learned early on to deprecate his own artistic opinions in deference to his father's eminence. In high school and beyond, his career ambition was to design switchboards for stage lighting.

The consequences for me of Jack's emotional ambivalence were several-fold. First, at some point when I was still quite young, Jack conceived the notion that brilliance of the sort his mother and her sisters associated with his father had skipped a generation: He himself was without distinction in matters that counted, arts and letters; but I, his son, was certain to become the vessel of C. J.'s intellectual heritage.

Secondly, when C. J. was facing retirement from the *Chicago Daily News* in 1948, Jack offered him a home with us in Rockford and bought, with his financial help, a large house suitable to the physical needs of an obese, lame, toothless, and diabetic retiree, and capacious enough for his collections. The books, pictures, records, and curios that crammed his Majestic Hotel apartment and his *Chicago Daily News* office arrived in due course in Rockford. Then C. J. abruptly announced he was marrying again – to a younger newspaperwoman he had met thirty years earlier rather than his longtime artist mistress. He told Jack he could henceforth consider the collections his own. When C. J. died in 1952, the rest of his books and papers arrived at the house. And there they sat.

Jack had neither the time nor inclination to go beyond perusing an occasional stack of C. J.'s old correspondence; but he could not bear the idea of throwing away any of his dad's things. My mother resented the vast clutter bequeathed by her father-in-law and occasionally disposed of things surreptitiously. I recall her destroying a garish – in her view obscene – watercolor painting of a nude; and she worried that her cleaning lady would disapprove of our nude etchings and lithographs by the likes of Renoir, Maillol, and Picasso. My sister Nina evinced no interest in the stuff either.

I, however, spent the decade of my adolescence prowling through the contents of this family shrine to C. J. Bulliet, thereby developing not only a historian's taste for archival dust and the smell of mold, but a conviction that serendipitous discovery is the essence of historical study. My parents never pressured me to find a summer job so long as I was engaged in cataloguing C. J.'s collections. Thus Jack's conflicted filial piety led inexorably to my finding my calling and fitting myself for his dream.

Thirdly, back to the dream, Jack's unsatisfied longing for paternal approval of his own achievements in technical matters led him, for some years after his retirement in the early 1970s, to look upon me as someone who could grant that approval. In essence, I became a kind of reincarnation of C. J. Bulliet, thereby offering Jack a second chance for "paternal" validation of the course of his life. Though I had known little about his employment while growing up, I enjoyed asking him to go through his several patents with me and explain exactly what he had invented.

It is in light of these perceptions that I interpret Jack's dream. It is conceivable that the aged man living alone in the residential hotel in New York is actually C. J., that Jack is the professorial son. But this would lead to an overall interpretation that Jack in his dream had finally attained higher recognition than his father and abandoned him in lower Manhattan to teach classes uptown at Columbia. However, nothing else in Jack's personality or expressed attitude toward his father would encourage such a triumphalist interpretation.

It is more in keeping with Jack's generally pessimistic outlook – at least at that time – to see him as he ostensibly is in the dream, a lonely old codger on a park bench. But I am inclined to think that the professorial son is actually C . J., or rather C. J. reincarnated in me. Just as C. J. lived apart from his son and ignored his accomplishments while basking in the adulation he enjoyed as a man of arts and letters – this would be Jack's interpretation – the professorial son in the dream is an intellectual eminence who is aloof from his lonely old dad. Yet the old man nevertheless seems to find his identity in their relationship: being the father of his son is who he is. A real life in the imagined shadow of C. J. thus becomes a dream life in the imagined shadow of C. J.'s avatar, me.

Bulliet Is a Peculiar Name

C. J. WAS BORN CLARENCE JOSEPH BULLEIT in 1883. Note the order of the final vowels of his surname. Likewise, my father was christened Leander Jackson Bulleit in 1908. In recent years, Bulleit has become widely known as the brand name of excellent bourbon and rye whiskeys distilled originally by one of C. J.'s distant cousins. Regardless of spelling, both the whiskey and my name are pronounced "bullet."

By the spring of 1913, C. J. had changed the sequence of vowels in his name from *ei* to *ie* and begun identifying himself as *Bulliet*. Consequently, my sister and I, and now my son, acquired a family name that is nearly unique.

Within the family, we have long wondered why C. J. changed the spelling of our name while retaining the "bullet" pronunciation, instead of switching to three syllables (e.g. *Bull-ee-ett-*) or to something Frenchy (e.g. Boule-*yay*). He was already publishing poems in southern Indiana newspapers by the time he entered Indiana University in 1902. Editing *The Daily Student* in his senior year and opting for a journalism career after college graduation in 1905, he had fully established his byline as a crime reporter and drama critic by the time he left the *Indianapolis Star* in 1913 to become the publicist and advance man for Robert Mantell, the aging Irish star of America's last touring Shakespeare company.

The Mantell Company stationery of 1913 documents the change in spelling. At the start of the year, C. J.'s name is *Bulleit*, but a new letterhead first appearing on a missive postmarked April 14, 1913, has the spelling *Bulliet*, and the colleague addressing the letter uses that spelling in his salutation. The next surviving documentation of his name change comes in 1915. After a long recuperation from typhoid fever forced him to leave the Mantell Company, he found work as one of the regional press agents for the famous D. W. Griffith movie *Birth of a Nation.* His business cards give his name as *C. J. Bulliet.*

In later years he explained the change in spelling to my father. Jack, in turn, explained it many years later to a second cousin:

> I want to refer to this apparent feud about the spelling of our name. As you certainly know, the family papers show a variety of spellings and that "*eit*" was the settled spelling at the time of our fathers' early maturity.

My father proposed changing [the spelling] to "*iet.*" It should be recalled that this occurred at the time of World War I when "pro -German" was an epithet fully as onerous as "pro-Nazi" was in World War II. At that time, Dad was traveling over the whole country as a theatrical press agent and he felt (rightly or not) that he was carrying the baggage of a linguistically German name when he knew that the name was ethnically French. I think he was quite disappointed that his brothers would have nothing of his argument. [Jack was unaware that C. J.'s younger brother Straudeth did adopt the new spelling.] I have always thought that they thought Dad was trying to be elitist. That this was an error showed up clearly later when he acquired note as an art critic and a denizen of the art scene in Chicago in the thirties and forties. The effete members of that scene at first insisted on calling him "*Booyay.*" He vehemently resisted all tendency to elitism—[Jack's Methodist horror of boastfulness is speaking here]—and insisted [on "*bullet*"] (even, perhaps, to the point of rudeness). I recall his referring to himself as a "country jake from Corydon."

While this seems unequivocal, Jack elsewhere recorded another memory that tells a different story.

When Dad went to Chicago and began his newspaper writing on art, the art community there began referring to him by the name "*Booyay,*" but he quite firmly resisted the tendency and "corrected" the pronunciation when it was used in his presence. When I became employed at Rockford, Illinois, my father's name was well known in that city because the Chicago newspapers were widely circulated there, and there was an active art/music community in Rockford. These people were using the French pronunciation, but they gradually shifted over to my business name as we became acquainted with them.

One day I was in Chicago with Fred Johnson [a business associate], and there was some reason for me to go to the *Daily News* office to see my father about something, and Fred went with me. This must have been the first time I went to that office because I remember being a bit tentative about getting around the building. We took the elevator to the proper floor and found a clerk in the elevator lobby. I asked how to find Dad, using my normal pronunciation, and he assured me there was no such person there. For some reason, it occurred to me to use the French pronunciation. The fellow smiled and directed me through the proper door and to his desk. I still don't understand how this could have happened, and it almost seems like something I dreamed up. However, I had a telephone conversation with Fred a couple of years ago, and he brought up the incident, and we had a laugh about it.

C. J. clearly used the war as an excuse to avoid discussing with his son the real motivation for changing the name. There was a public outcry against Germany's assault on Belgium in 1914, to be sure, but America's purge of German names did not set in until we entered the war in 1917. So why the deception of his only child about so trivial a matter as transposing the vowels in his surname, a deception that would have succeeded but for the chance preservation of a telltale piece of letterhead datable to 1913, which I did not uncover until after Jack's death?

Compounding the mystery is a letter C. J. wrote to his mother in 1918. After a long presentation on what he had discovered about her Revolutionary War forebears that would qualify her for DAR membership, he concludes with the following:

> In the French Dictionary of Universal Biography, a great work of dozens of volumes printed in French, I have been able to find what might be a trace of the Bulliet family (*"Bulliet"* is the best up-to-date spelling). I have found the account of an Abbé Boulliette, which according to some of [family friend] Mr. Soudry's papers is the old spelling of the name. This Abbé Boulliette was a grammarian and language scholar, born about 1720 in Burgundy. He entered the church, and became canon of the chapter at Auxerre, a rather important educational center, in the department of Yonne. An early work of his on the proper spelling and pronunciation of French geographical names attracted the attention of the French Academy.... He also published a religious work entitled "A Pacific Elucidation of the Essence of the Sacrifice of Jesus Christ." There is no record of the time of his death. Since the name Boulliette is uncommon, even in France, I have thought, probably this old abbé might be a relation. I wish we had some papers on this side of the family.
>
> Well, that's about the extent of my genealogical researches to date. If I find anything more, I'll write you.
>
> Your loving son,

The explanation of the name change here is simply that it is "up-to-date." Though the war was still raging, there is no hint of the story he later told my father about avoiding a German name. Rather, C. J. is firmly announcing his determination to be French. For his mother's eyes, he appears convinced that the vowel sequence he arbitrarily adopted in 1913 provides crucial evidence of his father's descent from an elite French family. He was essentially saying that his real father, the man his ancestor-proud mother married, was not the insignificant son of a Catholic immigrant who, in all likelihood, abandoned his family, but rather the descendant of French literati.

Yet beyond citing unspecified papers from an old family friend, he apparently never explored the question of the family name with other Bulleits in southern Indiana. Augustus, their common immigrant grandfather, was an innkeeper who supposedly devised the whiskey recipe that Bulleit Bourbon later commercialized. He seems to have immigrated to the United States by way of New Orleans in 1836. Once settled among French-speakers in the village of Lanesville, Indiana, he married Marie Julia Dulieu, a woman of unquestioned Belgian birth, and sired four sons and perhaps two daughters before disappearing without a trace around 1860, either abandoning his family or—the family's preferred explanation—falling victim to a murderer while returning with gold from New Orleans, where he had sold a boatload of farm goods. His sons went on to father at least twenty children, C. J.'s first cousins. Not only are these cousins rarely mentioned in C. J.'s writings, but in a letter written when he was twenty he mentions being introduced to an aunt he had never before heard of. Evidently the Bulleits were not a close family.

If C. J. had ventured to consult other family members, he would have discovered records of three spellings of Augustus' last name, each attested after his settlement in Indiana: *Beoyeelat* on Augustus and Marie's marriage license, *Boilliat* on the grave of an otherwise unknown young daughter, and—lo and behold!—*Bulliet* on acquisition papers for property in southern Indiana. But no Boulliette, beyond whatever Mr. Soudry may have suggested. The side of the family that preserved or hunted out these records believes that Augustus "apparently was from Brussels."

Was C. J. "correct," then, in transposing the vowels? If so, how could his abandoned wife Marie have been "incorrect" in adopting the spelling *Bulleit* and transmitting it to all her children?

The bizarre spelling *Beoyeelat* is best understood as a phonetic rendering of something like *Boillat*. Augustus was very likely illiterate, though his wife was from a rather refined family, her brother becoming at one point a government functionary in Belgium. Since they used the name *Boilliat* on a daughter's gravestone, the switch to *Bulliet* and then *Bulleit* would seem to represent stages of assimilation into Indiana life in the course of Marie's life.

The awkward French vowel sounds of the original name gave way to the pronunciation "*bullet*" still used by almost all family members.[1] This process was doubtless helped by the local eminence of a well-known, but unrelated, Bullitt family. Captain Thomas Bullitt laid out a plan for what later became

---

1. A cousin named Jim Bulleit, who in 1945 founded Bullet Records, a Nashville label that recorded such musicians as Chet Atkins, Ray Price, and B. B. King, pronounced his name "Bulay" before changing the pronunciation to match that of his company. I am ignorant of the history of that pronunciation in his branch of the family, whatever branch that may be.

the city of Louisville and was the eponym of northern Kentucky's Bullitt County. Thus there were known to be Bullitts living just across the Ohio River from where Augustus and his family settled. The order of the vowels in Augustus' name probably mattered little once the "*bullet*" pronunciation had been established, but why Marie (if not Augustus) finally settled on *Bulleit* remains obscure.

Significantly, when C. J. changed the spelling of the name to *Bulliet*, unwittingly returning to a documented early spelling, he seems not to have tried to change the pronunciation within the family. Yet one of his correspondents from his years traveling with Mantell regularly opens his letters with "Dear Bully." Was this a nickname? Or was C. J. experimenting with a new pronunciation for professional purposes? To be sure, his son's recollections attest to C. J.'s determination to retain the "*bullet*" pronunciation after becoming the editor of the *Chicago Evening Post*'s *Art Magazine* in 1922. But Jack's recollections also show that his father persistently lied to him in linking the change of spelling to the war. Hence, his behavior when Jack was around may not be a reliable indicator of his professional practice. After all, by the time Jack and Fred Johnson paid their visit to C. J.'s office at the *Chicago Daily News*, he had been a reviewer for that paper for at least five years, and more likely ten, and had been a major figure in Chicago art circles for a decade longer. Plenty of time, one would think, for his colleagues to have learned to pronounce his name.

Returning to C. J.'s claim that anti-German feeling inspired the spelling change, it is odd that he did not tell Jack that he made his decision on the basis of Belgian rather than French ancestry. His grandmother was certainly Belgian, and probably his grandfather Augustus as well. (One indicator is that French usage would have preferred the name *Auguste* to the Latinate *Augustus*, but Latin endings are well evidenced in Belgian naming of that time.) Moreover, the greatest beneficiaries of American popular sentiment against Germany in 1914 were the Belgians. C. J. himself spent the summer of 1918 working as a publicist for Mlle. Hendrica A. C. Van der Flier on her tour of the northeast United States and Canada for Holland-American Homes for Belgian Widows and Orphans. He was also proud of owning a copy of *Raemaekers Cartoons*, a Goya-esque collection of lurid lithographs detailing Germany's "rape" of Belgium.

But a claim of Belgian ancestry seems never to have crossed his mind. In a highly romanticized biographical sketch of grandfather Augustus, C. J. maintained:

> He was a native of Alsace-Lorraine, and of a good family, but records of his birth and ancestry are lost. In his late teens, he, like many other young

men of his day, left his native province to escape the irksome military service required of all youths, and came to the United States.

These lines are pure invention. The hyphenated provincial name Alsace-Lorraine became common only after the Franco-Prussian War of 1871, when Alsace and the eastern part of Lorraine, the regions of northeastern France adjoining Belgium, were seized by Germany. Recovery of Alsace-Lorraine subsequently became a French rallying cry, and this goal was achieved at the end of World War I. An attribution of Augustus' origin to a province that did not exist as such during his lifetime, therefore, could hardly have been a part of family lore stretching back two generations. Yet it fits quite well the World War I period, when C. J. was inventing his excuse for changing his name. His story was eminently plausible. German armies had overrun Belgium and invaded France, which had been lamenting long and loud the loss of her stolen provinces. Turning a German-looking name into a French-looking name might well have seemed wonderfully patriotic to someone who claimed a forebear from Alsace-Lorraine.

This was merely a story, however, like the equally duplicitous claim that Augustus might have been related to a priest named Boulliette from the department of Yonne in Burgundy, not Alsace or Lorraine. What was C. J. really thinking? What was the real reason for concealing the truth on a matter as ostensibly trivial as reversing the vowels of his name?

In his 1918 letter mentioning Abbé Boulliette, C. J. adds a discussion of one Pierre Bullet—note the absence of the *ie* vowel sequence that justified the inclusion of the Abbé—a seventeenth-century architect of Paris; his son Jean-Baptiste Bullet, also an architect; and another Jean-Baptiste Bullet, this one an eighteenth-century antiquarian and professor of theology. He concludes: "The name Boulliette, with its variations, has found its way into the annals of France, usually in connection with literary and artistic pursuits."

This repeated and expanded portrayal of an imaginary Boulliette family as long-time contributors to French culture strongly suggests that C. J.'s objective in changing his name was self-invention—"elitism"—just as Jack felt the family suspected. Enter an ambitious young drama critic from southern Indiana; exit the distillate of centuries of French literati. Goodbye Corydon, Indiana; hello Paris and the world. Goodbye to the country jake Clarence "*Bullet*"; greetings to C. J. "*Booyay*," the French champion of modern art. Strange behavior on the surface; but given the depth of turn-of-the-century midwestern snobbery, this effort at self-creation does not seem particularly extraordinary.

Nevertheless, one hint survives as to what may really have prompted the 1913 spelling change. Theatrical advance men at that time were mostly

Jewish, but, sometime during C. J.'s childhood, his parents had stopped attending a Catholic church and become Methodists. C. J. himself became an
avowed atheist and as an adult never attended a church service and never
voted.

Against this background comes this excerpt from a letter to his wife
Katharine dated July 1918:

> Mantell hasn't decided yet whether he is going to play in New York [or
> go on tour]. I haven't seen any of the outfit, except [Si] Conner. I hope I'm
> through with them for good. Ethel [Mantell's daughter] is going to marry
> her Jew [Ira Seymour Platky]. Both families are "cut up" over it, but Ethel
> and the boy are both of age, and they say they'll marry whether their par-
> ents consent or not....

Considering that C. J. changed his name from Bulleit to Bulliet and
thereby abandoned his well established newspaper byline only a few months
after joining the Mantell Company, it seems possible that he did so to accommodate a boss's objection to having an advance man whose German-looking
name might be thought to be Jewish. (I remember Jack saying his dad described himself, or heard himself described, as looking like "a Belgian Jew
banker.") Mantell's daughter Ethel married her Jewish boyfriend despite her
father's disapproval, but Mantell may have insisted on C. J. taking a French-
looking name, possibly as a condition for getting the job. This is pure specu-
lation, but it might explain why C. J. never told anyone the real reason for
changing his name.

Within the Chicago art scene that he entered almost a decade after
changing his name, C. J. became a champion of many Jewish artists. But how
did he feel about Jews in 1913? This is perhaps the sole point of intersection
between C. J.'s life and the subject matter that became the focus of my career
more than half a century later. In 1902 he wrote the following Longfellow-
esque poem:

LAY OF THE MIDIAN MINSTREL

While light-hearted and contented
　　Thus we dwelt a happy nation,
Out of Egypt came a whirlwind
　　Bringing death and desolation.

Came an army of fanatics
　　That with sword and fiery brand,
Desolated first our neighbors;
　　Desolated then our land.

Came an army led by Moses,
　　Captain stern and terrible,
Chosen by their god Jehovah
　　Some dire purpose to fulfill

And they fell upon our cities,
　　Slew our nation's guardian host
Every warrior of our armies,
　　Fighting bravely at his post.

　　· · · · · ·

Thus was wrought our demolition;
　　Thus our race as nought became
None are left except our daughters,
　　Dragging out their lives in shame.

Curséd be the sons of Jacob!
　　May their wives unfruitful be!
Curséd be their god Jehovah
　　Author of our misery!

Here, where once our splendid cities
　　Proudly reared aloft their spires,
Now remain but blackened ruins
　　Remnants of the Jewish fires.

Mid these scenes of desolation,
　　Where my kindred's ashes lie,
Weary, broken-hearted wanderer;
　　Let me lay me down and die!

Creativity

C. J. HAD A NEWSPAPERMAN'S EAR for the arresting anecdote and diguised his voluminous reading and thorough research beneath an engaging, even breezy, writing style. Yet he was not creatively gifted. His high school and undergraduate poetry notebooks preserve some intriguing ideas, but few memorable verses. One pair of sestets illustrates both his turgid style and his deep commitment to flouting conventionality. They are dated "7:10–7:20 AM (N. Y. time) Oct. 29, 1901," the moment of execution of President William McKinley's assassin, Leon Czolgosz:

CZOLGOSZ

The lightning current through his frame hath sped,
And the red-handed anarchist lies dead;
Law triumphs over Anarchy too late
For the reversal of our Chieftain's fate;
One treads the vale of death besmirched with shame
The other with an ever during name.

ANOTHER
Cruel-eyed a nation stands, a servile host,
To see one wretched man yield up the ghost;
And for what cause? Forsooth, with fatal ball
He wrought relentlessly a tyrant's fall –
Relentlessly as duty bade him to,
The man he pitied but the tyrant slew.

During his years traveling by railroad from one Mantell Company engagement to the next he wrote numerous short stories and plays, mostly dark tales with grim titles like "The Little Traitor," "A Midnight Episode," and "Marie's Confession." "The Crime of Dr. Vibert," like Edgar Allen Poe's "The Murder of Marie Roget," offered a fictional solution of a real murder – in Poe's case that of New Yorker Mary Cecilia Rogers in 1841. C. J. identified Jack the Ripper with a fictional Dr. Vibert who had a compulsion to handle the internal organs of disemboweled women. It was his best effort, but like the others it remained unpublished.

Surprisingly, considering the career as an art critic that he embarked upon as he was turning forty, he seems never to have drawn so much as a doodle and never visited Europe after the post-graduation eclipse expedition. He initially considered painting to be a feminine grace unsuited to the virile sex. In college he wrote a letter to his fiancée, Katherine Adams, a passable but uncreative painter of flowers and southern Indiana landscapes, reporting his encounter with a real artist. "I got acquainted with him yesterday and he seems to be a fine fellow. He completely changed my opinion about boy artists, which you remember I expressed somewhat strongly to you when I was there Xmas." The artist in question did Norman Rockwell-style magazine covers.

So despite Jack's conviction that I was C. J. reborn, the creativity that I have drawn on as a historian, novelist, and painter seems not to have come from my Bulliet or Adams DNA. The Williams clan, my mother's side of the family, looks more promising, but also more problematic, since Williams family gifts blend so easily with outright crazy.

My mother Mildred may or may not be the place to start, depending on how one looks at the mystery of creativity. She unquestionably doted on me, her overfed growing boy. But though good-hearted and of cheerful disposition, she was a woman of impaired affect: no facility with serious conversation, no taste for discussing the issues of the day, no sense of humor, zero physical warmth. Nor did she tolerate disagreement. So my sister and I, at our father's urging, always agreed with her to avoid making her "cross." Neither of us can remember ever quarreling with one another. Mildred seldom reminisced or told family stories; but she was devoted to, and took a not-always-appreciated managerial approach toward, the lives of her children, her three younger sisters, and their offspring. Today, I suspect she would be seen as edging toward Asperger's syndrome.

Nevertheless, in 1934 Mildred earned a PhD in physics at Indiana University. As unlikely as that seems for a woman in the midst of the Great Depression, it gets stranger. As my father wrote, "After graduation [from Valparaiso University in northern Indiana] Mildred enrolled at Indiana University for a master's degree in English. But, before classes started she encountered Mr. Hershman who had been her physics teacher at Valpo and who was back at IU to complete his Ph.D. He told her that the physics department needed a teaching assistant and that she could be it if she would apply. She did apply and started her journey to a Ph.D. in physics."

How many students of any gender set out to get an advanced degree in English and then get diverted into physics by a chance encounter on campus? Jack himself never finished a PhD because he had had such a struggle to learn French that he could not face learning German, the other required language. But what of Mildred? I rarely heard her utter a word of either

French or German. When I asked her how she had passed the German exam without taking a course in German, she replied that as an undergraduate English major she had taken the required course in Anglo-Saxon ... "and they are more or less the same." Apparently she had a prodigious memory for numbers, though I never quite believed my father's claim that she knew the logarithm tables.

When I was five, Rockford College expanded its physics offerings to accommodate returning soldiers taking advantage of free education under the GI Bill. That is when my mother started a teaching career that lasted for twenty-five years. Yet I only once recall her talking about physics in a family setting. I asked her at dinner about the electron shells around atomic nuclei. She gave me a succinct and satisfying response ... and then passed me the mashed potatoes.

The consensus within the family and without[1] is that Mildred was phenomenally intelligent. But so far as I could see, all she really cared or talked about was family and homemaking. As a child, I could please her by memorizing poetry, using a large vocabulary, and being dutiful. (I could recite at age seven that a mass spectrograph – whatever that was – could separate the uranium isotopes U-235 and U-238 so that the former could be used to make atomic bombs.) Somewhat later in life I found that despite her weak sense of humor, I could make her laugh, usually at her own foibles; and I noticed that on social occasions she sometimes kept her eye on me to see when it was appropriate to laugh.

Did my robust sense of humor develop this way? I don't know, but I do remember that as a child I would fall into uncontrollable and exhausting paroxysms of laughter that lasted for several minutes.

Mildred was a better mathematician than Jack. He went to her for help in solving difficult problems. This was a Williams family trait. Her grandfather, Isaac Greenbury Williams, had settled as a farmer in central Illinois and been taught to read and write by his wife. He was skilled at estimating the number of board feet that a felled tree could be sawn into. Among his sons, one became a civil engineer and then president of Lehigh University, while another became a mathematics professor and then vice president of Valparaiso University. The magnitude of the single-generation leap from

---

1. One of her early students wrote: "To complete my degree, I was forced to take some subjects that I had never thought much about. One such subject was Optics. Again, like everything in physics, it was largely mathematical. Because of the math connection I could easily understand what was happening in Optics.... My teacher was Dr. Mildred Bulliet and she made the subject particularly fascinating. Occasionally Dr. Bulliet would invite me to her house for parties. Her husband was also an extraordinarily interesting person.... I had never met a person of such broad interests before." Scott J. Harden, *Of Bullets, Bombs, and Armored Cars, My Life Adventures*, [n.p.]: Xlibris, 2017, ch. 12.

illiteracy to university president can be judged from an interview given by Isaac Greenbury's brother Presley to a Canton, Illinois newspaper in 1909:

> I grew to maturity on the farm, attended for a short time the primitive schools of pioneer times where I obtained a limited education. Father and mother were typical representatives of that sturdy pioneer class that came here when Illinois was practically a wilderness and their names are closely connected with the pioneer history of Fulton County [Illinois]. After we were fairly established in our new home near Monterey, we actively entered upon the arduous task of felling the trees and preparing the land for cultivation. I have made thousands of rails, grubbed, cut cordwood, and later, made many railroad ties. Father was a shoemaker by trade and I am a tanner and worked at my trade in Monterey for a number of years for a man named Eli Lyons.
>
> Politically, father was a Democrat and both he and mother were members of the Christian church.
>
> Throughout Banner and Orion townships wild turkey, wolves, and wild cats and catamounts abounded in great numbers and rattlesnakes were found everywhere. The wolves used to make night hideous around our cabin with their howls, snaps and growls. Coming up the Illinois River one time while I was working on Beebe's Island, I was pursued by two big lynx and I am here to tell you the grass did not grow under my feet until I reached a place of safety. On Beebe's Island, I worked at logging with oxen, felled great trees with the ax and labored part of the time in the steam saw mill operated by Little Brothers....
>
> In the summer of 1854 I broke prairie with oxen and a big breaking plow near Galva. In 1855, I returned to Utica [Illinois] and worked at logging for 13 years for a man named Calvin Tompkins. I had a big strong wagon to which was hitched seven yoke of oxen and I often hauled from two to three logs from 15 to 20 feet in length and from 4 1/2 to 5 feet in diameter at the butt end.
>
> Buckwheat cakes and cornbread were the staff of life then, but our suppers often consisted of mush and milk and occasionally biscuits on Sunday morning....
>
> Oh! How I would like to go back to the good old days of Fulton County, when there was no pride nor selfishness, when everybody was on an equal footing and when everybody was your friend and neighbor.
>
> I moved to Canton [where Mildred was born] about 17 years ago; have worked in the P. & O. shops for about 10 years; am a peaceable and law-abiding citizen and have tried to do my duty all through life.[2]

2. "Recollections of Presley Dennis. A Rambler's Notes. Some Things Seen and Heard in His Travels To and Fro in Fulton County," printed in the *Canton Daily Register* of May 7, 1909.

Unusual talent for mathematics apart, Williams family creativity is most tellingly represented by two of my mother's first cousins. Deirdre, the daughter of the Valparaiso mathematics professor and his rigidly puritanical wife, who headed the local chapter of The Women's Christian Temperance Union, was a secret (from her mother) flapper in the 1920s, taught elementary school, and wrote dozens of songs and musical plays. But she was too paranoid to see anything to publication since anyone she taught her songs to would – and in her view frequently had – copyright them in their own names. She claimed that she had written but not gotten credit for many hit songs.

The only song I remember her playing was the patriotic number she composed in her seventies and wanted to donate to the Republican Party. Since playing it for the society ladies who ran the party locally would have allowed them to steal it, she hit on the scheme of getting my mother to accompany her to Indianapolis, where the two of them would lurk in a hotel lobby waiting for Richard Nixon to appear, and then hobble up to him and present the song. Sensible Mildred quashed the idea. Here are the lyrics that accompanied a vigorous pounding of ten-finger piano chords:

> Why, a Republican, am I?
> Why, for democracy, I'd die?
> Why, on no other creed, rely?
> Why, a Republican, am I?
>
> CHORUS
>
> I am a Republican,
> In the great U.S.A.
> Champions of right! Purveyors of peace!
> Oh I'm so proud to say,
> "I am a Republican!
> I am a Republican!
> My party leads all the way!"

Old age sapped the tunefulness of her earlier songs and aggravated her paranoia. She believed her electrician's helper was casing her house on behalf of his father, whom she thought was none other than Saddam Hussein, in order to spy out where she hid her precious antiques. Fortunately, once she decided that she was under twenty-four-hour audio and visual surveillance by the corrupt local police, she stopped complaining about such nefarious activities because she would be overheard and accused of craziness.

My mother's other creative cousin, Dorotha, the daughter of a farmer brother of Deirdre's mathematician dad, painted rather well. Her later canvases were populated by gauzy angelic entities that she may have thought she was actually seeing. Her fantasies and out-of-body excursions were remarkable. They ranged from a conviction that the husband she divorced around 1950 had been a secret Nazi spy, to the tale of waking up at midnight and seeing the glowing, naked male torso of the Olympic diver Greg Louganis hovering at the door of her bedroom. Once she pulled her blanket up to her chin, the apparition disappeared. But soon an invisible dog jumped on her bed and struck her ankle with its beating tail. The next morning a chronic pain from an earlier ankle injury had miraculously disappeared.

My sister and I discussed from time to time whether I had inherited some of these Williams family qualities. We agreed that I had but disagreed about whether I also had inherited some of the family nuttiness. I said no; my sister said yes.

PART TWO

Ways Forward

W HEN RICHARD MAURICE TINKLER was mustered out of the British army after World War I, the prospect of humdrum village life did not appeal to him. So he answered a recruiting advertisement for the Shanghai police force. The story of his life put together by Robert Bickers in his remarkable biography *Empire Made Me: An Englishman Adrift in Shanghai*[1] fleshes out the double entendre of its title. The British Empire made Richard Tinkler in the sense that without it he would not have become the man he became: fluent in Chinese, absorbed in a self-image drawn from American hard-boiled detective fiction, and boastful of hobnobbing with White Russian countesses at Shanghai's baccarat tables.

Yet just as empire "made" him as a man with a career, it also compelled him, "made" him, do things. He brutalized the Chinese who crossed him so ferociously that he was dismissed from the police force. And when he went on to being a strong-arm guy handling labor problems for European factory owners in Shanghai, he ended up confronting a detachment of Japanese soldiers bent on taking control of an employer's property. They shot him dead. In the minds of some folks back in Britain, this made him the first British casualty of World War II.

The genius of Bickers' rendition of Tinkler's story is that it points up the connections between what brought him to China in the first place and what he did there as a servant of the British Empire. True, inasmuch as he always worked for Europeans and hated and demeaned the Chinese even while mastering their language, he seems like a Saidian Orientalist. But that does not define him as fully as the stories about his personal life and the letters he wrote to his family back home.

For myself, the likelihood that I would have thrown myself into the study of Arabic if policy-makers in Washington had not decided to jump-start American university programs focused on non-European societies in the 1950s is approximately zero. My upbringing in Rockford affords no hint of such an outcome. Thus, in a sense, American visions of Cold War "empire" made me the Middle East specialist that I became. But did they also make me do what I subsequently did with respect to Islam and the Middle East?

---

1. New York: Columbia University Press, 2003.

The Saidian formula offers useful analytical insights at the level of societal confrontation, but it fails at the individual level. Many Orientalists who served imperial purposes did so by choice, not axiomatically. To believe otherwise is to strip them of historical agency, just as it disserves historical reality by ignoring the innumerable Orientalists whose lives had nothing at all to do with Western imperialism.

My Grandfather's Library

I SHALL START MY ACCOUNT of those things that coalesced in my decision to study the Middle East with my grandfather's library because that was the topic I chose for the admission essay required by the two colleges I applied to, Harvard and Yale. (As a seventeen-year-old I was nothing if not supremely confident of my intellect.) Though my family expected me to go to law school, I think I always saw that as a back-up plan for something yet to materialize. Needless to say, the following account of the library is not the one I sent to the college admissions committees in 1957.

As already mentioned, the library began to arrive in 1949 as C. J. confronted retirement. The last materials arrived after his death in 1952. I was then twelve. The quantity of material involved was substantial. My father always quoted the number of 8000 books, which was certainly too high, unless one included the hundreds of booklets, pamphlets, and art show and auction catalogs. But there was a good case for including even the ephemera. C. J. prowled bookshops with an eye out for anything that appealed to his eccentric tastes. Since these included Nazism and Communism, and my father reported that C. J. did not believe in neutral or balanced accounts, he bought stacks of radical tracts and pamphlets. He also gobbled up seemingly every booklet produced by the free-thinking Haldeman-Julius publishing house. Indeed, extremist literature in general appealed to him – philo- and anti-Black, anti-Semitic, anti-Mormon, anti-Catholic – along with anything purporting to be serious scholarship about abnormal psychology, sex, women, crime, and race.

Books on these topics ended up in our basement because my mother was embarrassed by the subject matter, but she respected my father's determination that nothing should be discarded. Not surprisingly, the basement became my favorite place for prowling around. One room, about thirty feet long, contained a large billiard table my father bought cheap from someone in Rockford who wanted to turn his own basement into a chinchilla ranch. There were three bookcases in that room and a wall of cupboards filled with art magazines. One of the bookcases had three photo-illustrated books on European nudism that were a revelation for adolescent male eyes. There was also a large trunk containing a jumble of C. J.'s correspondence going back to around 1910.

The laundry room had one large bookcase and a tall cabinet crammed with pamphlets. There were even several shelves of books in the small adjoining closet devoted to storing mason jars and canned fruits and vegetables. Best was the furnace room, which had a venerable workbench from my grandmother's home in New Albany on one wall and about 300 shelf-feet of books lining two others. Here is where the hundreds of true crime books ended up, along with the books on women, race, and sex, and a lot of art books, not to mention my own paperback science fiction collection. There were also numerous trunks, suitcases, boxes, and satchels filled with correspondence, clipping files, magazines, art catalogues, sheet music, and more books. One small trunk, thought to be well-buried in the mess, held what my father's lawyer called the "dirty French books," which were mostly dreary books of "curiosa and erotica," except for an illustrated *Fanny Hill* and a tattered copy of *Letters of a French Schoolgirl*. Stenciling on the trunk showed that it was the very one that C. J. had used for lobby cards and publicity while on the road in advance of "The Birth of a Nation."

The books on the main floors of the house were generally organized by subject matter: art, music, religion, and biography on the ground floor, along with some sets with nice leather bindings that my mother kept for show in the living room (unknowingly including some with racy subject matter by the likes of Aretino and Boccaccio). Plays, poetry, novels, and translations of French fiction were in the upstairs hallway while history covered two walls of my bedroom. Portfolios of art prints and reproductions filled several drawers in the linen room I used as my study, and six large etching boxes started out in closets off my bedroom and ended up under my bed for easier access.

My early explorations of C. J.'s library were largely connected with sex. In a puritanical household that was never sullied by a copy of *Esquire* or *Playboy* or the sort of newsstand photography magazine that could be depended upon to contain some artfully posed nudes, a couple of thousand art books, plus a sizable collection of works on sex and abnormal psychology, amply repaid the efforts of the adolescent investigator. Books on drawing from the nude model or featuring artists like Felicien Rops or Egon Schiele were well worth the hunt. Havelock Ellis's multi-volume *Studies in the Psychology of Sex*, of which we had two sets, was endlessly fascinating – he didn't use so much Latin for the off-color parts the way Krafft-Ebing did – as were bound "artist's model" magazines devoted exclusively to airbrushed black-and-white photos of undressed young women. I learned few facts of life in covert conversations with my teen friends that I had not already read about, and memorized the Latin terms for, in our basement.

I don't wish to overstress this aspect of C. J.'s library, but it was my initial focus of attention, leaving whole sections that I essentially ignored for quite a few years: drama, crime, pre-World War II books about Adolf Hitler, proceedings of the Moscow purge trials, and fiction – we had no best-sellers – to name a few. It was not that these collections were not of interest, but they called for serious reading rather than leafing through. I was not an avid reader, except where science fiction was concerned. Nevertheless, I did take an interest in some history books, particularly ones with illustrations or in a reference format conducive to retention in memory.

Not long after I took up painting and woodcutting at the end of junior high school, I took it into my head to compile a card catalogue of the family art collection. This was fairly simple since it required only 400 or so cards and most of the items were either stored in the etching boxes and portfolios or tucked away in a closet in my parents' bedroom dedicated to the storage of paintings. But I kept adding to it as I discovered original etchings included as frontispieces of art books or enclosed in letters and greeting cards sent to C. J. I added the last card to the catalogue in 1987 when I uncovered a rather nice watercolor sketch of a nude by a Chicago artist named Salcia Bahnc while cleaning out the billiard room for the people who had bought our house. Though to this day I am uncertain about the signatures on some pieces, I identified several items my parents were unaware of, most memorably an etching by Henri Matisse contained in a book Matisse had autographed to C. J., and three drypoints by Max Beckmann. I was over seventy when I made my last discovery, an unsigned pencil drawing by the cubist Ossip Zadkine, whose name had been misspelled in the Russian dedication penned by some earlier owner.

There always seemed to be more to discover. Only six months before the house was emptied and sold, I looked for the umpteenth time at a peculiar mimeographed book with a taped-on binding hand-tinted in watercolor. It was by Richard B. Fuller and contained some text and drawings relating to housing, along with copies of a lot of letters from famous people saying how bright and innovative Mr. Fuller was. During this final perusal I thought the drawing style looked somewhat familiar. Could the B. in the author's name stand for Buckminster? It turned out that Richard Buckminster Fuller had lived in Chicago before he became famous and had produced this work at home as a sort of self-promotion. He apparently sent a copy to C. J., who responded by giving him his first newspaper write-up; and that, in turn, launched Fuller in the public eye. The book was a genuine rarity; I sold it for $2000 to Columbia University's Avery Library.

So this was the trajectory of my explorations: I began looking for naked women and ended up looking for rarities and items of value. In the process, I became intimately familiar with what must have been one of the most distinctive American private libraries of the period. My effort at producing an author, title, and subject catalogue of the books flagged after about 4000 cards. I never reached the basement. But then there was never the slightest prospect that anyone would ever use the catalogue. My father encouraged the effort, I believe, not because he wanted to find out whether we had a particular book or where it was located, but because it was a form of worship at the shrine of C. J.

C. J.'s collections went far beyond books. He had several hundred 78-rpm record albums, mostly classical. I listened to many and quickly developed a particular fondness for Stravinsky's "Rite of Spring" and Khatchaturian's "Violin Concerto." Along with canes, some of them gifts carved by Chicago artists, there were hundreds of photographs of art works and, from his earlier theatrical career, stage actors; boxes of newspaper and magazine clippings in small white Daily News envelopes, with penciled labels bearing words like "Hitler" or "Stalin" or "Transvestism" or "Freud;" masses of fliers and catalogues from art exhibits and auctions; and piles of correspondence.

As the years progressed, I looked through everything and read many of the letters C. J. had received. This huge archive was mine to do with as I wished, and I found it fascinating to make connections. Two examples will suffice: as C. J. the crime reporter might have put it, the stories of the murderess and the model/mistress.

"Satira" was the stage name of an exotic dancer from Ohio named Pat Schmidt. According to a *Time Magazine* article in 1947, "she had wiggled her way along the honky-tonk circuit from Chicago to Trinidad."[1] She lived on the same floor of the Majestic Hotel as C. J. and was a friend to him and my grandmother. The gist of her story as I heard it from my father was that she accepted a dancing engagement in Havana and went out one evening with a Cuban playboy. When he made unwanted advances and wouldn't take no for an answer, she shot him dead. The actual story, according to *Time*, was decidedly more tawdry, and the dead man was an American. Satira was tried, convicted, and sentenced to prison. The Chicago arts community contributed to her defense, but to no avail. During the trial and from the Cuban prison she wrote C. J. many letters, and he kept newspaper clippings of her case and copies of a number of "true crime" magazines featuring her story. Putting together the story from pieces scattered throughout the library, and then getting my father to share his (inaccurate) recollections of the incident, was a fascinating endeavor.

The story of the model/mistress, a subject C. J. focused on in his book *The Courtesan Olympia* (1930), arose when I opened an envelope and discovered inside several nude photographs. The accompanying letter was from a girl named Sophie, who wrote to say that she had returned to Indiana and

---

1. www.time.com/time/magazine/article/0,9171,793674,00.html

didn't want her mother to find the photos. She asked "Butch," her nickname for C. J., to support her claim that she had worked for him as a secretary. Elsewhere in the art collection I had already found a rolled up painting that a woman by the name of Sophie had sent to help him recuperate during some hospitalization and remind him to think about her. Delving deeper I eventually found a number of letters sent by Sophie from Los Angeles telling of her impending marriage and begging C. J. to acquire and mail to her (postpaid envelopes included) certain photographs taken in someone's studio. She cautioned C. J. to communicate with her only at her business address and not send anything to her home.

As evidence accumulated over a period of years, I went from being convinced that C. J. had a young mistress, possibly in her early twenties when he was over sixty, to believing that Sophie was simply a young woman who had modeled nude while studying art in Chicago, become a friend of C. J., and trusted him to help clean up the evidence of her bohemian youth when it came time to marry. Since I was uncertain as to what the real story was, I gathered the temerity to speak to my father sometime during my college years.

"Daddy, did Granddaddy have a mistress?"

"Well, I guess you're old enough to know. Yes, he did."

"And was her name Sophie?"

"No. Her name was Macena Barton. Who's Sophie?"

So I still don't know the truth of the matter and I can see no benefit in tracking down an octogenarian matron in Los Angeles, if Sophie is still alive, and asking her to set the record straight. As for Macena Barton, she was a prominent Chicago painter. An MA thesis was eventually written about their two-decade relationship.[2]

Like so much of what I immersed myself in during my years exploring C. J.'s library, the stories of Satira and Sophie ultimately had no point or significance. Indeed, I came eventually to think – though I do not still think – that C. J.'s entire life and career, and all of his collections, were simply dustbins full of rubbish. But how I loved poring over and burrowing into his things! Nothing was predigested; nothing was in order; nothing was "normal." And no one oversaw what I was doing, although my father was happy to hear of any new discovery, and my mother was eager to find out whether I had found something of monetary value. I could put things together and speculate in any way I wished ... then prospect for more evidence.

I could be a historian.

---

2. Jean Campbell Macheca, "A Critical Relationship : Macena Barton and C. J. Bulliet in the 1930's," MA thesis, School of the Art Institute of Chicago, 2001.

A Harvard Education

"IF MAX WEBER HAD LIVED long enough to complete his book on Islam, this course would not be necessary." Thus spoke the noted sociologist of religion Robert N. Bellah in 1959 in the first meeting of the first course I took on Islam. It was the most theoretically elevated remark I remember hearing during my eight years studying the Middle East at Harvard.

I didn't know who Max Weber was and would not find out what his views on Islam were until 1978 when I read Bryan Turner's scathing denunciation of them in *Weber and Islam*, and I don't remember any of Bellah's actual teachings. My greater concern in that first session was his announcement that the readings for the course would include the French priest Louis Gardet's *La cité musulmane*. "Is there anyone here who does not read French?" I don't recall seeing any hands raised. Mine certainly wasn't even though my two years of French at Rockford's West High School had barely gotten me past "la plume de ma tante."

Yet there is a certain stripe of Harvard man who will never admit to not knowing something, and that was the stripe I aspired to in that long ago September. My stock-in-trade at West High had been a show-offy store of what is now known as trivia. I doted on a little book from C. J.'s library titled *A Dictionary of Dates*, published, in the edition we had, in the year of my birth, 1940. I didn't learn anything specific from it, but it showed me how much amazingly obscure stuff there was to discover about the past.

How did I happen into Professor Bellah's classroom? A vague recollection from the spring of my freshman year is that someone offering guidance to freshmen on choosing a major mentioned that scarcely anyone in the country knew Arabic. (Except Arabs, of course, but who cared about them?) Law school being my presumed career objective, history seemed like a good major, and medieval history offered endless opportunities to expand my store of arcane knowledge. After that talk, however, I decided to make that medieval *Arab* history. I knew nothing about Arabs, Islam, or the Middle East – I remember being surprised to learn that Lebanon was the name of a country – and I had no personal connections with the region beyond Great-Aunt Grace once winning a Fulbright to Iran to study elementary education and on her return giving my parents a lovely mosaic box as a souvenir. But when fall came, I confidently signed up for Bellah's full-year course on "Islamic Institutions" and for "Social Sciences 127: The Middle East," a full-year introductory course taught by a dog-and-pony show of half a dozen faculty. I would eventually inherit teaching the latter course after joining the faculty in 1967.

From then until my departure from Harvard as an Assistant Professor in the summer of 1973, I was increasingly a denizen of the Middle East Area Studies program shaped by Professor H. A. R. Gibb, who became the Director of the Center for Middle East Studies (CMES) in 1957. First an undergraduate, then a doctoral student, and finally junior faculty, I immersed myself totally in studying the Middle East, though I also audited a lot of art history courses. Yet in terms of historical thinking, I learned more from Oscar Handlin (American social history) and Robert Lopez (Italian cities in the Renaissance), who was visiting from Yale, than I did from any Middle East course.

While my choice of a field of study fully satisfied my yen to learn what no one else knew, it struck me even at the time that Harvard's course offerings were mediocre. Eventually I discovered that mediocrity was the norm in American Middle East studies, partly because the half dozen or so universities that had been encouraged by the US government and the Ford Foundation to create such programs in the mid-1950s were drawing on too small a pool of talent to hire a consistently first-rate staff, and partly because the Area Studies vision they were attempting to fulfill had, and still has, intrinsic flaws.

Apart from Bellah, few Middle East faculty members of that era commanded intellectual respect in the Harvard faculty universe. Gibb was the principal exception. Hired away from Oxford with the supreme, extra-departmental rank of University Professor, Sir Hamilton – nobody I knew ever called him that – was the program's czar despite his red-faced shyness and understated manner. I never encountered the side of Gibb that led Richard N. Frye, a young Iran specialist who had been instrumental in bringing him to Harvard, to liken him to Hitler and Stalin. An even younger faculty member in the Government Department, Nadav Safran, told me that he had had a permanent falling out with Gibb over what book he should write. This effectively got him barred from CMES affairs until well after a stroke forced Gibb into retirement in 1966.

Building on his University Professor rank, Gibb created a Standing Committee on History and Middle East Studies with himself as chair. This committee enabled him to admit doctoral candidates, direct their studies, and approve their dissertations without going through any History Department procedures. The Department of History did not maintain files on doctoral students in the Middle East field and rarely recognized their existence. After Gibb's retirement, this proved a problem since neither the Department of History nor the Department of Near Eastern Languages and Civilizations took responsibility for the committee's affairs, and Gibb had no successor of comparable rank and fame. In later years, as junior faculty, I got the committee to vote its own dissolution, but we were informed that no matter how dysfunctional it became, a standing committee could only be dissolved by a vote of the entire Harvard faculty. So doctoral students of Middle East history were doomed to second-class status on campus.

Gibb had a masterful command of classical Arabic. Students normally took his course in Advanced Arabic twice and topped it off with his poetry seminar. However, he was not really a historian. I reached this conclusion by twice sitting through his lectures on Islamic history, but I later read the same appraisal in the memoir of Bernard Lewis, a much earlier Gibb student. Gibb was, rather, an Orientalist, and the unspoken goal of his standing committee was to produce Orientalists.

But this was decidedly not the goal of the CMES Area Studies MA program. When I began Intensive Elementary Arabic in my junior year, I was the only undergraduate in a class designed for master's degree students. The instructor, Professor George Makdisi, tried to bar me from the class because Arabic was "too difficult" for undergraduates, but the course catalog designation allowed me to enroll without the instructor's permission. The truth of the matter was that unlike Harvard College, which then admitted the cream of the crop from elite prep schools, along with a sprinkling of public high school graduates, the Middle East studies master's program attracted a disparate and decidedly non-elite group of students who had an interest in becoming "Middle East specialists" for government agencies, NGOs, businesses, and, a bit later, the military. They were expected to take no more than two years of Arabic – though four was the absolute minimum for a prospective Orientalist – as well as a potpourri of courses that would impart basic information about the history, politics, ethnography, religion, and economics of the Middle East. Two years were felt to be enough to make Middle East specialists out of studious (and not so studious) American boys and girls with a BA from anywhere and no prior knowledge of the area. This at a university that did not then believe that a graduate student could become a true specialist on the history, politics, or economics of, say, France or Germany in less then five years.

Of the several dozen graduate students who took Intensive Elementary Arabic when I did, only one, Jere Bacharach, proceeded on to a PhD and a professorial career. The others, having learned next to nothing about the European tradition of Orientalism that Gibb represented, went directly to work with their smattering of language and area knowledge. Some of them were quite successful; but what they imbibed at Harvard was not classical Orientalism. It was the hot new idea of modernization.

As Edward Said would point out in *Orientalism* in 1978, British, French, Spanish, German, Dutch, and Russian scholars had diligently pursued the study of Islam in relation to their governments' colonial interests from the eighteenth century onward. Said's blistering diatribe against the British and French versions of Oriental studies would eventually become a turning point in the field of Middle East Studies and a landmark work in the rise of post-modernism, post-colonialism, and cultural studies. But that was far in the future. For me as a first-year Arabic student, Edward Said, the only non-faculty Arab I even slightly knew of at Harvard, was simply the person I turned to one evening in the Adams House dining hall to find out how to curse in Arabic. His response was informative (*il'an abuk*) but did not encourage further contact; and fortunately, by the time we became colleagues on the Columbia faculty, he had long forgotten my naïve inquiry.

The only Muslims the United States ever held colonial sway over were the so-called Moros of the southern Philippines, the military suppression of whose yearnings for independence we inherited from Spain after the Spanish-American War. So the branch of Orientalism devoted to Islam and the Middle East was barely visible in American academia prior to World War II. Edward Said's later evisceration of Orientalism being all-inclusive, he assumed that Middle East area studies, a distinctly American post-war enterprise, was fully the creation of European Orientalists who came to the United States to escape Nazism in the 1930s, and of others who were recruited from abroad in the 1950s to staff the fledgling programs at Harvard and elsewhere. H. A. R. Gibb at Harvard, Gustave E. von Grunebaum at UCLA, Joseph Schacht at Columbia, and later Bernard Lewis at Princeton headed a cast of dozens. Said mistakenly believed that their students were all apprentice Orientalists.

In fact, the students in the Middle East MA programs, that is to say, almost everyone studying the Middle East in America in the 1960s, learned little or nothing about the European Orientalist tradition. The real architects of American Middle East Studies were homegrown social scientists who were in thrall to the idea that the entire world was on the path to modernity and that it was vital, particularly in the context of the Cold War, that the new countries born of decolonization should follow the Free World version and not the Communist version of that path.

Robert Bellah rightly stressed the theoretical vision of Max Weber, who loomed in American Cold War thinking as the anti-Marx because, to over-simplify, his *Protestant Ethic and the Spirit of Capitalism* saw capitalism arising from religious belief, the "superstructure," rather than from Marx's class struggle and mundane economic activity, the "infrastructure." As the modernization process moved forward ineluctably, those social scientists who sought to chart its direction wrote books that had much greater impact on MA students, myself included, than anything penned by Gibb or von Grunebaum, whose writings were not widely assigned. The introductions and acknowledgements of these social science books reveal how closely this group interacted.

Within the group, a few were educated before the war – J. C. Hurewitz (Columbia, b. 1914), Daniel Lerner (MIT, b. 1917) – but most of them right after, including Dankwart Rustow (Columbia, b. 1924), Manfred Halpern (Princeton, b. 1925), Nadav Safran (Harvard, b. 1925), William Polk (Chicago, b. 1929), and Malcolm Kerr (UCLA, b. 1931). It would be a stretch to call any of them Orientalists in either the traditional European sense, or in the Saidian sense. For them, the Middle East was not peopled, as Said would have it, by indolent, craven, lubricious, backward "orientals" deserving only domination by their imperial masters, but rather by "traditionals," whose day was past, and a few pioneer architects of a modern, democratic, free enterprise-oriented future. These heroic figures were variously referred to as "change agents" and "men on the move" (Lerner) or "the new middle class" (Halpern). They saw anti-imperialist America's role as illuminating the path forward, granting benevolent assistance, and blunting the perverse appeal of communism. But they had little need for classical Islamic studies as expounded by older immigrant Orientalists like Gibb (b. 1895), Schacht (b. 1902), and von Grunebaum (b. 1909).

A. J. Meyer, the professor who taught Middle East economics at Harvard, exemplified the new social science outlook when he brought to class the paternalistic Lebanese entrepreneur Emile Bustani, a founding partner of the dynamic engineering and construction firm CAT, so we could hear first-hand from someone who was building the modern Middle East. This was an uncommon opportunity, however. The impact of the modernization vision on Middle East studies at the classroom level was more often conveyed indirectly in perfunctory lectures that resembled briefings one might give to government or business trainees than it was directly through magisterial professorial pontifications of the type that characterized Harvard education at that time. In a word, the classes were dull. One lecturer, Joseph Upton, then still unidentified as a participant in the CIA coup in Iran, simply read aloud the manuscript of his book *The History of Modern Iran: An Interpretation.*

Modernization theory revealed itself as much in what was not spoken of in class as in what was. Western-trained military officers being identified by the theorists as science-minded agents of modernization, there was little or no criticism of military rule ... except when misguided revolutionary officers leaned toward the Soviet Union. The oil industry was also sacrosanct, but rarely discussed. European colonialism was bad and obsolete, but everything the United States undertook in the region was done for the most benevolent of reasons. Prior to the 1967 war, Israel was virtually a taboo topic. And most fatefully, current streams of Islamic religious thought were deemed of zero interest since the secular modernization process would inevitably retire religion from the public arena and relegate it to the humble sphere of private observance.

I listened intently because I was determined to learn everything possible – all that trivia – about the Middle East. But medieval history was my real interest, and in courses on contemporary topics, medieval Islam was briefly and simplistically summarized as the "tradition" part of "tradition and change." All MA students would acquire some knowledge of Islam as necessary background to understand "tradition," but detailed discussion of Islam essentially stopped in 1839 when the Tanzimat reforms began in the Ottoman Empire. That was the beginning of modernization – real history – and Bernard Lewis' *The Emergence of Modern Turkey*, published in 1961, was deemed the most exciting history book we were asked to read.

A trio of professors shared the course on Ottoman history: William L. Langer, an age-mate of Gibb, and Robert Lee Wolff, both pillars of the wartime Office of Strategic Services and polished lecturers, and thirdly, Stanford Shaw, the only one who knew Turkish. According to Langer, Mahomet II conquered Constantinople in 1453. According to Wolff, the conqueror was named Muhammad II. According to Shaw, he was Mehmet II. It grieved Shaw, who was then in his thirties, that he was not a member of the History Department. But such was the reputation of Middle East Studies: second rate. His professorship was in Near Eastern Languages and Civilizations, a department that did not enjoy a stellar reputation.

A. J. Meyer, who had no PhD, taught regional economics but did not have a voting membership in the Economics Department. His role as one of the two associate directors Gibb recruited for the CMES was to maintain the Center's corporate fund-raising and graduate placement links with the oil industry. In later years he boasted about how many graduates he had placed. The other associate director, Derwood Lockard, taught anthropology, likewise without a PhD, but did not have a voting membership in that department. He had left the CIA, to which he had shifted after wartime intelligence service, and volunteered to administer the Center for a dollar a year

– that, of course, was not what he ended up being paid – and he remained the contact person for MA students who were looking for careers in government and the intelligence community.

Gibb himself had been knighted for some undisclosed role he played in Britain's wartime intelligence service. So the vision of the fledgling field of Middle East Studies that gave structure to the Center's program in the 1960s was very much a product of World War II, and of a strong conviction that academic talent would be needed to train and inform the people who would devise and implement policies designed to help the Middle East move forward into the modern world and resist global communism.

As I have already said, Middle East Studies attracted and was designed for graduate students who would not have been admitted to Harvard's doctoral programs, much less to Harvard College. I initially had little personal contact with those students outside of Arabic class. I took the same lecture courses, but they were older, and I had my own life in the college. Outside the classroom, that life had nothing to do with the Middle East. I studied, I read twentieth-century fiction, I conversed avidly with friends, and I played endless hours of pool, my only major social commitment. For two years I took art classes in my residential house and pondered the notion of becoming an artist.

The only other undergraduates I knew of studying the Middle East were part of a junior-year history tutorial group taught by William Polk. They were John Damis, who became a professor of political science and a Middle East area specialist at the University of Oregon; Bill Mares, who co-authored an Arabian travel narrative with Polk and later commented on all manner of subjects for Vermont Public Radio; and Frances Fitzgerald, who in 1972 won a Pulitzer Prize for her book *Fire in the Lake: The Vietnamese and the Americans in Vietnam*. None of them took Arabic with me. Another classmate, David Mack, rose high in the Foreign Service as a specialist on the Middle East. He took the plunge into studying the area in graduate school and years later gave an internet interview about learning Arabic at the CMES:

> It was a regional studies program where you had the language but you also had a full set of economics, history, politics and culture, etc. in the area. There was a Middle East center at Harvard which was pretty good. Later on, I found that they did a terrible job of teaching languages. They used a very old fashioned approach. In fact, we started out Arabic using a French grammar [Charles Pellat's *L'Arabe moderne* in George Makdisi's mimeographed English translation] because the head of the Arabic program [Makdisi] had his doctorate from the Sorbonne and felt that it was the only place where they really knew how to teach Arabic. The [State

Department's] Foreign Service Institute would not believe that anybody would make a native speaker of English study Arabic via a French grammar. But that's the way he did it, and it was a very stilted kind of Arabic at that.[1]

One thing that was missing from both my undergraduate and graduate experiences was contact with students from the Middle East. To be sure, Arabs taught discussion sections in language courses. (My first-year section instructor, Hanna Mikhail, was a gentle doctoral student and a Palestinian patriot who was later killed in the Lebanese civil war.) For a real-world Middle East experience, students could eat Lebanese food at the Nile Restaurant in Boston, or go to the Museum of Fine Arts to see antiquities. But otherwise the Arab Middle East was very far away and our learning was taking place in a vacuum.

Iran was even farther, despite being an object of American imperial interest in the anti-Mossadegh coup of 1953. When I began taking Persian as a first-year graduate student, there were two students enrolled; the next year I was the only one. My first teacher, Heshmat Moayyad, was a fine literary scholar, but having just arrived from teaching in Naples, his English was less than adequate. He quickly moved on to Chicago. My second teacher, Iraj Afshar, another fine scholar then visiting Harvard to assess the library's Persian holdings, taught only in French. I finally got one semester of excellent instruction from a fellow graduate student, Roy Mottahedeh, whose Persian name belied his upbringing in New York City.

Roy became a good friend and sometime rival. Another graduate student, Ira Lapidus, who had finished his BA three years before me, was assigned by Gibb to direct my senior thesis on the life of Muhammad. When I finished, Ira allowed that someone would probably have to go to the trouble of refuting it someday. Though the three of us became known as Gibb's last significant students of medieval Islam, only Ira worked closely with Gibb before his stroke. I wrote my dissertation under the direction of George Makdisi, with whom I did not get along terribly well. Roy wrote his under Richard Frye.

As was the prevailing practice at the time, I planned to spend a year abroad in the Middle East to do research for my thesis and then write it up in the year following. To fund this I received a government Fulbright-Hayes Fellowship that allowed me to visit fifteen different countries. So in the autumn of 1965, my wife and I boarded a plane for Istanbul. Aside from a brief visit to Canada, I had never been outside the United States nor been exposed to a non-English speaking environment.

1. www.adst.org/OH%20TOCs/Mack,%20David%20L.toc.pdf

Art and Romance

THE ALERT READER will have noted that I acquired a wife before I set off on my maiden trip to the Middle East. How this happened involves an aspect of my life that I have thus far only adverted to, namely, painting and drawing.

One bright, balmy day in the summer of 1955, when I was fourteen years old, my sister arranged a ceramic bust by Alexander Archipenko and a plant in a bronze vase on a table on our front porch. She then produced paints, brushes, and a piece of canvas-board and began to paint a still life. It seemed she had received instruction in drawing and painting in the studio component of her freshman art history course at Wellesley.

Since I always took guidance from my older sister, I asked for my own piece of canvas-board and began to paint alongside her. Her picture did not turn out well, and that was the last time I saw her paint until she took brush in hand again in her retirement years. My own picture, on the other hand, looked pretty good, at least to my eye. So for the rest of the summer I was in a fever to produce art works.

This was surprising because my worst grades in elementary school had always been in art and penmanship. I simply did not have the disciplined hand control of a skilled draftsman. I did have enthusiasm, however, and, through C. J.'s library, familiarity with every landmark and byway in the history of modern art. I retrieved grandmother Katherine's paint box from the basement and found that some of the paint tubes were still soft. I also found a set of woodworker's chisels and fished some hardwood scraps out of the woodbin. Add a tube of printing ink and a roller, and my first woodcut soon followed my first painting.

Making images became such an absorbing activity that I imagined becoming an artist. Many years of hit or miss effort, however, taught me that there was a deep gulf between the way I made images and the way an artist does. Time and again I found that sitting before a blank canvas or drawing pad was a recipe for nothing good to happen ... or nothing at all. Trying to draw or paint whatever I was looking at commonly produced dismal results. On the other hand, when I was absorbed in doing something else, like listening to a lecture or a discussion, the idle marks I made on the paper in front of me often turned into arresting images. In other words, my most inventive drawings emerged when my hand and eyes were toying around but my mind was deeply preoccupied with something else.

In high school and college this worked best with woodcuts. Designs I produced haphazardly with pencil or pen turned into interesting artworks once I traced them onto a piece of wood, carved around the tracing, and printed them out. German Expressionism afforded me a stylistic model. Courtship provided a purpose.

The summer after my first year in college, I was enlisted as the escort for a friend's Pomona College roommate who would be visiting Rockford for a week on her way from California to Europe. As soon as I set eyes on Lucianne Cherry, I was smitten. I spent as much time with her as was feasible during her visit and was devastated when she left. Fortunately, her glasses turned up in my car so I had an excuse to enclose a note when I sent them back to her. Our correspondence (I've never had the guts to reread the letters I wrote) would continue for two years before we finally got together during a summer I spent at Berkeley ostensibly learning German and dabbling in art. We were married shortly after I graduated from college the following June.

Since my relations with girls had been a model of ineptitude throughout high school, I feared that every letter I sent to Lucy would be the one she didn't respond to. But I reckoned that she would at least have to acknowledge any missive that contained a work of art. So in lieu of dating in college, I produced a woodcut every couple of months to accompany my latest letter to Lucy. This made my emotional biography similar to Jack's and C. J.'s. We didn't date in college, but right after graduation married sweethearts from years before.

Aside from woodcuts, my best high school paintings ranged from a portrait of my friend Karl to a fantasy derived from Lewis Carroll's "Jabberwocky."

But now, back to my journey into Orientalism.

Karl, 1960

College room, 1961

Woodcut, 1957

Woodcut, 1962

Going There

TWO MORE INNOCENT WAYFARERS would be difficult to imagine than Lucy and I traveling to the Middle East in 1965–66. We spent many weeks in Turkey, Iran, and Egypt, the latter only because a growing stomachache on a train from Luxor to Cairo climaxed with an emergency appendectomy that kept me hospitalized for a while. Visits to Lebanon, Syria, Jordan, Jordanian-occupied Jerusalem, Iraq, Afghanistan, Uzbekistan, Turkmenistan, and Azerbaijan were briefer. The specter of war and terrorism being unimagined at that time, Americans could travel pretty much everywhere without difficulty or danger. At times our routes intersected those of the derisively named third-class youth travelers, meaning twenty-somethings heading east for the Afghan and Nepalese hashish. In Iran, we also connected with American missionaries, who gave us lodging in Tehran and contacts in Nishapur, where we rented a room from a high school English teacher and hung out with Peace Corps volunteers.

My ostensible purpose in these wanderings was to search for manuscripts pertaining to my projected doctoral thesis on Nishapur. I was poorly prepared for this task, so, with a couple of exceptions, my visits to libraries were frustrating and fruitless. I did luck out in Iran, however, when I acquired a source that would eventually prove of great value, to wit, a set of aerial photographs of Nishapur, including the ruins of the medieval city, taken in 1956. An American civilian cartographer serving with a US Army military assistance mission heard the senior American officer curtly dismiss my request for help and offered to introduce me to the commander of the geographical department of the Iranian army. Four hours later I had the precious box of photographs in my hands.

By their very nature, first visits to foreign lands create strong impressions, but the visitor is too inexperienced to appreciate which impressions will mean something and which will prove mistaken, ephemeral, or silly ("Look at that! Contrast old and new!"). My memory now has so thoroughly edited the experiences of those months, turning some into favorite stories and forgetting or misremembering others, that an effort to recall my candid observations on first exposure would be self-serving and anachronistic. Nor do the letters I wrote home to my parents contain much more than updates on itineraries and pleas for money.

Nevertheless, here are some of my more vivid recollections:

- Eating our first meal in an Istanbul restaurant. My slight knowledge of Turkish suddenly vanishing, I didn't realize we had ordered sheep's head until Lucy pointed to the spherical things on my plate, one of which I had already eaten. I boldly ate the other eyeball.

- Designing a toilet seat that would fit the bathroom space in the apartment we shared with a fellow graduate student and his wife. Dolores was well into her first pregnancy and quailed at using a squat toilet. My rapidly improving Turkish proved up to the task of telling the carpenter down the street what we needed and showing him my drawing. The delivery of the foreigners' toilet seat was an occasion of public amusement in our working class Aksaray neighborhood.

- Seeing in Ankara my first ballet, a visiting troupe from Russia. Former president Ismet İnönü was in the audience.

- Arriving at the railway station in Kayseri and discovering horse carriages instead of taxis waiting for customers to detrain.

- Being driven without crossing any border from Amman, Jordan, to Jericho and Jerusalem by a fellow Arabic student from years past.

- Going to a casino-nightclub with Jewish hosts in Beirut; spending a bleak Christmas in Damascus; celebrating the New Year with hamburgers at the YMCA in Baghdad.

- Hating Iran's rigid class structure, despite the fact that as a foreigner I was given preferential treatment.

- Playing on the Peace Corps basketball team in a game against Nishapur's all-stars. "Don't touch the ball," our captain told me, having seen me warm up without managing to hit even the rim of the basket. "Stay behind the center line and throw your shoulder into whoever brings the ball downcourt. Iranians will always take the shot rather pass the ball." He proved right. I became a hero.

- Becoming aware that two men in suits – I assume SAVAK secret police – were watching me trying to deter local treasure hunters with pickaxes from destroying a medieval pottery kiln in Nishapur's ruins. The men, who had one of the handful of cars that existed in Nishapur, apparently concluded I was harmless, if not idiotic.

- Seeing a weeping shepherd beat a sick or injured sheep to try to keep it moving with the animals he was driving to market in Nishapur.

- Watching Lucy sit in our little room and work on learning the Sanskrit alphabet and composition rules, a first sign that her passion for Sanskrit grammar, conceived in a post-graduate course at Berkeley, would ripen into work on a PhD and a fascination with India. She despised having pebbles thrown at her when she walked to the public bath without a head-scarf. She would never return to the Middle East.

- Waiting days in a border village for the broken-down International Harvester bus that carried the mail from Afghanistan to Iran. The rugged trip back on the unpaved and unmarked desert track took us, a few Afghans, and an unsavory clutch of third-class youth travelers to the wonderful city of Herat, which seemed to belong to an earlier century.

- Arriving at the Intourist hotel in Tashkent after flying from Kabul and reveling in our return to the modern world. We gleefully rode up and down the escalator in the GUM department store.

- Taking a boat on the Caspian Sea from Baku, Azerbaijan back to Iran. We didn't speak to the American officials on the boat, who carried their own canned foods with them.

- Meeting a high school girlfriend married to an Egyptian who told us how to make substitutes for American products like breakfast cereal. As if we hadn't painfully adjusted to living on the local economy.

When I took my second long trip to the region in 1971–72, I kept a journal for the only time in my life. This trip took me back to Turkey, Iran, Lebanon, and Syria and, for the first time, across North Africa. My two goals were to collect information on the history of camel utilization and on the possibility of a pre-Islamic spread of Buddhism into Iran. I achieved a good deal relating to the former project, though huddling in the desert wind with an army friend to see whether a Zippo could ignite camel dung was not a high point. As for Buddhism, what had I expected? A village out in the desert where no one had previously noticed a centuries-old statue of the Buddha? My army friend got leave time and an army vehicle, and we ventured along desert tracks into several villages that I suspected had forgotten Buddhist pasts. But nary a trace remained.

The journal of my four increasingly lonely months abroad serves an autobiographical purpose apart from its particular observations about camels and Buddhists. It reflects an apprentice Orientalist's mindset at a time when Edward Said's eviscerating attack on Orientalism had not yet been conceived. I was still for the most part a lapsed Methodist from Rockford, albeit one who had lucked into a teaching position at Harvard, and my journal entries can thus be read for what they do or do not reveal about the Saidian interpretation of Orientalism at a pre-Saidian moment.

Said would eventually propose, of course, that beneath the minutiae of personal experiences there lies an invisible current that for generations propelled and guided people who studied the Orient. This current embodied the will to domination manifested by Western imperialism over at least three centuries. Western portrayers of the Orient, he would maintain, relentlessly characterized the people of the region as passive, perverse, exotic, backward, and cruel. Furthermore, they based their judgments on subjective, fragmentary, and misinterpreted readings and experiences. They invented the Orient in this way because they had unknowingly absorbed, from every aspect of their upbringing and education, a mindset predicated upon, and devoted to maintaining, the dominance of West over East. Some of Said's followers have gone so far as to say that the entire notion of Western civilization arose from a denigration of Muslims.

Since my 1971–72 journal precedes Said's revelations, whatever I wrote represents who I was then and who I was becoming. The selections from it that follow include my personal interactions with the people I encountered but leave out those entries that are of strictly scholarly concern, such as the discoveries I made about the history of harnessing and camel saddle design. To be sure, a case can be made that my very choice of research interests reflects an Orientalist interest in exotica rather than more important matters. But since I subsequently pursued similarly idiosyncratic research on European and American history, primarily in my books *Hunters, Herders, and Hamburgers: The Past and Future of Human-Animal Relationships* (2005) and *The Wheel: Inventions and Reinventions* (2016), I strongly contest the notion that an imaginative and malign creation of "the Oriental other" was a determining factor in my research.

The selections that I have chosen deal with places I was visiting for the first time, first eastern Turkey and northwest Iran, then Tunisia, Morocco, and Algeria. I have made no changes in my original text.

ॐ

September 24 – Sivas, Turkey
It took twenty-six hours for the Turkish version of the Orient Express to creep from Istanbul to Sivas. After twenty-two hours I was suddenly and completely overcome with loneliness. For what cogent reason am I separating myself from my wife and my home for five months? I don't

know. I have no wanderlust. I feel a professional imperative to travel in "my area," but many are the orientalists who never left their libraries or, if they did, did not so much travel as live in a foreign land for a period of years. Only in recent years has the "study trip" become obligatory for young American scholars, an effect, no doubt, of the immense amount of money released into the academic world in the period just past. But I suffered through a "study trip" once. Why am I doing it again?

It is striking how seldom any mention of loneliness finds its way into published travel accounts. Hindsight, of course, can be expected to edit it out, but even daily journals don't mention it. To be sure, it is without scholarly interest, and mention of it violates the convention that a travel narrative is about the travel and not the traveler. Yet it must strike most travelers at least in the early part of a long journey, that is, if they are truly traveling alone. Whether it finds you in a train compartment facing foreign faces for whom your presence is a burden and an embarrassment, or whether it comes during one of the long interstices between the order and the fulfillment of the order in a nearly empty hotel dining room, it takes hold of you completely and forces into your mind against your will images of loved faces, memories of familiar touch. The sudden thought that you will never return comes and cannot be dispelled. And then the storm is past. The memories have been made to return to their cages where you cautiously survey them once again just to make sure they have been tamed. You can only wonder when they will escape again.

September 28 – Tabriz, Iran

It is another long creep from Sivas to Erzurum.... In the railroad station sat a sweet-looking young German traveler looking like a fallen angel with his enormous halo of golden hair and surrounding throng of gawking Turks. After his departure on a train to Samsun where he hoped to retrieve a broken-down VW bus originally intended to bear him to India, I acquired a goodly portion of his audience although my pedestrian appearance and ability to answer the simple questions they had to ask soon dispersed most of it. Left with me were a high school student and an elementary school teacher named Ehsan. For the next twenty-six hours I was never without Ehsan's company and I shall never be without his memory.

Traveling alone by available means robs you of more than your health, comfort, and peace of mind. You are confined by lack of mobility. Obscure villages, refreshing stops by mountain streams, removing oneself from the beaten track, these are pleasures reserved to the automobile traveler. But to compensate there are the special experiences to be gained from knowing those who beat the beaten track. For nineteen hours as the train rattled along the broad valleys that greatly facilitate penetration of the mountains of eastern Turkey, I talked to Ehsan and other passengers who for brief times joined our compartment to share through the countless tunnels our allotted portion of coal gas and smoke. There was a stout farmer from Kars who had labored for five years in a German factory and managed to pick up a smattering of English. There was a group of elementary and secondary schoolteachers eager to learn about American educational practices, especially with respect to salaries. And there was Ehsan.

Ehsan was a farmer's son from near Konya and had at his blunt, thick fingertips the exact number of farmer's sons schoolteachers in Turkey. Aside from his hands, he looked like most young Turkish men from provincial cities: cheap-looking trousers and jacket, white shirt, necktie reaching the fourth button of his shirt, fancy-looking square-toed shoes poorly adapted to the variety of rough and unpleasant walking surfaces favored by Turkey's departments of roads, water, and electricity but helpful toward understanding Turkey's fantastic proliferation of shoeshine men, and, most of all, the slightly tense, conscientious facial expression that seems to broadcast individual desire to succeed in an increasingly Westernized society and at the same time a recognition that Western-style success is beyond the reach both of individual and society. He was traveling to Erzurum to sit for a four-day examination in science. I asked him if he was prepared, and he said that farm work had prevented his studying but that the minimum mark needed to pass was low enough to relieve him of any anxiety over the exam. He took concerned interest in my welfare, leaping from the train at various stops to buy bread, grapes, cheese, or melon and carefully scrubbing off my seat with an old newspaper to prevent me soiling my filthy clothes.

We talked about many things. He had great tolerance of my poor Turkish. Although he clearly knew the difference between a PhD and an MD, he asked me as a doctor and an American to prescribe for his chronic cough. When we reached Erzurum, he accompanied me through the surprisingly modern museum and into the Twin Minaret Madrasa and Yakutiya Madrasa, beautiful remnants of Seljuk rule in eastern Turkey and the following period of Mongol suzerainty. Although he knew I was a specialist on the history of the period, he never asked a single question nor displayed the slightest interest in his country's past. The past for young Turks is the past, nothing more. In the midst of expressing concern for my insufficient appetite he saw my exhausted body off on a bus to Dogubayezit on the Iranian border.

For six hours by bus and then by minibus, for which read fifteen men in a Ford panel truck, I could barely summon up the energy to view the landscape ... The Sarihan hotel, as good a flophouse as the little town [Dogubayezit] possesses, slept that night at least eight non-Turks, about half its capacity. I slept in a room with three Turks who rolled out of bed at 4:00 AM to hawk and spit and get the day underway before the sun rose. Perforce I rose too.

During the three-hour wait for a minibus to take us the last 45 kilometers to the border I met some of my fellow passengers. Robert was from California and had lots of blond hair on head and face, a shiny countenance, and a year to wander about before his return air ticket expired. Salik was also a Californian. A musician turned Sufi, he was on his way to Pakistan to sit at the feet of the Sufi master of his Sufi master. He regretted that he would have to return to the US in five months when his girlfriend had his baby. His ingratiating and slightly childish manner seemed to win every Turkish heart. They kept saying that he was a "beautiful child." There was also an Uzbek returning to his home in Kabul from visiting friends in Germany, but in particular there was Memduh.

I'm sure that Memduh was a dealer in some kind of goods usually subject to restrictions of international law. He was from Van, well but not expensively dressed, thirty-six years old. This was his fourth trip to Iran "as a tourist," and he had also visited Europe, Syria, and Lebanon. He talked incessantly to anyone and everyone, a great taker of hands and locker of arms. As we strolled about like lovers he told me what great friends we were and how he admired Arab women and American whisky. Did I happen to have any American cigarettes? Once in Iran, he retained his ebullience and confidence. He had been there before. Twice he dragged me to restaurants and ordered meals; twice I paid. Once he admired an Iranian ten-riyal coin I received in change and pocketed it. Six hours of travel and wait brought us to Tabriz where I ditched him.

October 3 – Tehran, Iran

The number of camels seen along the road peters out steadily from Tabriz to Tehran in inverse proportion to the increase in Mack trucks and burgeoning industrial parks. In Tehran camels do appear in the spring, and camel dung is peddled door to door in the wealthy districts as garden fertilizer; but the bewildering pace of modernization in the city renders them a distinct anomaly. On the way to Tehran the bus stops for the passengers to get out and view the fresh wreckage of a bus-truck collision. It's my first introduction to the traffic horrors of modern Iran.

Ensconced in complete American comfort in the home of an old friend on military assignment here, my pace of life diminishes considerably....

For the most part I sit around, read, play chess, and chat with Americans – scholars, tourists, businessmen, and old friends. It all seems rather strange....

One night my hosts and I attend a dinner party given by an old American friend married to an Iranian architect on the brink of success. The descriptions they give of life on the brink of success sound like an amalgam of New York City in the 1890s and La Dolce Vita. The distance between the elegant hairdos and catered service of the party and the Sarihan Hotel in Dogubayezit, between the German businessman talking about hunting mountain sheep in the Elburz mountains and the unshaven Turkish stock buyer staying in the hotel talking about the 27 cattle he had just purchased for shipment to Gaziantep, is staggering. I feel neither like a bridge between their experiences nor like an observer of them. Like the trip itself, they seem to come about without a clear chain of causation. I feel a bit like a stranger in my own life.

December 3 – Tunis, Tunisia

Should I compare Tunis to Beirut? From a traditional orientalist point of view it would be bad form to say they differed in any essential way since both are part of the supposed seamless web of the "Islamic world," and it would be equally offensive to nationalist feelings to go on at too great length about the overwhelming French character of both places, although Tunis definitely has the edge in this. Nor can I compare the character or attitude of the two populations since I have never been here before, although a day and a half of walking about the streets is enough to show anyone that shared Phoenician/Punic blood from the days of Sidon, Tyre, and Carthage doesn't amount to much any more. So I won't try to compare them, at least not now.

I had forgotten how different it is to go to a country for the first time instead of the second. I have no feel as yet for Tunisia. It's still the trivialities of a new country that catch my attention, such as the public display of kosher food signs and the fact that the coinage bears European Arabic numerals and not real Arabic numerals.

December 7 – Tozeur, Tunisia

Tozeur is an oasis of several hundred thousand date palms and a small town just inside the northern edge of the Sahara desert. It was dusk when the bus arrived so I have seen little of the oasis, but it is dry and warm and has a comfortable ambiance. Even a long conversation with a young guide willing to show me around tomorrow was pleasant. My only regret is that for the first time in a Muslim country I admitted to the hangers-on at the Hotel Splendid that though a nominal Christian, I did not believe in God. For the last hour and a half I have been discussing religion in a very halting mixture of French and Arabic and have been getting decidedly the worse of it. I was requested pointedly to read aloud passages from the Qur'an dealing with unbelievers and other low-life, and while I did so, a most self-satisfied young man with a prosperous waistline encased in a three-piece blue suit gave me such looks as to indicate that I had best take heed. Then we got onto whether Jesus was the son of God, and after a few minutes I pled exhaustion and gave up.

December 9 – Tozeur, Tunisia

Another day in the life of the village atheist. Fortunately, the theological discussion did not set in until after a pleasant day's promenade around the oasis, in part on camel back....

When I started writing this journal, I expected it to record the gradual working out in my mind of a number of questions of educational philosophy and policy within the framework of a scholarly journal, which itself seemed to me to typify a sort of malaise in scholarly life in general. Alternatively, or perhaps simultaneously, I considered the possibility of the journal becoming pure fantasy. Now, of course, it has become something rather different, an apologia, not for making this trip, but simply for being in this place on this day. I grasp at and record the wisps of purpose that blow my way almost fortuitously, and when the wind is still, the pointlessness of being here is almost overwhelming. Am I becoming a broader person? Of course. Better informed about the subject I teach? Naturally. Restocked with cocktail anecdotes for the next few years? Beyond question. Then this should make me a better history professor and, indeed, a better historian. Yet this is all a round dance in limbo if I do not gradually come to see better why I am a scholar and why the realms of scholarship and fantasy seem to me so terribly close.

December 16 – Paris, France

Coming here was a strange psychological experience. My last day in Tunis I puttered around visiting the zoo and trying to consume my Tunisian money down to the last *millième* in order to avoid the hassle of changing it to something else when I left the country. Then I boarded the ship bound for Marseilles. I had seat number 20 in a room for 70 people; the other seats were occupied by Tunisians. There appeared to be no more than half a dozen Westerners among the several hundred economy class passengers. For three months the ratio had been roughly this, and I was quite accustomed to being foreign, and to that extent being handicapped, a mild but definite encumbrance on the society around me.

On the sun deck in the dark one passenger with a drum and another with a Tunisian double-reed woodwind instrument made music for others to dance and sing to. In my compartment bread and oranges and all sorts of eatables were consumed, and rather early most people shed their shoes, propped their odoriferous feet high in the air on the seat back in front of them, and went to sleep. Only towards morning was I able to join them.

The next day started out much the same, but as it wore on I felt a change take place either in me or in the other passengers or both. By evening we would be landing in France. I would be in a major Western country, one I had never visited before, but one whose culture I not only knew, perhaps not even as well as I know Muslim culture, but also shared. They would be North African immigrants or visitors, in either case members of an unpopular and even despised minority, despite their fluent French which put mine to shame. I found myself enjoying the conversation of a young Austrian merchant seaman, blonde and bearded, and wondering about the nationality of another Westerner who looked exactly like an Edward Gorey character, with pointed beard, far-off look, and gaunt greyhound dog. A month or even a week before I would more likely have disclaimed interest in either of them.

By noon the music had stopped and the passengers became much quieter. I now saw them as a crowded mass of dark, anonymous people with a very few belongings done up in cloth bags and cheap suitcases. If I were enthusiastic about the idea of territoriality, I would say that we were about then passing from their territory to mine and that there consequently took place a shift in psychological dominance from them to me. And yet I was to be as fresh a newcomer to France as any of them and would have a poorer grasp of the language. I'm sure that all of this change in perceiving the situation was mine alone, and that I was preparing to leave the non-Western world behind.

In Marseilles I found a cheap hotel and a good restaurant. For no obvious reason I had been eager to become parted from the Tunisians, from the long line at the passport control, separate from my own, forlornly waiting to undergo what I take it was entry procedure for immigrants. The main streets of Marseilles were decorated with lights for Christmas, and I walked up and down them filled with emotion simply at being there. The next day I boarded a train at St. Charles station for Paris and was joined in my compartment by three Tunisians from the boat. They recognized me, and we said a few words. Two of them seemed genuinely frightened. They mispronounced the names of towns along the way, such as Arles, because they had not internalized these names as part of their cultural background. They got off at Orange.

This left only one. He was tall, thin, dark, very handsome with Berber features and crisp hair. He wore a red shirt and a black leather jacket that contrasted with the winter clothes of the Frenchmen who now filled the rest of the compartment. He looked very brave, but the timorous way in which he murmured *"neige"* when we passed a light dusting of snow betrayed the insecurity he felt beneath the facade. He got off at Lyons; he would look for work there. A few minutes later two young Canadian girls got on wearing hiking boots and carrying big orange backpacks on featherweight magnesium frames. They were having a wonderful time traveling.

January 5 - Rabat, Morocco

The power of French culture is amazing. Since Morocco was only comparatively briefly under French control, I hadn't anticipated quite such a degree of French influence as there is. Coming here is like revisiting Tunis or Beirut despite the centuries of political independence, not to say isolation, of Morocco from the more eastern Muslim countries. Porticoed avenues, sidewalk cafes, French pastry, prix fixe menus, even caution signs on the highway showing the profiles of a mother and daughter in flounced skirts crossing the road despite the fact that women here are long-robed and veiled and present an altogether different profile.

January 6 - Rabat, Morocco

Is it my saucy blue eyes or my dewy complexion?

Chella is a combination necropolis-Roman ruin just outside the walls of Rabat and quite near the U.S. embassy.... It is one of Rabat's main tourist attractions and is really quite pretty with its reddish walls spilling down a hillside covered with grass of a spring-like green. Inside are gardens and tombs and excavated Roman ruins. A charming site for a small imperial outpost (*Sala colonia*) it was, too, built on terraces looking out over the broad river valley that separates the city of Rabat from the city of Salé.

So I was poking about looking for interesting potsherds among the ruins when I noticed a negro watching me from nearby. I was uncertain who he was, but there was always the chance that he was a guard or gardener, so I ostentatiously threw down again every sherd I picked up so as not to be accused of pilfering antiquities. Presently he drew close, keeping furtively next to a wall, and beckoned me over. Then I knew what he was. He was a peddler of illegal antiquities to tourists. I was interested to see what treasure he was concealing and went over to look. I had half expected a Roman lamp; alas, it was only his penis.

Uninterested in his treasure, I walked determinedly away. No sooner had I gone a few steps, however, when I was grabbed strongly from behind and subjected to lewd advances, to be coy. I broke away, but he was at me again in a few moments. I was a bit incredulous up to this point since I beat him by about eight inches and forty pounds and since despite his appreciable strength, I was obviously stronger. One simply doesn't go about raping grown men in this manner. But as I tried to break away again, it became clear that in another few seconds we would be seriously fighting and that one of us, not inconceivably me, might get hurt. To make things more awkward, he got a hand on my camera and was about to rip it from my coat pocket. If he couldn't have sex, at least he could have money, and for a dollar or so in hastily proffered change I regained my liberty.

I do not, on careful consideration, believe that all Moroccans are homosexual muggers and rapists. Nevertheless, I did not linger much longer, as I would have liked, at Chella; and for the rest of the day I kept to well-peopled areas....

That makes two assaults in little over two months. Female [in Iran], I felt embarrassed, awkward, rude, and caddish. Male, I felt frightened, angry, shaken, and again embarrassed. Is it the gender or the mode of approach that makes the difference? I daresay the latter. But I hope I can get through without any fresh opportunities to find out.

January 10 - Oujda, Morocco

Actually, it's four in the morning on the eleventh. I have just arrived here from Fez in a Volkswagen with two Americans and two Canadians I got into a conversation with in a restaurant in Fez. I wonder if they will ever ask me my name.

January 11 - Tlemcen, Algeria

We reached Tlemcen after dark, had a good meal, and while Penny and Matthew returned to the hotel to go to sleep, Francine, Kathy, and I walked around a bit. By and by we wound up having a very amicable beer with the members of the championship Tlemcen volleyball club. So far, so good.

Meanwhile, back at the hotel, Penny, a sloe-eyed beauty who appears to be the epitome of the North African concept of female beauty, had gotten locked out of her room. The hotel did not have another key. Her luggage was inside. This time it was the Tlemcen soccer team that showed up and after Herculean efforts climbed through a kind of transom and unlocked the door. This in turn led to an invitation to the room of some of the soccer team members, and the effort to extract the girls from their clutches stopped barely short of fighting. It was a very ugly scene, and even now we feel a threat lurking in the corridor.

January 15 - Ghardaia, Algeria

This morning I said good-bye to Matthew and Kathy and Francine and Penny. Traveling with them for four days was like visiting another country, the everywhere-in-the-world country where countless European and American youth travel constantly and almost aimlessly. I had looked over the borders before but never myself visited it.

Matthew is nineteen, thin, and bushy bearded, almost entirely aimless. His parents are wealthy; we traveled in his car, which he was planning to store in Tunis to proceed by less encumbering means. He is seldom interested in where he is, but he becomes enraged if an Algerian hotel charges more than a comparable hotel cost in Morocco. I really have no idea why he is going to the trouble and pain to travel except that he apparently has nothing else to do. My intuitive judgment is that he is remarkably intelligent, but this would seem to be more a burden than an asset to him.

Kathy is eighteen. She has been keeping company with Matthew for three years. The high intelligence that Matthew buries in neurosis, Kathy almost feverishly spews forth in books read, arts learned, philosophies understood, and especially images created. She is a talented artist and is aggressively aware of it. Much of the time she wore a white turban and black burnoose and looked for all the world like an even tinier Lawrence of Arabia.

Kathy will probably leave Matthew soon, which will propel him into an emotional crisis. She is on the trip because Matthew's parents thought she would be able to take care of him and keep him from spending too much money.

Francine and Penny have been living together in Toronto for several years. They are two nice Jewish girls who, all round-eyed, have been living totally serendipitous lives. On this trip they have worked as bar-girls and go-go dancers, and in the summer they will be back in Toronto selling flowers to tourists. They have never slipped into prostitution, but they have flirted with it. Yet for all this, they are very different individuals.

Penny is black-haired and looks better in a form-concealing Moroccan jallaba than she does without it. Her make-up is excellent; she may be the only youth traveler who religiously puts on her false eyelashes every morning. Local males find her breathtakingly beautiful and usually believe she is a liberated fellow-countryman. Her manner is forward in an almost old-fashioned sultry way. As with Matthew, I cannot see why she is traveling. She can't either and may not last too long on the circuit.

Francine is large and healthy-looking. Were they practicing rather than only sentimental lesbians, she would be a fine masculine foil to Penny's coquettishness. She seems much better suited to bumming around the world. When it's all over, she will most likely go to law school and go into her father's real estate business. For now life is full of adventure, and the only problem is a lack of contact lens wetting solution. The two of them are 23 or thereabouts and only met Matthew and Kathy half a day before I met them.

So that was the carload. Matthew drove very fast; I drove conservatively. General conversation was sparse. Drugs were a rare topic of general interest, but it flagged. Kathy and I did intellectual talk. Penny and Francine talked about Ron, and Bob, and Hamid and so forth, mostly to each other. Life stories came out in bits and pieces. Matthew rarely spoke. He was upset about Kathy.

After Tlemcen I diverted everyone southward on the argument that the desert would be more interesting than Algiers and a no more time consuming way of reaching Tunis. The night before last we stayed in Tiaret in expensive and unsatisfactory accommodations. To save money I slept in the same room with Penny and Francine. Rather to my surprise, nobody (including me) tried to break the veneer of Platonic comradeliness.

From Tiaret we drove yesterday to Laghouat. It was not a long drive, but it took us out of the coastal mountain area, through the flat steppe of the *tell,* over the ridges that mark the border between the *tell* and the Sahara, and through a bit of desert to the first of the Saharan oases. Laghouat was not very impressive. Again we felt victimized by the Algerian tourist industry and paid a lot for a little. I slept with Penny and Francine, and decorum was again observed. Matthew was feeling paranoid; Kathy was fed up with him. I listened a long time to Penny and Francine talking about Ron and Bob and Hamid and so forth.

This morning we parted.

I Write a Novel

THE FINAL PART OF MY TRIP, which took me in airplane hops from Laghouat to Tamanrasset in the middle of the Sahara Desert, led to the writing of my first novel. Just as I had long mooned over whether I had what it took to be an artist, a yen to write fiction had been germinating in my mind ever since Maude E. Weinschenk's high school class in creative writing. This, I've found, is not unusual in the academic profession. I have discovered that many professors have at least one unpublished novel sitting around in their files. A much smaller number, including one-time Columbia University colleagues like Carolyn Heilbrun and George Stade, actually see their works published. Many of these professorial tales are couched in elegant prose, take place on college campuses, and garner warm praise from fellow academics.

My own first efforts were not so elevated. One day during my freshman year I sat down and typed a few pages of a story. My Mozart-loving roommate returned from somewhere and asked what I was doing. I told him I was writing a science fiction novel. He read what I had written and asked what I had in mind for the second chapter. We discussed a few things, and then he started pounding on his own typewriter. We alternated chapters and soon had finished a post-apocalyptic thriller: *And the Omega*. Post-apocalyptic plots were still uncommon in 1959, and I like to think that that was the reason our effort was rejected for Ace Doublebook publication. After that first rejection, by a publisher we agreed was at the low end of the genre, we hadn't the courage to try elsewhere.

A decade later I tried again, this time with a pornographic novel. It, and another that soon followed, were actually published. The small fee I received helped mollify Lucy's disgust by paying her Harvard tuition since she had commenced a graduate program in Sanskrit. Then the publisher sent me a formula with the assurance that they would publish anything I wrote that followed their plot outline. I had thought my lubricious fantasies were strikingly original, so I was deeply insulted and forthwith abandoned the genre. By good fortune, I can no longer remember either the pennames I used or the name of the publisher. Nor is any further discussion of sexuality consistent with the Methodist and Muslim sensibilities this book is addressing.

A few more years passed until January, 1972 when I found myself in the oasis town of Tamanrasset, Algeria's southern point of entry in the middle of the Sahara desert. As discussed previously, I had been traveling alone for four months and was tired, bored, and cold. I had scrapped my plan to continue on to Niger, Mali, and Senegal and resolved instead to fly home at the first opportunity. In the meantime, however, I was stuck in this remote outpost of French colonial expansion. Since one of the rationales for my journey was to collect information on camel use in different lands, I was happy to photograph the beautiful white *méhari* camels owned by the local Tuaregs and to study the construction of their saddles. I also joined with several other travelers in arranging an excursion.

January 18 – Tamanrasset

6:00 this morning found six of us waiting for the Land Rover to take us into the mountains – I, the Italian painter, a French nun, a German social worker who had just completed several years work in Niger, an old Frenchman, and an Algerian editor of an automotive magazine whose project to take a fancy new Citroen back and forth across the Sahara had somehow gone awry.

The Land Rover was open, so four of us were exposed to the cold and the ever increasing billows of dust as we followed the track across the plain. We slowly took on the aspect of actors caked with flesh-colored makeup without any rouge or mascara to distinguish our features. The landscape was incredibly bleak. The Hoggar [also Ahaggar] is an area of volcanic mountains and outcroppings. It is almost devoid of vegetation. It hasn't rained in three years. Nothing acts to break down the lava fields and basalt projections but temperature change, which over time has created broad expanses of jagged, fractured rock, and the constant sand-blasting of the dust-laden wind.

Our destination was Assekrem – three buildings beside the road – and far above it by a winding footpath the hermitage of Père de Foucauld [a French Catholic priest assassinated by Tuaregs in 1916]. At 9000 feet and two to three hours from the nowhere of Tamanrasset, the hermitage must be one of the remotest spots in the world excluding the polar regions. But the view of the Hoggar Mountains must rank as one of the most beautiful in the world. Shrouded by the dust in the air they look like Chinese paintings of imaginary mountains as rank after fancifully shaped rank of them recede into the ever-dimmer distance.

The wind speed at the hermitage was fifty miles an hour. We ate bread and oranges in one of the huts at Assekrem, and then we started back. But there was still the plain and again the thick coating of dust.

We reached Tamanrasset again at 3:45, just in time for me to change money and buy my air ticket. The trip had cost us $15 apiece, but no one was complaining. The bus for the airport leaves at 4:30 in the morning.

No one keeps late hours in Tamanrasset.

So much for what was in my travel diary. Idling around in my head, however, were thoughts of what Agatha Christie might do with a handful of unconnected people of various nationalities just happening to cross paths in an isolated oasis where none of them has contact with the local population of blue-veiled Tuaregs. I don't remember whether I jotted down the outline of a plot while I was there, or whether it came to me over the following few days I spent in England. By the time I returned home to Cambridge, however, I was determined to shape a murder mystery around the trip to Assekrem. Gino, the delightful Italian painter, would be my victim.

When I finished writing *Kicked to Death by a Camel*, I asked an aspiring writer friend what I should do with it. She told me that Joan Kahn at Harper & Row was the foremost mystery editor in the country. So I got her address and mailed off my manuscript, totally unaware of the fact that over-the-transom novel submissions, thousands every year, never, ever, get published. So naïve was I that it did not seem to me all that strange when Joan Kahn wrote back to say that she wanted to publish my work. She didn't like the ending, but I was more than willing to rework it to make it acceptable.

In the meantime, my fourteen years at Harvard were coming to an end. Though I had one book published, *The Patricians of Nishapur*, and a second pretty much completed, what would become *The Camel and the Wheel*, I was never formally considered for promotion. I was simply told that there was no provision in the Department of History for a senior appointment in Islamic history. This despite the assurance from a previous chairman three years before that the department had decided it wanted to fill precisely such a post by internal promotion.

Angry, humiliated, and bitter at being unceremoniously discarded after six years on the faculty, I accepted the first opportunity to leave that presented itself: a two-year job at the University of California at Berkeley to fill in for Professor William Brinner, who was to spend that time in Israel. I had already decided to publish my novel under a penname, though I had failed to grasp that my insistence on holding the copyright personally, instead of through the publisher, would result in my real name appearing on the copyright page. So I became Clarence J.-L. Jackson, a conflation of my grandfather's given names, Clarence Joseph, and my father's, Leander Jackson. My concern, of course, was that publishing a mystery might detract from my credentials as a scholar and should therefore be concealed.

At Berkeley, two things transpired quite quickly. First, the acting chairman in Brinner's absence, was Mounah Khouri, a Lebanese Arabic teacher and lover of poetry who was delighted to welcome me as a published novelist. Second, my new colleagues disabused me of the notion, which had been hinted at when I was offered the fill-in job, that Brinner might choose to stay in Israel and relinquish his Berkeley position. Such a development, it was suggested, would have left me as a possible inside candidate to succeed him.

Kicked to Death by a Camel was nominated for an Edgar Award in the category of Best First Mystery. I was thrilled by this and never considered that the Joan Kahn imprimatur might have been the key to the nomination. (Years later, a bookseller specializing in mysteries remarked to me, not knowing who I was, that the best thing about my novel was its title.) The prospect of becoming a successful mystery writer buoyed my spirits, which were otherwise much depressed by the absence of any prospects for gaining a tenured position as a historian of medieval Islam.

Accordingly, I started a new novel, retaining the same central character: Roger Allenby, an obtuse, culturally insensitive, self-important specialist on the history of camel saddles who gets everything wrong but nevertheless convinces himself in the end that he has solved the crime. I called it *Tehran Traffic*. Joan Kahn didn't like it. So back to the typewriter. My third effort found Allenby and his wife in the Galapagos Islands, where Lucy and I had actually gone in the company of her parents. It centered on a felonious collector of rare eggs. I couldn't decide whether to give it the title *Poached Penguin*, or *The Purloined Egg*. But it made no difference. Joan Kahn didn't like it.

In later years I had occasion to recall the Galapagos story when I realized that Janet Reno, President Clinton's Attorney General, was the daughter of the outrageously profane old lady whom I had settled on as my villain. At Secretary Reno's request, I sent her the novel, and she reported back that her mother would have been tickled by the villainous characterization.

Joan Kahn's second rejection ended my dream of being a mystery writer. But my hope of becoming a tenured historian at a time when there seemed to be no posts available in my field anywhere in the country gained an unexpected boost when I was awarded a Guggenheim Fellowship for the academic year 1974–75. My project was to devise a quantitative technique for analyzing the process of conversion to Islam during the medieval period.

Five years would pass before I again got the yen to write a novel. But my initial efforts had implanted several dos and don'ts in my mind. First, always make your villain a Westerner lest you stereotype and insult the people you travel among and associate with. Second, accept that American readers cannot distinguish one Arabic-Persian-Turkish name from another. The names Ali Reza and Rauf, for example, look and sound exactly alike to people whose minds go blank when they see words in exotic languages. And third, if you are going to portray someone as a fool, make him your alter ego.

PART THREE

Things Happen

"**H**APPEN" IS A WONDERFULLY PASSIVE VERB. Irrespective of whether one is trying to accomplish a particular goal, many things just happen. And they happen more often in New York City than elsewhere. Though I have known scholars who sketch out a plan for their careers and seek to draw their colleagues and students into that plan, I have never had a plan, or at least none that took priority over things that just happened serendipitously.

The memorable episodes of my life do not cohere. Some things just happened, from advising Nevada camel jockeys on getting the IRS to waive a tax on a retiring rancher's proposed transfer to them of a herd of camels, to reviewing dozens of videos seized in two British police raids on suspected terrorists; from devising a new algorithm for setting faculty rent levels in Columbia owned buildings, to discussing on a trans-Atlantic call with a Dutch philologist whether the word "dildo" comes from the name of Muhammad's mule *duldul*; from reviewing and appraising Middle East studies and history programs at ten universities in the United States and Israel, to co-sponsoring back-channel talks between Americans and the Iranian Foreign Ministry during the Clinton administration. The episodes that follow stand out in my memory as ones that may reveal something about living one's life as an Orientalist.

Changing Sides of the Desk at Harvard

I WAS A HARVARD GRADUATE STUDENT during my first trip to the Middle East. By the time I returned to the area and wrote my journal, I had become an assistant professor. Does that mean I won first prize in a nationwide search? Hardly. University jobs were filled very differently in 1967, and my elevation to the Harvard faculty was intertwined with the career of a man I had never met until he offered me a job.

Nadav Safran was one of several students who completed their doctoral dissertations during H. A. R. Gibb's days at Harvard and then became junior faculty members. The historians all moved on to other universities, William Polk to Chicago, L. Carl Brown to Princeton, and Ira Lapidus to Berkeley. Safran, in the Government Department, was the only one who managed to gain a tenured post. Ironically, this occurred after a rupture in his relations with Gibb had made him persona non grata at the Center for Middle East Studies (CMES).

Born in Cairo, Safran emigrated to Palestine in 1946 and served as a lieutenant in the Israeli army during the Arab-Israel War of 1948. He completed his PhD in 1958. In a conversation about his career, he told me that Gibb had thought very highly of him and hoped to groom him as his successor. But Safran preferred to work on the modern rather than the medieval period. Gibb accepted this and directed the dissertation that became Safran's first book, *Egypt in Search of Political Community: An Analysis of the Intellectual and Political Evolution of Egypt, 1804-1952* (1961). Gibb then instructed him to write a similar study of Iraq.

In the meantime, Harvard University Press had invited Safran to write a short, and much needed, primer on Israel. This was published in 1963 as *The United States and Israel.* With two books in print within five years of completing his doctorate, Safran was fulfilling the promise Gibb had seen in him. But Gibb rebuked him for disobeying his instructions by writing a book on Israel instead of Iraq. That was the end of their relationship.

When a stroke forced Gibb into retirement in 1965, the CMES was in a quandary. Gibb was its only scholar of international repute. Marshall Hodgson and Albert Hourani came as visiting professors, but neither offered a lasting solution. In the spring of 1967, therefore, as I was completing my own doctoral dissertation, a decision was made to allot the equivalent of a visiting professor's annual salary to Safran to underwrite a year-long graduate colloquium dealing with the entire sweep of Islamic history, religion, and government. Each weekly meeting was to feature a major Orientalist flown in from wherever he might be teaching. To administer the colloquium, Safran could nominate someone to serve for three years as a junior faculty member with the rank of instructor.

I knew nothing of these plans until Safran, whom I had never met, much less studied with, called me in and offered me the job. Scuttlebutt later told me that he had first offered it to one of his own newly fledged PhDs, but she had turned it down. So he had asked around to see whether there was any other recent PhD who might do the job, and my name came up. The upshot was that after a dispiriting job search in a year when there were no openings anywhere in the country for medieval Islamic historians, I suddenly and unexpectedly became a member of the Harvard faculty. No public announcement of an opening, no search, no job talk. Just being in the right place at the right time.

Together Safran and I made a list of scholars to invite to the colloquium, and the $500 honorarium we were offering in return for preparing and presenting a paper was generous enough at that time to guarantee a high proportion of acceptances. On the student side, the CMES declared that every first-year MA student would be required to take the course for double credit, making it half of all of their work for the year. Second-year students had to take it for single credit. The difference in workload was that the second-year students only had to write a lengthy research paper while the first-year students had to write the research paper in addition to a five-page précis of every colloquium session.

The workload was so heavy for the first-year students that after three months they revolted and petitioned for relief. In addition, the budget was significantly overspent as more scholars were invited than had been planned for. My role as colloquium factotum was overwhelming. I had a dream in which I was wandering naked through Harvard Yard with colloquium papers stuck to my body. Every week I met the visitors at the airport, settled them in a room at the Faculty Club and saw to their needs (General John Bagot Glubb, "Glubb Pasha," was keen to find an Anglican church and a supply of laxatives); arranged for the duplication and distribution of the papers they had prepared; selected 300 pages of reading for the students to do in preparation for the colloquium session; served as maître d' for the reception and dinner arranged for each guest; graded all of the papers, both the short and the long; and held office hours to respond to the complaints of disgruntled students. For his part, Safran chaired the sessions (sitting on the foam donut I carried for him to ease his recovery from hemorrhoid surgery) in pontifical fashion and hosted the receptions and dinners.

Despite the titanic workload and the unhappiness of the students, the colloquium was nothing if not memorable. The class developed a camaraderie that increasingly focused on resentment of Safran. As for me, I had lucked into a job on the Harvard faculty that gave me a chance, at age twenty-seven, to meet and talk with an array of the best-known Middle East scholars in the world. Some, like J. N. D. Anderson, Peter Avery, Jan Brugman, W. B. Fisher, John Bagot Glubb, Gustave E. von Grunebaum, Manfred Halpern, Joseph Schacht, and Harry Wolfson, I never saw again. Others, like Ernest Gellner, J. C. Hurewitz, Halil Inalcik, Kemal Karpat, Malcolm Kerr, and Maxime Rodinson, I had other opportunities to interact with in the years that followed.

After the first semester, I showed Safran a budget projection for the entire year that made it clear that we were spending too much. He instructed me to keep the figures to myself, but I showed them to the CMES Associate Director D. W. Lockard anyway. (I do not take instruction well.) Safran couldn't chastise me for this, however, because I was doing too many other tasks for him. Most onerously, I abridged several chapters of his manuscript in progress, which was as prolix as the title he gave it when it appeared in print: *From War to War: The Arab-Israeli Confrontation, 1948–1967; A Study of the Conflict from the Perspective of Coercion in the Context of Inter-Arab and Big Power Relations* (1969).

As the colloquium was winding down, Safran proposed a process that he was convinced would lead to solving the Arab-Israel dilemma. He had commented to me once, when looking at the long table in the dining room of the Harvard Faculty Club where professors entering alone found luncheon companions, that he was acutely aware of his status as a peer of famous minds like David Riesman and John Kenneth Galbraith. And he spoke often about a grand theory he was gestating that would combine the dynamism inherent in the Marxist theory of class struggle with the more static analysis of social structure associated with Talcott Parsons, Harvard's preeminent sociologist. Hence it did not seem to him to be overly ambitious to think that with his twin personal roots in Egypt and Israel, he could be instrumental in bringing about peace.

What he had in mind was modeled on the Pugwash Conferences on Science and World Affairs, founded in 1957 by the physicist Joseph Rotblat and the philosopher Bertrand Russell. Focused on nuclear disarmament, the conference meetings in Pugwash, Nova Scotia brought together scholars and men and women of affairs for informal and private discussions of some of the world's most pressing problems. Safran proposed a similar program of high-level intellectual deliberations focused on the Arab-Israel conflict to the American Academy of Arts and Sciences, a society of scholarly luminaries based near Harvard in Cambridge. The Academy agreed to fund the project and issue invitations for the series of sessions, over which Safran would preside.

I helped Safran compile a long list of eminent invitees from a variety of academic disciplines, and I carved a manageable paper out of his book manuscript to be used as the initial focus for discussion. The first meeting was unremarkable, but shortly thereafter a noted Palestinian scholar named Ibrahim Abu-Lughod, then teaching at Northwestern University, contacted the secretary of the Academy to ask why his organization was supporting a peace project conceived and chaired by an Israeli. Abu-Lughod noted a paucity – or was it a total absence? I can't remember – of Arab invitees; and in truth, the scholars who had agreed to participate in the sessions came disproportionately from the subset of invitees who happened to be Jewish. At that time, only a year after the June War of 1967, most non-Jewish American intellectuals had yet to focus on what was to become a major national concern.

Safran and the secretary – I don't recall his name – had a tense lunch at the Faculty Club with me as a silent third party. The secretary told Safran that the Academy was pulling the plug on the project. Ibrahim Abu-Lughod had declined an invitation to become a co-chairman, and without significant Arab participation, no further sessions could be held. Safran replied that the Academy's withdrawal was unwarranted, cowardly, and severely damaging to his reputation. He completely rejected the idea that the sessions would be tainted by a pro-Israeli bias. Nevertheless, the deed was done, and no more was ever heard of Safran's project.

After a tumultuous year running the colloquium and a revelatory summer witnessing the rise and fall of a grandiose professorial enterprise, I was happy to spend the remaining two years of my Instructorship teaching ordinary courses. Though I was promoted to Assistant Professor and served on the faculty for a subsequent three years before departing from Harvard, my contacts with Safran became few and far between. Nevertheless, the chance to meet so many luminaries at the very outset of my career, and the months of intense involvement with Safran's Arab-Israel project proved to be of great value in later years.

Coming to Columbia

MY TWO YEARS in Berkeley began to cure my severe case of Harvarditis, though fantastic imaginings of Harvard's campus architecture still roil my dream-life while seeing the fog roll in every evening over the Golden Gate Bridge and climb the Berkeley hills is only a placid memory. As visiting faculty, I was not deeply engaged in departmental affairs, which were strongly polarized on the Arab-Israel issue. Years later I realized that Harvard too suffered from the polarization, but managed to conceal it under its all-enshrouding blanket of self-regard.

My most consequential Berkeley experience took place in a classroom. The topic was Syrian history between the fall of the Umayyads and the advent of the First Crusade. Never having done my own research on the matter, I pulled out Gibb's lecture on the subject and glanced through it before class. But the shifting politics of the Syrian tribes were difficult to remember. Thus during the class, I paused to find my place before continuing with a boring account that I didn't really understand.

During the pause, a student in the front row said: "Why are you giving this lecture?" Definitely not what I wanted to hear, and definitely not a Harvard question.

After quelling my instinct to give a barbed response, I said: "I'm giving this lecture because I have the notes for it." That was the last time I gave a lecture from written notes. Extemporaneous speaking had been my forte on my high school forensics team – fourth place in the state tournament in 1956, hooray! – and reacquainting myself with speaking off the cuff proved to be liberating. Harvard history professors gave well-composed set-piece presentations that did not change from year to year. This had always annoyed me because it left no opening for an ambitious student historian to find his own voice. Henceforward the hallmark of my classes was to be improvisation. At the cost of a certain degree of incoherence, as a few students invariably pointed out in course evaluations, I found that I made much better contact with the class; and every year I would surprise myself with three or four lectures that unexpectedly advanced my thinking on some subject. The hours saved on not doing much preparation for my lectures also gave me time to teach overload courses that did not concern the Middle East.

Overall, I was not enchanted with Berkeley. After so many years in the Cambridge pressure cooker, I wasn't ready for the relaxed lifestyle of backpacking and brown rice and the more tepid intellectual atmosphere. So I spent my Guggenheim year back in the Cambridge vicinity where my wife was striving to write her doctoral thesis on the role in the Rig Veda of the serpent demon Vrtra.

In November, 1975, after my first meeting with the Columbia search committee looking for a tenured professor to teach both modern and pre-modern Middle Eastern history, the chair of the Department of History, Professor Malcolm Bean, took me aside and stressed that if I were to get the job, he would expect me to exert a strong hand in the area of the modern Middle East. He was determined that the department should no longer have to depend upon Professor J. C. Hurewitz of the Political Science Department for graduate supervision in that area. I assured Professor Bean that I would carry out his wishes. However, I concealed from him that the star of one of my classes at Harvard had been Jay Hurewitz's bright and talented daughter, Anne. In fact, several years earlier Hurewitz had written me a letter raising the possibility of my teaching someday at Columbia. Jay never let on to Professor Bean that I was his preferred candidate for the position, and I suspect he eventually regretted my joining the faculty.

The interchange with Bean made it clear that even though my doctoral work had been on the medieval period, and I considered myself a medievalist, I would have to take the later centuries of Middle Eastern history seriously if I won the Columbia job. I had taken a number of courses on the Ottoman and modern periods at Harvard, and had prepared Ottoman history as one of my fields for doctoral examination, but I had never focused closely on the modern period except in terms of the work I did for Safran. Nor had I ever lectured on the modern period before my two-year stint at Berkeley. Nevertheless, I was essentially unemployed after Berkeley – a situation agreeably disguised by my Guggenheim fellowship – and I was more than willing to teach whatever Columbia wanted me to. Over the next four decades, about half of the forty-five-plus doctoral dissertations I supervised at Columbia dealt with post-seventeenth-century topics.

When I moved into my office at Columbia's Middle East Institute in September, 1976, I wrote an essay to set in order my thoughts about the contemporary Middle Eastern matters that I was expected to teach. I did not intend it for publication. Much of the essay diverges from the views I would adopt after the Iranian Revolution. At the time, I was still in thrall to the modernization theories that were just as voguish at Columbia as they had been at Harvard and Berkeley. Some parts of the essay are worth relating, however, to demonstrate how one American specialist on medieval Islam viewed contemporary Middle Eastern affairs at the point when he was about to start teaching about them. I have made only minor editorial changes in what I wrote in 1976, two years before my new Columbia colleague Edward Said published *Orientalism* and attacked precisely this kind of scattershot opinion-mongering perpetrated by scholars of the Middle East.

§▲

In 1928 Reza Shah Pahlavi, the father of the present Shah of Iran, abolished the wearing of the chadur, a kind of all-concealing shroud-cum-veil, by Iranian women. In accordance with her husband's decree, the Shah's wife appeared in public with her face uncovered. In reaction to this violation of Islamic tradition, a mullah in the important shrine and pilgrimage city of Qom, fifty miles south of Tehran, preached a sermon denouncing the Shah's wife. Reza Shah, who before his rise to the throne had been a colonel in the Russian-officered Persian Cossack regiment, reacted in turn by speeding to Qom with an armored car, striding into the mosque with his boots on, and whipping the insubordinate mullah.

In 1966, in Mashhad, an important shrine and pilgrimage city in northeastern Iran, I went into an unpretentious barbershop for a haircut and a shave, the latter an indulgence I reserve for travel in the Middle East. In response to my request for a shave, the barber said, *"trash ya masheen?"* [razor or machine?]. Startled, I looked and saw that he was proudly holding a brand new electric razor. His evident disappointment in my choice of the former offering was matched by my feeling after being shaved by his now obsolete and quite dull razor.

As improbable as it may seem, particularly given the fact that Iran is not an Arab country, these two events exemplify two elements in the attitude toward Israel of cosmopolitan, educated Arabs, two elements that have seldom been mentioned in the flood of writing about the Arab-Israeli conflict. These two elements are secularism and cultural imperialism....

In political terms, secularism is normally taken to be realized in the effective separation of church and state. Separation of church and state was not the product that was being peddled to the peoples of the Middle East by their European and American mentors in the nineteenth and twentieth century, however. What was enjoined upon the Middle Eastern peoples by a succession of English, French, Russian, and American ambassadors, consuls, and advisors went beyond the political separation of church and state. What they urged was the transformation of a society which they viewed as oppressively dominated by a moribund religious system, that of Islam, into a society in which the dead hand of religion would be removed entirely from political and cultural life. What was visualized, in fact, was the restriction of religion to the areas of personal conscience and private observance.

It is of utmost significance that this vision was neither a reflection of the political and social reality in the ambassadors', consuls', and advisors' homelands nor a prescription that the ambassadors, consuls, and advisors would feel comfortable giving to their own governments. The Jews of England, for example, did not attain full parliamentary rights until the middle of the nineteenth century, nor did the government that sent Sir Stratford Canning to Istanbul to bully the Sultan into granting religious equality ever give a thought to disestablishing the Church of England.

Two questions grow out of this peculiar effort to persuade Muslim rulers to do as the Europeans said rather than as they did. First, how did the policy arise? And second, what result did the policy have on the people who were subject to the persuasion?

The first question could involve one in a tangled skein of personalities and diplomatic history. Several relevant threads run throughout, however. To be sure, there must have been enlightened prophets and peddlers of secularism as an ideology who truly believed in the value of the wares they had on display; but for the most part, this does not appear to have been the case. A great number of these ambassadors, consuls, and advisors were Bible-quoting, church-attending Christian gentlemen whose government service was predicated to some extent upon Christian ideals which they would have been loth to see disappear from public currency. For this latter and larger group the underlying feelings appear to have been fear and loathing of the Muslim religion and a clear perception of Middle Eastern society as being backward and debased due to the influence of its odious religion.

An excellent analysis of the mentality of the nineteenth-century agents of imperialism is provided by Norman Daniel's book, *Islam, Europe, and Empire* (1966). The main components of the European attitude toward Islam were several: hatred, based upon the idea, of medieval origin, of Islam as a potent competitor of Christianity; fear, based upon centuries of crusading propaganda followed by additional centuries of Turkish military conquest up to the gates of Vienna; loathing, based upon the utter collapse of Middle Eastern economic power and war-making potential in the face of rapidly industrializing Europe; romanticism, based upon the idea of the noble savage and the lure of Arabian Nights eroticism. Nowhere in the mental equipment of any but a very few Europeans was there a sound knowledge of the actual functioning of Islamic religious institutions in Middle Eastern society.

Under ideal circumstances this defect in the education of European men of affairs would have been made up by the diligent research of scholars into just such questions as the real character of what was seen as a backward and stagnant Muslim society. Unfortunately, works by specialists on Islam and Middle Eastern society in the last century and a half have only rarely served to plug this educational gap. The discipline of Orientalism – which, essentially, is the name applied to what scholarly knowers of peculiar languages do with their knowledge – functioned superbly in resurrecting and making available to a scholarly public the literary high culture of the Islamic world up until roughly 1400.

For later periods, the editing and publishing of literary, philosophical, and theological monuments gave way almost entirely to narrating the military and diplomatic history of European-Ottoman relations. The high culture of the Ottoman Empire was ignored, and there are still Orientalists who claim that one never existed. Whoever wanted to find out about the Middle East had no other recourse than to consult the Orientalists and their writings on the serious, scholarly level, or peruse a mushrooming library of travel memoirs, ranging from superb to abysmal, on a more popular level. From none of these sources could one get a dependable picture of the nature and structure of Middle Eastern society and the role of religion in that society. And it may have made little difference if better information had been available anyway since the Orientalists and travelers were more often than not as filled with assumptions of Islamic vileness and Christian superiority as the ambassadors, consuls, and advisors who read their works.

The upshot of this combination of negative stereotypes of Islam inherited from the European past and ongoing scholarship that stressed medieval poetry, theology, and philosophy while ignoring the seemingly decadent contemporary society was a mental attitude that said several things. It said that it was perfectly all right to advise the disestablishment of Islam while not urging the disestablishment of the Church of England or of the Roman Catholic hierarchy because Islam was both an inferior religion and one that had fallen into deep decadence.

It said that this advice, if acquiesced in, would result in a freeing of society, a rebirth of mental and cultural vigor, and an acceptance of the modern ideological views circulating in Europe and America. Consequently, the advice was not only proper but was a downright favor, compelling, as it did, the Middle Eastern peoples to do things that were genuinely in their own best interest.

Finally, it said that the dark night of Islamic decadence had had much more negative effects upon the Muslim populations in countries under Islamic government than upon the non-Muslim populations. Hence, however benighted in their customs and outlook the Christians, Jews, and other non-Muslim inhabitants of the Middle East might be, they were potentially salvageable; so it was perfectly proper to give advice that would result in a specific improvement of the lot of the non-Muslims and, at the same time, to favor those same non-Muslims in economic and legal ways.

Much more could be said about what went into the mental makeup, indeed, what still goes into the mental makeup of European and American men of affairs who seek to prescribe correctives for what they perceive as the backwardness of Middle Eastern society, but this subject is not only depressing but it misses the central point concerning secularism. That point is that in the fullness of time there evolved in the Middle East a class of Western-educated Turks, Arabs, and Persians who were largely emancipated from the more obvious bonds of traditional society and who believed strongly in the exaggerated brand of secularism that several generations of ambassadors, consuls, and advisors had been preaching.

The new secularist intelligentsia appears in different parts of the Islamic world at somewhat different periods because of the varying rates of Western penetration. Only very recently, for example, can traces of it be found among the younger generation in Saudi Arabia. However, it exhibits the same characteristics everywhere. The secularists accept as a fact the notion that what is bad and backward by European Christian standards in Middle Eastern society is the product of a decadent religious organization. At the level of government policy, the acceptance of this notion normally leads in one of two directions:

One direction, most notable in the case of Turkey, is that of religious repression. Repression may seem like too strong a term, and it is too strong if by repression is meant an attack upon personal religious observance. Given the overwhelming interpenetration of religion and social structure in Islamic societies of the eighteenth century, however, repression is certainly not too strong a term to describe the abolition of religious law and religious social institutions under the Turkish Republic.

The other direction is Islamic reform. The reform movement, about which an enormous amount has been written in European languages, has several branches, but its underlying premise is the abolition of the benighted social and religious forms of the eighteenth century by rethinking Islam on the basis of the supposedly purer religious observance of some much earlier time, usually the time of the prophet Muhammad himself and his immediate successors. That the accommodation of Islam to the moral standards and ethical norms of Christian Europe – often simply referred to as modern civilization – was the goal of the reformers is not open to serious doubt. The publicity given to the Islamic reform movement by European Orientalists reflects the hidden yearnings of many Orientalists, who are steeped in medieval religious lore but prevented from expounding upon it in a prescriptive manner because they are not themselves Muslim, to show the Muslims the right way, to teach them how to become good Europeans without sacrificing their religious belief.

Those rulers who were most firm in power, such as Atatürk, adopted secularism as a basic tenet of government. Less autocratic governments have had to endorse some form or other of Islamic reform as an expedient way of achieving their essentially secularizing ends. Politicians of either stripe share the idea that government and society must be free from the dead hand of a decadent Islam. Yet they also realize that the overwhelming majority of the Muslim population in every Middle Eastern country still lives according to the social outlook of precisely that form of Islam that was dominant in the eighteenth and nineteenth centuries. It is the sincere hope of the secularizing leaders that European-style education will ultimately redirect the thinking of the population and make religion properly subordinate to secular citizenship; but in the meantime, potential popular opposition to secularism must be defused by the expedient devices of the Islamic reformers.

To see how this century-long train of development affects the Arab-Israeli dispute one must remember that the secularist doctrine that has come to be an article of faith for a significant portion of the governing class in the Arab countries is much more extreme than that commonly accepted in the Western countries that promoted the idea in the first place. A Mu'ammar Qadhdhafi in Libya appears to be a deranged fanatic when viewed within a group of secularizing, modernizing Middle Eastern rulers who believe religion has no legitimate business in the workings of a modern government. Yet from a different perspective one could argue that Qadhdhafi's religiosity is no more extreme than Jimmy Carter's.

Take now this substantial discrepancy in perspective toward religion and view the state of Israel first through Western eyes and then through the eyes of the secularist Arab politician. From the Western viewpoint, Israel is a state based upon religious foundations, but essentially secular in its separation of church and state and its forbearance from limiting on a religious basis the civil rights of non-Jewish citizens. Such things as the Law of Return, which grants automatic citizenship to any Jew who comes to Israel, and the influence in the perpetual coalition government of the National Religious Party, are regarded from the standpoint of Western secularism as anomalies that are justified by principle or by political practicality but that do no vitiate the essential secularism of the state.

From the point of view of the secularist Arab leader, however, the Israeli state appears quite different. In fact, Israel bears a striking resemblance to the type of state that generations of European and American ambassadors, consuls and advisors taught was thoroughly backward and reprehensible. The Law of Return and the National Religious Party appear as primitive and decadent remnants of an era when religion held primacy in political affairs. The Zionist movement as a whole smacks of the same benighted fanaticism that the secularists now regard as so deplorable in their own recent history. Indeed, it is quite possible that the state of Israel would be better understood, and found, at least theoretically, more acceptable by a Muslim religious scholar of the eighteenth century than it is by a Westernized Arab of today.

The vision of the future propounded by the Palestine Liberation Organization and other Westernized Arabs sees a secular state of Palestine, a state in which Muslim, Jewish, and Christian citizens live in equality under a government in which religion plays no essential role. This vision has been attacked from several directions: It has been asserted that it is simple eyewash intended hypocritically to disguise vicious designs upon the Jews of Israel. It has been maintained that Muslim domination would be a demographic fact in a Palestinian state and that the secular ideal would be unattainable because the views of the majority would inevitably color the outlook of the government. It has been observed that those who preach a secular state receive financial support from religiously conservative regimes such as that of Saudi Arabia.

The list of types of attack could be extended, but what is important about the ideal of the secular state is that many Arabs truly believe in it, not just as an ideal for a future Palestine but for other Arab states as well. Hypocrisy and political expediency may exist in certain quarters, but in others the idea of secularism burns with a brighter flame than is normally realized. In the light of that flame Israel appears to be a state predicated upon the worst of principles. The distinction between Zionism and Judaism, the former evil and the latter perfectly acceptable, is precisely the fact that Zionism represents an unwarranted intrusion of religion into politics, an anachronistic assertion of a political principle that progressive circles in the Middle East have now learned to despise. This is one of the sentiments underlying the idea that Zionism is a form of racism, racism in this sense being equatable with religious community as a basis for state formation.

Yet the secularist Arab viewpoint toward Israel is almost completely unappreciated in the West. Non-Arab Muslims who share the same secularist philosophy can see it quite easily, but it appears completely nonsensical to most Europeans and Americans. Only when one realizes how deeply the European image of a decadent Islamic society, which can be cured solely by total secularization, has sunk in in the thinking of progressive Western educated Arabs can one understand why Israel appears so different to them than it does to Westerners. The call for a secular Palestinian state and the equation of Zionism with racism are not hypocrisy disguised as idiocy; they are largely the expression of an extreme secularist viewpoint that was initially inculcated by Europeans and Americans who despised the Islamic religion as practiced in the Middle East in the nineteenth century.

It is quite possible, of course, that the secularist views of the progressive, Westernized Arabs are dangerously out of touch with the views of the population at large. It is also quite possible that insofar as secularism is a doctrine inculcated by the West it will eventually be seen as such and rejected in favor of a renewed closeness of relationship between Islam and political life. There is a great deal of evidence pointing toward both possibilities. Regardless of the eventual fate of secularism in the Arab countries, however, it is a present reality in the thinking of many of the people who run the Arab governments, and it is a real component of the attitude of the Arabs toward Israel.

Now it is time to turn to the second element in the attitude of the Arabs toward Israel, namely, cultural imperialism. The action of cultural imperialism in the Arab-Israeli conflict can best be seen against the backdrop of economic imperialism. Time and time again the anti-Israeli position has been argued from the standpoint of imperialism, and particularly of Lenin's analysis of imperialism. Perhaps the most expert proponent of this view is Maxime Rodinson in his book *Israel and the Arabs* (1968).

Simplified, the imperialist thesis sees Israel as a colony of Europeans bent on exploiting the lands and resources of Third World peoples. Analogies are drawn between Israel and South Africa, with the Jews playing the role of the whites obviously, and between Israel and Viet Nam. The prognosis for the Arab-Israeli conflict from this point of view is quite dim. Imperialism must be fought through a movement of people's liberation, and the cancerous growth of Western colonialism must be eradicated.

Without going into the merits of this argument from the economic side, one can still see that it has one glaring weakness: if the Jewish religion, which is not a creation of capitalism, did not exist, the state of Israel would not exist. In other words, when everything has been said about the role of non-religious ideas in the origin of Zionism and about the economic structure of the state of Israel and its economic ties with the West, the fact will remain that were it not for religion, a cultural phenomenon, this particular economic entity would not exist. In a very basic way, then, Israel is a cultural phenomenon and not just a political and economic entity.

Compared to the rigorous, if, in this case, insufficient, analysis of Israel from the standpoint of the Leninist theory of imperialism, an analysis of Israel's position from the standpoint of cultural imperialism is squishy soft. What is cultural imperialism, anyway, other than a snappy bit of jargon?

Cultural imperialism is the mode of interaction between two cultures that share a belief that one of the cultures is superior to the other. It only occurs when there is a loss of self-confidence on the part of one of the parties. If self-confidence is maintained throughout a period of transference of cultural characteristics from one culture to the other, the result is cultural borrowing but not cultural imperialism. What is important is not so much the fact of dominance as the belief in the superiority of the dominating culture.

In economic imperialism it is relatively easy to tell the good guys from the bad guys. After all, the latter – using the Marxist analysis – are stealing the food from the mouths of the former. In cultural imperialism, however, this sort of black and white identification is extremely difficult to make because there is a willing and enthusiastic collaboration between the imperializers and the imperialized. The opponents of the cultural dominance of the imperializers are reviled by imperializers and imperialized alike as backward and stupid agents of a thoroughly outmoded traditional society.

Historically, perhaps the best example of cultural imperialism, and one that is still of great importance today, is the phenomenon known as Hellenism. Hellenism represented a collaboration between Greeks and non-Greeks to spread ancient Greek culture to the ends of the earth. This collaboration was predicated on the shared assumption that Greek culture was superior to any others. This assumption was not shared by all non-Greeks, needless to say, but the cosmopolitan ruling classes of a great many non-Greek areas slavishly adopted Greek ideas and institutions. The opponents of Hellenism generally lost. In time Hellenism became a kind of cultural soup in which bits and pieces of various non-Greek cultural traditions floated to the surface here and there but in which the basic flavor was set by the enveloping broth of Greek ideas and institutions. The non-Greek bits and pieces were merely the last pickings from carcasses that had once been quite alive and independent.

On the one hand, it is possible to analyze the triumph of Hellenism as a product of the force of Greeks arms, and the conquests of Alexander the Great in particular. On the other hand, military or economic conquest cannot alone bring about a shared belief in the superiority of the dominant culture. No conqueror, for example, has ever been able to exert cultural dominance over China because the Chinese have never believed that the culture of their conquerors has been superior to their own. They have borrowed from their conquerors, but they have not been imperialized at a cultural level.

Military and economic strength may be a signal that one culture is superior to another, although the enormous spread of Buddhism is a good example of cultural imperialism, in this case Indian cultural imperialism, taking place without military or economic conquest. In any specific case, however, it is problematic whether the dominated people will buy the notion that the impinging culture is superior to their own. For this to happen it would appear that in at least some important areas the superiority must be patently manifest.

In the case of Hellenism, it seems to have been perfectly evident that rationalism was a superior cultural quality greatly to be emulated. Buddhism, similarly, provided a religious insight that was clearly more rewarding than those provided by competing religions. In the case of Western culture, the obvious arena of superiority is science and industry.

Western cultural imperialism in the Middle East did not begin the day a European army for the first time soundly defeated a Turkish army. In fact, the Ottoman Empire lost wars to European nations on a regular basis for over a century before the first glimmerings of true cultural imperialism began to appear. Initially, around the turn of the nineteenth century, the perception that European military success was increasingly enhanced by modern industry led to vigorous but unsuccessful efforts to establish European-style arms industries in the Middle East. Cultural imperialism only began when some people began to perceive, rightly or wrongly, that European-style industry presupposes European culture. Ergo, European culture is superior and its adoption will lead to industrialization which, in turn, will lead to a restoration of military and economic might.

As in the case of Hellenism, once the initial assumption of Western cultural superiority was made, the floodgates fell and virtually all aspects of Western culture took on a brilliant luster. Western cultural imperialism progressed rapidly both in the number of people affected by it, initially through Westernized educational institutions and subsequently through mass media, and in the areas of life that were touched by it. The opponents of Westernism steadily lost ground because they were defending a traditional Islamic culture that was increasingly regarded as an anachronism in a modern world. While religious customs and scruples steadily gave way, Coca-Cola and Gillette razors penetrated deeper and deeper into the society.

Chronicling the course of Western cultural imperialism in the Middle East would be an exhausting task, and for present purposes it is quite unnecessary. What are important are not the specific steps taken on the road to Westernization but the attitudes that have built up regarding the road itself and the destination towards which it is leading. Paradoxically, as Westernization increases, the thought of becoming completely Westernized becomes increasingly revolting in the minds of precisely those Middle Easterners who are most involved in the Westernizing process. To a varying extent, Westernization has become a pernicious habit in the opinion of cosmopolitan, Western-educated Middle Easterners. By upbringing, education, and career choice they have become substantially attuned to a Western way of life. They would not wish to forsake the benefits of Western science and industry, which they recognize as genuinely good things. Still, there is much about the Western way of life that disgusts them.

Earlier generations did not see the negative aspects of Western culture because they were blinded by the brilliance of its achievements. Only when these achievements have come to be taken for granted can a more complete view of Western culture emerge, a view that takes in faults as well as successes. Those Middle Easterners who are far enough into the generations-long process of cultural imperialism are now able to see Western culture through untinted glasses; and, seeing it in its naked reality, they cannot but ask themselves whether in buying the good things of Western culture they have not unavoidably and irretrievably bought the bad things as well.

Here are the horns of the dilemma thus posed: If one rejects Western culture, one is not only rejecting the good things of that culture, but one is committing oneself to the only apparent alternative, namely, some sort of return to the traditional Islamic culture that one's Western-style education has taught one to regard as inadequate for life in the modern world. On the other hand, if one commits oneself wholeheartedly to Western culture, one may not only lose one's feelings of social identity and self-respect, but one may be opting for crime in the streets, destruction of family ties, libertinism, and domination by infantile telecasting.

Struggling to avoid being impaled upon these lethal horns, Western educated Arabs, Turks, and Persians think long and hard about their own culture and their own society vis-à-vis the West. Communism is one way out because it is of Western culture while at the same time damning those qualities in Western culture that seem so vile. Yet further reflection sometimes brings the realization that Communism, too, is a form of Western cultural imperialism that threatens one's social identity and self-respect.

Another way out is Islamic reform, the present continuation of the turn-of-the-century movement that sought to find the seeds of the modern world in tortured interpretations of ideas and events from the seventh century. Initially, and with a certain amount of success, this movement sought to make Einstein a good Muslim in the same way that Thomas Aquinas made Aristotle a good Christian. Nowadays, however, the premises of the reform movement seem less than sure. Is it not, after all, an attempt to ignore a millennium of history and social and religious development instead of facing it and dealing with it?

Whether nationalism and special forms of socialism are ways out of the dilemma is more than a little doubtful. The ideological underpinnings of these movements are rather feeble. Moreover, when they do not stem from Western cultural imperialism, they appear to be simply secularized forms of traditional Muslim thought.

The point of all this is to show the kind of moral and intellectual quandary many Westernized Middle Easterners find themselves in. With rare exception, however, the people who find themselves in this quandary live on a day-to-day basis according to the patterns and norms of modern Western life that they have become accustomed to. This kind of existence cannot help but produce a potential for self-criticism and criticism of others in the same situation. This potential is realized much more strongly in some cases than in others, and in some cases it attains to the level of self-loathing.

Whether or not every Westernized Middle Easterner is aware of this quandary is not really important. What is important is that the quandary is a structural one set by the very process of cultural imperialism. It is inconceivable that the same feelings were not felt by early generations of Hellenized Egyptians, Persians, and Aramaeans. In the long run – one might estimate, on a comparative basis, another century and a half – one or more integral and distinctive cultures are likely to emerge in the Middle East from a synthesis of some aspects of Western culture and some aspects of Islamic culture. In the meantime, however, what exists is the dilemma.

It is the dilemma that affects the attitude of Westernized Arabs toward Israel. Basically, Israel is the nearest and most exaggerated example of Western culture. Although it is realized that non-European Jews and Muslim and Christian Arabs constitute a major part of the Israeli population, the image of Israel is overwhelmingly that of a Western cultural entity. Science, industry, military might, technology, discipline, know-how, a feeling of close kinship with the countries of Europe and America – the Western cultural attributes of Israel are obvious. Indeed, they are points of pride that are made much of by friends of Israel.

On the other hand – and these are points that are made much of by enemies of Israel – Israel embodies many of the negative aspects of Western culture as well. It is rude, uncouth, threatening, bullying, boastful, self-righteous, and unfair to the non-Western elements in the population, be they Muslim, Christian, or Jewish. All of this is part of the standard image of Israel propounded by many of its enemies. What is striking in this stereotype is that a century ago much the same terms would have been appropriate for describing European society at large if the person doing the describing had been a foe of European penetration. In other words, because of its proximity and its political history, Israel has inherited much of the opprobrium once directed toward the West in general. Israel has become a focus of the dilemma of cultural imperialism.

There is a secret and not so secret admiration of Israel's war-making capability as well as envy of her ability to deal as an equal with Western powers. It has frequently been stated, half seriously, that the Palestinians are becoming the Jews of the Middle East. By this it is meant that a diaspora beginning in 1948 is working toward the formation of an international

Palestinian community embodying the qualities associated with the ste-reotype of the international Jewish community. That is, the Palestinians are becoming self-reliant, rich, well educated, secretly influential in gov-ernment and business, etc.

What is interesting about this comparison is not its possible accuracy but the fact that it is not resented and refuted by Arabs who hear it men-tioned. This does not signify a hidden desire on the part of these Arabs to be Jews, but it does indicate a secret satisfaction in being thought of in the same terms as the stereotyped Jews. The stereotype, after all, represents the envy that some European non-Jews feel of the way in which a small minority of Jews succeeded in attaining the peak of Western cultural mas-tery. Cosmopolitan, Western-educated Arabs, who are quite numerous in the Palestinian diaspora, are not at all averse to being thought of in these terms.

Israel, then, is the physical embodiment of the force of Western cultural imperialism, and this without making the slightest effort to "convert" her neighbors to Western culture. The ambivalence about Western culture, the admiration and the guilt, the longing and the loathing, all become en-tangled in the Westernized Arab's view of Israel. Israel threatens the Arabs culturally precisely because the culture that Israel stands for is one that the Westernized Arabs believe to be superior – and hate themselves for believing it.

Is this not, however, the opposite attitude from the one discussed ear-lier that portrayed Israel, through secularist Arab eyes, as a backward and fanatic country? Yes. No one ever said that the Arab attitude toward Israel was a simple and consistent one. As a religiously based state, she is seen as an affront to modern civilization by the same people who are equipped to admire her Western achievements and castigate themselves for admiring them.

No. No one ever said that the Arab attitude toward Israel was a simple and consistent one. It has many components of which only two have been discussed here. The purpose of discussing these two, which are certainly not the most important, has been to illustrate the sort of complexity that is involved.

One of the ideas that becomes commonplace among the imperializers in episodes of cultural imperialism is that whatever true profundity of thought there is to be found within the imperialized culture resides in its classic pre-imperialistic tradition. The thinking of those people who are abandoning the old culture for the new one they regard as superior is nor-mally considered to be puerile and imitative, even though the individuals involved may be among the most intellectually gifted members of society. The reason for this is that the new recruits to the dominant culture have much more difficult questions to ponder than hereditary members of the dominant culture normally think. The answers are slow in coming, but they can be revolutionary when they arrive.

History has placed Israel at the crux of a long-term process of cultural imperialism (of which, after all, secularism is only a part). A normalization of political life between Israel and the Arabs may be attainable, but it would be idle to expect a normalization of life between the two to evolve before the dilemmas of cultural imperialism have found some sort of resolution.

I wonder today how much of this essay Said would have agreed or disagreed with. I suspect that my thinking was not entirely different from his own at that time. But I was never to find out. During the seventeen years we served on the same faculty, Edward and I never had a protracted conversation about the Middle East. Indeed, I can only recall a dozen or so brief exchanges, primarily about parochial Columbia matters.

Inasmuch as my office was in the Middle East Institute, which I came to direct after Jay Hurewitz's retirement in 1985, Edward understandably regarded me as an Orientalist. And Edward, as a rule, did not converse with Orientalists. Nor did he ever teach a course on the Middle East or participate, despite many invitations, in any activity of the Institute or, to the best of my recollection, of the Department of Middle East Languages and Cultures. As an English professor, the methodology he employed in thinking about Orientalism focused on interpreting published writings, not on asking those people who fell into his Orientalist category what they thought about the people and cultures they had chosen to devote their careers to, or how their careers related to the lives they led before and after first setting foot in an elementary Arabic class.

The Middle East Studies Association

WHEN PRESIDENT JIMMY CARTER took office in 1977, Professor William Zartman of New York University (NYU), who had been the secretary-treasurer of the Middle East Studies Association (MESA) since its founding in 1966, announced that he was stepping down from his post in anticipation of an appointment in the new administration. The MESA board had little time to recruit a new secretary-treasurer, and whoever was chosen would have to be able to come to the MESA office at NYU's Kevorkian Center at least once a week. I don't know who mentioned my name—I had been at Columbia for less than a year—but I was told that the choice came down to me and Professor Walter Weiker at Rutgers, a political scientist. Possibly I was offered the post because a commute from Morningside Heights in Manhattan was easier than one from New Brunswick, New Jersey.

I had attended a few of MESA's annual conferences, but I knew nothing of its inner workings. Thus when I took office I had no ideas about what I might do. This dilemma evaporated when I reviewed the annual budget and found an addition error that turned a balanced projection for the coming year into a $5000 deficit. MESA had no reserve fund to cover a deficit of even this modest size. So I decided that solving MESA's financial problem would be my primary goal as secretary-treasurer.

My first concern was the MESA Bulletin. Zartman had created and edited the MESA Bulletin as a publication of the secretariat. He was quite proud of it, and it gave him a personal means of reaching the membership. But the Bulletin's cost had never been factored into the MESA membership fees. Thus as the association grew, the Bulletin's printing and other costs grew apace with no budgetary foundation. So I called Professor Jere Bacharach at the University of Washington at Seattle and asked him whether his institution would cover those costs if he became editor. He made the necessary arrangements and proceeded to do a good job as editor.

The next problem was Cambridge University Press (CUP). Professor Stanford Shaw of UCLA had been the editor of the International Journal of Middle East Studies (IJMES) for a number of years and had accepted many articles that had not found their way into print. He liked to group articles in topical fashion in each issue and would therefore hold an article until its particular topic seemed right. This meant that some authors waited much longer than others, and they complained to CUP about editorial favoritism.

When Shaw's term as editor came to an end, the new editor, Professor Afaf Lutfi al-Sayyid Marsot, also of UCLA, found a full year's backlog of unpublished articles and announced that no new articles would be considered until the backlog was dealt with. The CUP journals people were furious and said that the announcement would doom IJMES. Yet at the same time, it became apparent that CUP had failed to reward MESA as per contract for its growing membership. To resolve the problem, CUP agreed to a contract renewal that benefited MESA, and Professor Marsot agreed for one (expensive) year to publish eight instead of four issues to clear the backlog.

In 1980, New York University gave MESA notice that it would stop providing space and administrative support in one year's time. This touched off a search for a new home for the association. After reviewing and rejecting proposals from several institutions, I telephoned Professor Michael Bonine, a geographer at the University of Arizona, and suggested that he solicit financial support from his administration and take my place as secretary-treasurer. This plan succeeded and brought stability to MESA's precarious finances. Mike provided excellent service as secretary-treasurer for many years.

My concern for saving money conflicted with the way MESA nominated its officers. At the association's 1976 business meeting, held in conjunction with its annual conference, Professor Kemal Karpat of the University of Wisconsin delivered a tirade about MESA being controlled by a clique and moved that nominations for the board be made by an elected committee rather than by board-selected nominators. This motion carried, and I had the responsibility of putting the new process into effect. The problem was that the new arrangement would greatly strain MESA's finances. I had attended Bill Zartman's last session with a nominating committee and seen that his practice was to bring its members—always living nearby until we started electing them—to New York, talk to them in the morning about MESA's needs, treat them to a nice lunch in Greenwich Village, and then discuss at length the pros and cons of the names put forward in afternoon deliberations. He freely gave his opinions on who would be a good president or board member, and who would not.

Once we had an elected committee, flying the members to New York and putting them up for a night became prohibitively expensive. I decided, therefore, to have the committee meet by conference call. I outlined MESA's situation on the phone, and then said that I would simply be the recording secretary during their deliberations over names. I did not comment on any of the names they discussed. I thought this worked well, and I recounted the event to Zartman with some pride. He responded by strongly upbraiding me for losing control of MESA, if not for totally destroying it. I thought that this pretty much confirmed Karpat's charge that MESA was being run by a clique, so I continued to keep mum during subsequent nominating committee conference calls.

The actual activities of the MESA secretariat during those years were minimal since the annual conferences were arranged by separate local arrangements and program committees, and MESA's publications were edited elsewhere. As for the meetings of the board, few important issues arose until the very end of my time in office, when the Alternative Middle East Studies Seminars (AMESS), a group of mostly younger scholars involved in a left-wing critique of the field, charged that MESA was still being run by a clique. Nothing came of this, but the leading AMESS members soon found themselves on the MESA ballot.

The only other matter worth mentioning is that my administrative assistant, who did most of the secretariat's work, was asked by a friend to supply the unedited minutes of MESA's Board meetings to the American Jewish Committee on a confidential basis. She told me about this effort to suborn her, and nothing came of it. To this day I find it bizarre that any organization at that time considered the MESA board worthy of surveillance.

Around the time that New York University told MESA that it would have to relinquish its office space and move to another host institution, I proposed a research project to analyze the evolution of MESA's membership over its first fifteen years. I requested $1500 from the Joint Committee on the Near and Middle East of the Social Science Research Council and American Council of Learned Societies. The Committee turned me down. I was told that a proper survey should include scholars who were not in MESA and cost a great deal more than $1500. Less formally, it was suggested to me that a survey that was likely to show a steady rise in the proportion of MESA's membership born or educated in the Middle East might lead me to conclude that Middle Eastern students were different from—possibly less capable than—American students. No one, until Said, suggested the opposite conclusion, that scholars from the Middle East might be more capable, or have a different and valuable outlook on the region. It seemed to me to be quite likely that this rejection reflected anxieties about scholars' personal backgrounds stimulated by the expanding impact of Edward Said's attack on Orientalists of the Euro-American persuasion.

The MESA membership file that I had intended to analyze was thrown away since Cambridge University Press had taken over keeping and updating the roster. Nevertheless, I did, toward the end of my tenure in office, write a personal appraisal of the Middle East studies field. That appraisal follows.

Reflections on the Study of the Middle East in Aerica

May 11, 1980

The segment of the American academic community concerned with the scholarly study of the Middle East is in a state of disarray so complicated and so severe that it is hard to perceive in all its aspects and even harder to prescribe for. My intent here is to present in summary form my own understanding of how and why this chaos arose, what its current dimensions are, and where a concerned student of the Middle East might expect the academic enterprise to go in the coming years.

I. Historically, one must start with the 1950s and the perceived need to create in the United States a capacity for understanding obscure parts of the world with which the United States was inextricably involved in the aftermath of World War II. It was a time of overall university expansion and democratization of higher education through the GI Bill, and federal and Ford Foundation financial stimuli brought forth major university commitments to study the Middle East. Enthusiasm with a world leadership role overshadowed problems of staffing and structure seemingly inherent in the new undertakings. There was an inadequate supply of competent scholars, and most of the existing talent was educated in a European tradition that stressed Orientalist values, even though major figures such as H. A. R. Gibb and Gustave E. von Grunebaum were as willing to prescribe for the modern world as the Oxford classical scholars had been to rule India a century earlier. Nevertheless, tenured appointments of mediocre scholars were made at that time at major universities and are only now beginning to be cycled through. In the meantime, a generation of students has been guided by professors who only rarely command widespread respect outside the sphere of the Middle East.

The structural problem compounded the staffing problem. Area studies centers were mandated with the mission to train broad-spectrum foreign area specialists possessing competence in language, culture, and modern affairs for their respective areas. The curricular demands of such programs, leaving aside the question of their intellectual validity, caused most Middle East specialists to devote the vast preponderance of their postgraduate, non-language course education to area-defined courses taught by marginally qualified faculty. Standards were established and patterns of snobbery emerged that put ever increasing emphasis upon broad-spectrum area studies with a strong Orientalist foundation.

The staffing problem in a time of rapid expansion led to Middle East studies gaining a reputation for mediocrity at the faculty level, and the structural problem caused this reputation to be extended to the student level. The reputation was well warranted, and the continued lack of penetration of Middle East scholarship into the academic world at large is testimony to this fact.

II. A second historical dimension has to do with the sociology of scholarship at both the faculty and student levels. The underlying motive factor here is the very inspiration of Middle East studies in the post-World War II period: US national interest. The atmosphere of Middle East studies in the late fifties, when I first became involved with it, was very clearly entwined with the ethos or temptation of government service, secondarily with commercial enterprise. Courses were designed and works of scholarship were written according to an agenda unconsciously set by the national interest. Insofar as the national interest was felt to be served by the development of the underdeveloped world (à la Walt Whitman Rostow's *The Stages of Economic Growth*), which would inevitably lead to pluralist, secular, democratic institutions, the agenda of scholarship was to discover this process as it was unfolding in order to help understand and guide it. Alternative directions of development were disregarded because they did not lead to desirable future outcomes, and actual Middle Eastern developments were given distorted interpretations for the sake of fitting the hopes of the world power. It is noteworthy, for example, that studies of modern Islam were done by scholars trained before World war II, but rarely by those trained more recently in this country.

At the same time that the national interest was guiding faculty and students toward the study of modernization in the recently created nation-states of the Middle East, the Arab-Israel conflict was engaging the emotions and thoughts of many area specialists. Yet it was an unspoken rule that one did not speak of the problem in a partisan fashion lest the veneer of academic civility be irremediably breached.

In sociological terms, the effects of this underlying national interest (understanding that Israel is regarded as part of that interest) were to divide students into two categories at the very same time that they were being trained to be universal area specialists. Within a deliberately unified curriculum, students who were drawn to the study of religion, high culture, and the continuity of tradition, or who were disinclined to involve themselves in modern political concerns, drifted into the most competently staffed segments of the program: classic Orientalist courses. Students who accepted the national interest agenda embodied in the area studies concept in its fullest sense tended to look upon Orientalist training as an unavoidable evil while concentrating on political science and modern history. Their programs did not have room for truly deep disciplinary training in the social sciences, and they did not usually pursue their Orientalist courses to an effective level of expertise.

The former group of students, therefore, selected academic tracks that gave them impressive language and cultural skills and a strong empathy with traditional society. The latter group concentrated on modern affairs, narrowly defined by the national interest agenda, and made little effort to gain cultural depth and understanding. Both groups, it is important to note, lacked disciplinary depth and were being taught by professors who were themselves poor in disciplinary background.

III. By the late 1960s the area studies concept had begun to come apart. Quantity was rapidly increasing, but low quality was built into the staffing and structure of the Middle East field. With increasing quantity came increasing specialization and a realization that disciplinary depth was important. Good students began to back away from the idea of being an area specialist in the academic world and moved into departmental programs that would give them a respectable training. Yet this also entailed an abandonment of some part of the old unified curriculum. Language expertise often declined, and broad-spectrum courses came to be recognized as the vehicles for disseminating intellectual pabulum. In 1960 a campus lecture on Iranian music would draw students from all branches of the Middle East curriculum; by 1970 it was drawing ethno-musicologists only.

With the reversion to traditional disciplines and the corresponding doubtfulness regarding the intellectual validity of area studies, faculty cleavages papered over by the rubric "Middle East studies" began to reopen. The strong Orientalists of European formation faded or passed away, and the newer luminaries were modernists of indifferent Orientalist skills and scarcely more impressive disciplinary talents. They were to be the new leaders of a Middle East studies field that was coming unstuck, but they themselves carried little weight in their nominal social science disciplines.

This crisis hit other area studies fields in the late sixties, as well, and there it exploded into loud and painful debates as to the intellectual validity and ethical propriety of having major academic enterprises determined in their scholarly pursuits by the national interest agenda. The Vietnamese war tore apart East Asian studies; decolonization and the civil rights movement did the same for African studies. The Middle East field seemed immune and prided itself upon its gentlemanliness. Yet the immunity was not real. In actuality, confrontation within the field was suppressed by the unspoken understanding that the keystone of national interest was Israel, a subject about which it was forbidden to speak. Instead of going through catharsis in the late sixties and coming out with sharpened minds and reexamined priorities, Middle East specialists stuck to business as usual and managed their consciences through other academic and non-academic outlets. The June War of 1967, a major event in

American intellectual history, had less effect within the field of Middle East studies than it did outside it.

Moving into the seventies, therefore, Middle East studies was drifting without strong leadership, beginning to fracture along Orientalist-modernist lines, losing its unified curriculum and common commitment, but still accepting the outmoded, disreputable, and ethically equivocal guidelines of the 1950's.

IV. Nothing has happened in the seventies to alter this state of affairs in a fundamental way, but much has happened to disguise it. The energy crisis added items to the modernist side of the agenda, and the ensuing US business involvement further enlarged the scope of the national interest agenda. These matters were increasingly handled outside the old Middle East studies curricula. The rise of Palestinian nationalism forced the Arab-Israel issue more intensively upon the Middle East studies community, but again the issue tended to be handled by new organizations and extra-curricular activities. The failure of liberal democracy—or to put it more precisely, the recognition that liberal democracy had never been in the cards for Middle Eastern countries—led to abandonment of simple modernization models, but the upshot was a new set of models demonstrating the value to the national interest of military dictatorship and other forms of authoritarian rule. This change in thinking provoked strong responses insofar as it seemed to be a betrayal of the ideals underlying the old modernization models, but these responses were muddled within the Middle East studies community and developed outside and along strongly leftist lines.

By the end of the 1970s, separate organizations had come into existence in support of Turkish studies, Iranian studies, Afghan studies, Middle East library science, Middle East economics, Middle East philosophy, Arabic teaching, etc., all under the benign auspices of the Middle East Studies Association although without formal connection with that association. There existed as well a revived orientalist group in the Middle East branch of the American Oriental Society, a pro-Zionist Academic Association for Peace in the Middle East, a pro-Arab Association of Arab-American University Graduates, a quasi-Marxist group of collectives known as the Alternative Middle East Studies Seminars, and a number of other less visible groups with deep concerns in the area. On the national organizational level, Middle East studies had become little more than a vague rubric around which people with more specific interests, both regional and disciplinary, gravitated. But the organizational structure of the university programs had changed little; indeed, new Middle East studies programs were still coming into existence as the national interest was perceived to grow.

The loss of focus implied by this profusion of new institutions was accompanied by striking new trends at the individual level. First, major statements of opinion or theory were increasingly being made by people who could in no way be called Middle East area specialists: Edward Said, Stanley Hoffman, Roger Fisher, Noam Chomsky, and others. Second, intelligent disciplinary specialists with area studies backgrounds ceased to identify with Middle East studies in a significant fashion: Nadav Safran, Morrow Berger, and others. Third, students became increasingly lost in their search for coherent programs and migrated toward disciplines or toward Orientalism.

V. Looking ahead, the prospects for Middle East scholarship are complicated but not very luminous. Academic departments at significant universities are moving away from area specialization toward disciplinary depth, and Middle East studies has been constructed so that disciplinary excellence is not available in quantity. While job opportunities of this sort do not abound, more and more Middle East specialists will be employed as isolated faculty in smaller institutions with meager resources. Middle East programs at universities seem likely to maintain their current constitutions because of the national interest imperatives that are still voiced and felt and because of funding that arises from such imperatives. Student anomie and faculty disharmony seem bound to continue with Orientalist-modernist cleavages remaining strong. MESA will continue to be a weak organization since it is no one's primary home, and the most it can offer are benign auspices. Disciplinary excellence is likely to become more abundant but at the cost of area integration, mutual contact and sharing of views, and language competence.

VI. Compounding the unattractiveness of this picture is the probable direction of real world events in the Middle East. The Iranian Revolution is part of a far broader current of Islamic political activity that is certain to become increasingly important in the next decade. The national interest agenda of the1950's, even as augmented in the last two decades, has militated strongly against the development of expertise in this field, not to mention empathy. The self-selection of Middle East scholars over the last quarter century has channeled the personalities most attuned to these developments away from the modern period and allowed the modern period to be dominated by people who are constitutionally disinclined to undertake such studies, as well as unprepared in their lack of good Orientalist credentials. The Muslim political movement as it grows will make its own definitions of quality with regard to Western Middle East scholarship and will not be as in thrall to the latest turnings of the paradigmatic Harvard political scientist's mind as were the Middle East elites of the decades recently past. In other words, the next phase of Middle Eastern history has already in its opening days demonstrated the poverty of thought and conceptualization in the modernist side of the field.

VII. What is to be done? New leadership is always a convenient answer, but how should leadership be manifested and where should it lead? Educational phylogeny suggests that the fracturing of an original concept into a whole set of descendant research directions is natural, irreversible, and desirable. But there is always a lingering awareness of the need to keep an eye on the concept as a whole and facilitate communication among its myriad wayward branches. MESA can probably aspire to no higher role in the academic world strictly speaking, as opposed to public education, etc. If MESA cannot undertake a more ambitious leadership role, what about the Joint Committee on the Near and Middle East of the Social Science Research Council and American Council of Learned Societies? Setting of collective research priorities and facilitating their fulfillment provides a reasonable leadership goal of some utility, but it does not address the major, underlying problems of the field and hence does not provide a broader sort of leadership. Perhaps it cannot address these problems, but the following are examples of what appear to be major problems:

- What is and should be the relationship of the American national interest to Middle East scholarship?

- How can the talents and insights of the Orientalist or modernist Middle East scholars be made available to each other without forcing either into the other's mold?

- How can the so often superior social science skills of non-Middle East specialists be integrated with area knowledge?

- How can fundamental theoretical work be fostered that is not foredoomed to failure by the built-in pattern of incompetence in the field?

- How can political problems be confronted openly without destroying the field?

- How can stimulating and mutually beneficial relations with non-American scholars and thinkers be fostered, and how can their benefits be mediated to a larger and better audience than that provided by existing Middle East studies programs?

VIII. Whether it will be necessary to destroy existing structures in order to reach a point where questions of this sort can be effectively addressed is problematic. What is not in question is that if these questions are not addressed, existing divisions will become exacerbated, new funding will reinvigorate and revalidate outgrown concepts of Middle East studies as a creature of the national (and business) interest, the penetration of Middle East scholarship into the disciplines and overall university communities will remain stagnant, mediocrity will continue unabated, and we will all find ourselves in one hell of a mess ten years hence.

A Columbia Education

WELL OVER HALF of the undergraduate and graduate courses I took at Harvard dealt with the Middle East and its languages. I boasted to friends and family that Harvard was a perfect environment for someone like me: highly focused on an unusual area of study and eager to take advantage of the university's wealth of offerings. As a result, when I got to Columbia a decade after finishing my PhD, I had published two academic books on the Middle East and one novel set in the Sahara desert. And I had read a very great deal about Islam and the Middle East ... and about camels. Yet unlike a traditional European Orientalist, I didn't know much else. I had no training in either classical philology – my Latin was mediocre, my Greek all but non-existent – or Biblical/Jewish/Christian studies. Nor did my two substantial trips to the region add up to even a year of in-country experience. And even when considering non-academic career options during my period of jobless-ness, I had never given thought to any sort of Middle East-related government or corporate employment. Lucy fancied the Peace Corps, but I did not.

Once I had landed a permanent job, however, I was pretty happy with my level of education. I felt that I had escaped the most stultifying part of Orientalist training, namely, editing Arabic manuscripts, even though I had used innovative quantitative techniques to cull information from them. That I might have known too much about the Middle East was not a question that I was inclined to entertain.

Columbia's idea of a basic college education differed from Harvard's, which had been based on *General Education in a Free Society*, a report and curriculum design put out by a faculty committee in 1945. It is a thoughtful document, but we undergraduates never had to read it. Instead, as it prescribed, we sat in large lecture halls twice a week to listen to a professor pontificate (blo-viate?) on some great work, and then (a few of us) spent a third hour in a discussion section where a graduate student would seek to elaborate on the professor's presentation.

I found the approach unutterably boring.

The corresponding core curriculum at Columbia was based on small group discussions of the Great Books (or art works, or musical compositions) that made up the canon of Western civilization. Down through the 1960s the university's most illustrious humanists proudly dedicated themselves to taking their turn as section instructors. By the time I arrived, however, most senior faculty had dropped by the wayside, and the teaching was done by graduate student preceptors and junior faculty.

When I first learned about the four required courses – Contemporary Civilization (that is, political and social thought from the Greeks on), Literature Humanities, Art Humanities, and Music Humanities – I thanked my lucky stars that I had never undergone such force-feeding of Europe's ballyhooed cultural tradition. I remember thinking that here I was, a ten-ured Ivy League history professor, and I had never read Homer, Thucydides, Virgil, Dante, Cervantes, Hobbes, Locke, Bentham, Kant, or Nietzsche. But I had read the Qur'an, al-Ghazali, Ibn Khaldun, Ibn Tufayl, Usama b. Munqidh, Hafez, Rumi, Naguib Mahfuz, and Sadegh Hedayat. Wasn't that just as good? Or even better? Even when I was sitting on the committee that oversaw the core curriculum, I made no secret of my disdain for its insistence on indoc-trinating undergraduates in the intellectual and artistic classics of Western Civilization.

Then one day Michael Rosenthal, the associate dean who chaired the committee, observed that maybe I was simply making a virtue of my igno-rance. I pondered this, chose to overlook the snide tone of his remark, and eventually decided that he might be right. Why was I disparaging some-thing that I had not directly experienced? Consequently I decided to teach a Contemporary Civilization discussion section for one semester ... on a "know your enemy" basis.

I eventually devoted fifteen semesters to core curriculum classes and taught all four courses, becoming the first of only two faculty members to do so. Two considerations won me over as a fan of the core. First, I was autono-mous in my section. There was no grand lecture by a professorial notable that I had to fall in line with, particularly since my tenured status allowed me to attend sporadically the "staff only" briefing luncheons designed to suggest some common themes from the week's reading. And second, I came to like knowing that in any undergraduate course I taught I could count on all of the students knowing at least a little something about the required library of famous books.

When I started out, I was on the same footing as most of my students. We were all reading the texts for the first time. True, I was forty and they were eighteen, and I was grading their work. But many of my ideas were just as jejune as theirs. By the last time I taught Contemporary Civilization, one bright but pugnacious young woman frequently found fault with my idiosyncratic approach to certain texts. But eventually she declared: "I have finally figured out how you are teaching this course. We are all reading the texts for the first time, and you want to be the smartest kid in the class." She was right. I always felt more like a student than an instructor. Plus I could demand that they read a graphic novel, Alan Moore's *Watchmen*.

My Columbia education did not stop there. With the dawn of the twenty-first century Theodore de Bary, an eminent Confucian scholar and former university provost, campaigned to add a new element to the Columbia core that he was firmly wedded to. He decided that nobility and civility were such universal and transcultural ideals that students should be offered discussion seminars focused on those concepts as they developed through time, not just in the West, but in a variety of cultures. I participated in several years of week-long planning sessions and co-taught the course with Ted once it was accepted by the curriculum committee. So now my exposure to classic texts expanded to include the likes of *The Lotus Sutra*, *I Ching*, *The Tale of the Heike*, the *Ramayana*, and *Cilappatikaram: The Tale of an Anklet*.

Yet a third component of my Columbia education came from my association with Columbia University Press. I served for about a dozen years on the Publication Committee that had to approve all proposals before contracts could be offered. And then I replaced the press Director as the committee's chair when a by-laws change elevated that role and made it include membership on the Board of Trustees. I remained on the board after I rotated off the committee. All told, this exposed me to the details of Press publishing, and entitled me to receive free books, for more than thirty years. Would I otherwise have ever read a history of Finland? A history of Poland? A biography of Darwin's rival, William Wallace? An account of hunters and gatherers in Amazonia? A history of rain-making experiments?

The question arises of whether my Orientalist training at Harvard – or anybody's Orientalist training anywhere – should be taken to define the parameters of my intellectual life? A career and a life, after all, are two different things.

Iran 1: *The Tomb of the Twelfth Imam*

THE PEDESTRIAN CONVENTIONALITY and perfunctory narratives that defined Middle East studies from the 1950s through the 1970s suffered
three devastating blows:

First, in 1979 the Iranian Revolution climaxed in the Shah's flight into
exile. American social scientists found it baffling that a religious upheaval
led by high level clerics wedded to beliefs that should have been disappearing in the global current of modernization could spark a revolution that
would root out royal autocracy, decimate the officer corps, drive the nou-
veau riche and other Westernizers into exile, and impose a religiously inflected regime structured around a constitution and electoral institutions.
Some scholars, such as my then Columbia colleague Zalmay Khalilzad, who
would come to play a key role in American diplomacy, simply denied that
religion had anything to do with the revolution. Many others discovered
that there was almost nothing written in English describing Iranian Shi'ism.

Rightly or wrongly, I felt I had a handle on what was going on.

Second, in 2001 the 9/11 attacks on the World Trade Center and the
Pentagon showed that the terrorism that had long been considered a ghast-
ly but localized aspect of the Arab-Israel conflict could inflict serious dam-
age on the United States. Yet the terrorists were not Palestinians. Nor were
they Iranian Shi'ites. Most of them were from Saudi Arabia, an American
dependency that was regarded as unassailable. What was happening with
Islam? Why had no one seen 9/11 coming?

Rightly or wrongly, I felt I had a handle on what was going on.

And third blow, the Arab Spring upheavals of 2011, came as a complete
surprise and totally overturned the existing political order in the Middle
East. Those, like me, who had predicted the emergence, through revolution
or otherwise, of moderate electoral regimes based on Islamic political parties, were dismayed by the onset of civil wars, bitter sectarian conflict, hor-
rendous atrocities, and intensification of military autocracy.

This time my attempts to understand what was going on proved to be
mostly wrong.

Though I think I did better job of analyzing these three cataclysms than
most Middle East specialists, my overall conclusion is that the Middle East
studies enterprise had abjectly failed as a vehicle for training people with
specialized understanding capable of guiding the United States in choosing
wise regional policies.

Did Middle East studies fail because of Orientalism? Or because the dead hand of the modernization theorists remained at the helm as one crisis after another spun out of control? Or because the task of understanding the political, social, intellectual, and economic currents welling up within a world Muslim community of 1.8 billion people was just too overwhelming for a small cadre of specialists drawing on scanty documentation, stultifying and inapplicable theories, and a network of tendentious and dysfunctional institutional structures?

In April, 1977, at the end of my first year of teaching at Columbia, the Director of the university's Middle East Institute, J. C. Hurewitz, offered to have the Institute pay for me to participate in a week-long "scholar-diplomat seminar" in Washington. Hurewitz had a long and fruitful relationship with the US Department of State, and I'm sure he felt that my teaching about the modern Middle East would benefit from observing its operations first-hand.

Iran was my primary interest. During my two years at Berkeley before coming to Columbia, I had become increasingly convinced that what we have come to call Islamic politics was a growing force that would soon overtake all of our scholarly concerns about Zionism, nationalism, socialism, and modernization. This conviction arose partly from looking at the long-term trajectory of Islamic history and partly from conversations with various colleagues, most notably Hamid Algar and Hichem Djaït. With that in mind, I asked Frank Huddle, a former student who was the Iran desk officer in the State Department's Intelligence and Research division (INR), whether he had any materials relating to Ayatollah Khomeini. He said he thought there were a couple of pamphlets, but he told me that the bank of filing cabinets devoted to the Tudeh, the Iranian communist party, was the proper archive for me to explore. I disagreed. My recollection is that when Frank received a posting to Nepal later in the summer, INR did not get around to filling the post of Iran desk officer before the revolution.

Six months after my Washington stint, I flew to Iran with my friend from Harvard, Roy Mottahedeh, the two of us being the most junior invitees to a conference devoted to the history of government administration in Iran. After a couple of days in Tehran, we traveled to Hamadan by bus. The conference offered little of intellectual interest, but it gave me a chance to listen to senior scholars like Bertold Spuler, Hans Robert Roemer, and Masashi Haneda whom I would never again meet. Of greater consequence on this first Iran visit since 1971 was the opportunity it provided to talk about social and religious ferment with various Iranians and to observe some of the obnoxious aspects of Westernization that were becoming apparent in

Iranian society, both in Tehran, where the Tehran University campus was being patrolled by the military, and in the provincial city of Hamadan. I was particularly struck by a reception at the Hamadan officers club at which the officers and their conferee guests stood in the center of the room and had drinks while the officers' wives, perforce dressed in stylish Western party dresses, sat silently on chairs around the room's perimeter, protected from contact with males by an invisible *cordon sanitaire*.

When I got home and read the news about disturbances in Iran, I recalled a poster of the Shah I had seen in certain stores selling military uniforms. Instead of a marshal's uniform or imperial ermine, he was wearing a plain dark suit and looking off into the distance with a lambent glow over his left shoulder. The text read: *Shahanshah, Zell Allah*, or King of Kings, The Shadow of God. The thought slowly grew in my mind that the Shah was too late in calling on God, and that a religious revolution was far from impossible.

To expand this thought into a novel that would see the Shah's rule imperiled by a religious revolution led by a white-bearded Ayatollah, I made use of an anomalous, clumsily carved tombstone I had discovered in 1966 in the ruins of Nishapur. The information on the stone clearly identified it as marking the last resting place of an early descendant of Ali ibn Abi Talib, Muhammad's cousin and son-in-law in whose cause the Shi'ite branch of Islam came into being. There was some possibility that the stone was a pious fraud from the 1960s, inspired perhaps by some Nishapuri's dream. ("Oh, ye of faith, my last resting place has been forgotten! Go forth and find it.") This at least was the theory of the eminent Shi'ite cleric I eventually corresponded with. My own theory was that it was a barely literate copy of a real stone that had been destroyed when railway builders working on the line connecting Tehran to Mashhad dug a trench through the ruins. The stone stood all alone next to the cut made for the track, and in a part of the ruins that I estimated had probably been an elite cemetery a thousand years earlier. I guessed that the builders had been reluctant to report their destruction of an important tomb and risk delaying work on the railroad, but also reluctant to ignore entirely what they had done lest someone find out and blow the whistle on them.

I finished the novel shortly before the pre-revolutionary Jaleh Square massacre of September 8, 1978, and messengered it off to Joan Kahn, the editor who had accepted *Kicked to Death by a Camel* but rejected my next two efforts. She gave a hesitant reply because what I had written was so close to what was actually transpiring, but she offered me a contract once I wrote an introductory chapter set in the eighth century to assure readers that my story was pure fiction. It still took fifteen months for Harper & Row to see

the book into print, and by that time the American embassy had been occupied. As the reviewer for the Los Angeles Times put it:

> Oooops. Talk about the wrong time and the wrong place.... One can picture
> [the author], visions of a best seller, not to mention movie rights, dancing
> in his eyes.... However, for reasons all too painfully clear, the current crisis
> hasn't prompted a great movement to plumb the Moslem mind. How often
> do you hear, for example, someone saying: "You know, I'd really like to
> take an Iranian to lunch to understand how they really think"?... It's not
> that bad, but we're not watching "War and Peace" go down the tubes.[1]

I had not been trying to compete with Tolstoy, and later intimations
I made that *The Tomb of the Twelfth Imam* predicted the Iranian Revolution
have been justly ridiculed. I had written a second-rate potboiler, and the pot
bubbled over before I could get it off the stove. Nevertheless, I would still
claim that in comparison to more successful books glorifying the Shah published immediately after his fall, mine was the only book published that year
that highlighted religious militancy and found the idea of Islamic revolution
both credible and logical.

Being prescient gets you only so far, however. In the months that followed, the *New York Review of Books* invited me to analyze some recent works
on Iran, and then paid me a kill fee when my essay was insufficiently critical
of the revolution. Likewise, the *New York Times Magazine* invited me to write
about the rising current of political Islam, though with the editor's explicit
stricture that they would not publish any sentences favorable to Iran. I ful-
filled my assignment, but my reward was again a kill fee. Thus my breakout
moment as a public intellectual came and went.

For the next two decades my contention that the Iranian Revolution
was as important as the French or Russian revolutions and its product, the
Islamic Republic of Iran, just as deserving of continuing and open-minded
analysis made me persona non grata in American policy circles. A KGB agent
working for the Soviet UN delegation came by every few months to chat
with me about Middle Eastern affairs, as did a Chinese military intelligence
officer, but the CIA stopped in only to ask me what the KGB agent had been
asking about. I eventually invited the KGB man to talk about Soviet Middle
East policy at the Institute and invited the CIA woman to sit in the audience.
My disposition was to answer the questions of anyone who wanted to know
my views, regardless of their affiliations.

---

1. "The Wrong Time, Wrong Place," *Los Angeles Times* (Dec. 10, 1979).

Iran 2: Islam in Ashkelon

HAGGAI RAM, A HISTORY PROFESSOR at Ben Gurion University of the Negev, wrote the following in his book *Iranophobia: The Logic of an Israeli Obsession* (Stanford University Press, 2009):

> The international ordeal ... began in Tehran on November 4, 1979, when some four hundred Iranian militant students stormed the U.S. embassy and took all diplomats and employees there hostage. In the midst of this crisis, in March 1980, the late Ze'ev Schiff, *Ha'aretz*'s expert on military and security affairs, reported on a conference held in Tel Aviv University in which Middle East experts from Israel and the United States convened to discuss the implications of the Iranian revolution and the hostage taking. Schiff was particularly impressed with Columbia University's professor of Middle East studies, Richard Bulliet, who "for quite a while ... talked enthusiastically ... about the positive aspects ... and the humane side of the revolution." "It is remarkable," Schiff wrote, "that you can always find Americans who think differently and raise question marks about the position of the mainstream." And yet in his essay, Schiff said not a word about Bulliet's "different" modes of thought. Readers interested in the assumptions and reasoning of the American professor regarding revolutionary Iran would find none. Instead, Schiff concentrated on the negative impression Bulliet left on "most Israelis" present in the audience, who, like Schiff, were shocked to discover that "what seemed insanely murderous to many of his countrymen, seemed perfectly sane and understandable to him." Paradoxically, although Schiff's declared intention was to introduce original and provocative views on the revolution and the hostage crisis, all he ended up doing was reproducing what he himself defined as "the position of the mainstream." The other stance, in this case the one voiced by Bulliet, was entirely absent from his account.

Since I had seldom written and rarely spoken publicly about matters touching on Israel, the invitation to attend the Tel Aviv University conference held at a pleasant resort hotel in Ashkelon came as a surprise. As I recall, only two other Americans were flown over for the event. My surmise was that Nadav Safran, who had given me my first job at Harvard and who was then spending a year in Israel, had proposed my name. I had been out of touch with Nadav since leaving Harvard in 1973, but he had recently asked me to suggest a plan for restructuring Harvard's Center for Middle East

Studies, to which he was expecting to be appointed Director. I had sent him my proposal – three boring pages predicated on my return to the Harvard faculty – but not heard back from him. My expectation, therefore, was that the conference would pay for my trip, but its real substance would surface in a private discussion with Nadav. That discussion never took place, and Nadav never said a word about my proposal. He also said nothing about the talk I delivered to the conference

My message was not exclusively about Iran. It was about Islamic politics. Speaking to the A-team of Israeli academic specialists on the modern Middle East, I maintained that new political currents identifying themselves as Islamic were so important that they would unquestionably become the primary concern for all of us for the remainder of our careers. Going further, I said that "Islamic politics" constituted a political spectrum that ranged from revolutionary and terroristic at one end to meliorative and democratic at the other, and that it would be the task of the policy community to recognize the different parts of that spectrum and to appreciate that all Islamic political tendencies were not necessarily evil. I cited student political currents in the West Bank Palestinian community as a case in point.

My speech did not differ much from speeches I had been delivering in the United States since the onset of the Iranian Revolution, but the reactions did. One by one, a series of well-known Israeli specialists took the floor to denounce my idiocy. Not only was the Iranian Revolution categorically evil, they informed me, but any young Palestinians who were waving the banner of Islam were simply revolting against their fathers and would inevitably mature after a few years into secular and militant nationalists. Rather than being simply a tool for adolescent rebellion, therefore, Islam should be seen as a conservative antidote to the Palestinian nationalism that threatened the security of Israel.

To compound matters, the organizers of the conference arranged for me, and me alone, to repeat my bizarre views at a press briefing. This was where Ze'ev Schiff and other eminent Israeli journalists encountered my opinions. Privately, I was told that my presence had become an embarrassment for Samuel Lewis, the American ambassador.

A day later, waiting for a plane home at Athens airport, I saw my picture on the front page of an Israeli newspaper being read by another passenger. I asked him what the article said, and he told me that some American had made a fool of himself by saying positive things about Iran.

It did not surprise me that the Israelis were either ignorant of, or in deep denial about, the rising current of Islamic politics. So were most Americans. Seeing their annoyance so vividly on display, however, helped me to understand the Israel government's benign attitude toward the founding of Hamas later in the decade. Islam was to be an antidote to the nationalist extremism of the PLO. I don't know which specialists supported the creation of Hamas, but it was a logical follow-through to their hostility toward the analysis I was proposing.

As for the public lampooning I was subjected to, it dampened whatever interest I might have had in revisiting Israel, and it left me with the impression, since confirmed through one Middle East crisis after another, that Israeli academics specializing on the contemporary Middle East, particularly those who make significant contributions to government policies, are no more astute than their American counterparts, and often less so. I believe they have consistently underestimated their Palestinian and Muslim activist adversaries, though not necessarily the front-line Arab governments, for many decades.

Some years later an Israeli diplomat specializing on Iran visited me at the Middle East Institute. He remarked that Iran's position on crucial matters defied analysis because they had been unable to identify the individual in the Iranian government who made the key decisions. I responded that conflicting currents of thought in the parliament, the security establishment, and the clergy did indeed complicate matters, but added that this was not unusual in countries with normal political institutions.

"We are a small ministry," he told me. " We can't do normal politics. We need a single leader on whose supremacy we can rely."

Iran 3: Islam in Honolulu

IN 1980 I RECEIVED AN INVITATION from the Department of Religion at the University of Hawaii to participate in a conference on Islam. A chance to visit Hawaii! Also attending would be Professor Mahmoud Ayoub, a highly regarded blind authority on Islam. We flew out together and were met at the airport by Lenn Evan Goodman, a professor of Islamic and Jewish philosophy, who filled us in on the murky rationale for the conference. It seems that a theatrical professor in the Department of Religion had taught a course in which he assumed the role, complete with costume, of assorted founders of religions. The presentations were videotaped for prospective dissemination to other universities that might be interested in such a dramatic introduction to comparative religions. Unfortunately for the professor, certain Muslim students took exception to his sword-wielding portrayal of Muhammad – allegedly containing the exclamation "I love my women and I love my wine!" Since I never saw the video, I can't confirm its contents.

Lenn told us that a group of Muslim students decided that the professor in question should be killed for his offense, and the assassination plot was moving forward when two Muslim professors reported it to the administration. The plot was promptly squelched, but instead of being thanked for coming forward, the two professors were disciplined for failure to specify the names of the individual students who were said to have committed themselves to carrying out the assassination and whisking the murderer out of the country in a private plane.

As news of the controversy spread, the Muslim community in Honolulu became concerned that the Department of Religion was not teaching about Islam in an appropriate fashion. In response, the Department decided on a peace-making gesture, namely, a conference on Islam to which the local community would be invited and given a chance to air any grievances. To get funding for the conference from the Hawaii Council for the Humanities, the Department had to invite at least two off-islanders: hence, the weekend junket for me and Mahmoud. But a junket that without forewarning landed us in a cauldron of outrage.

Happily, the conference went off without a hitch. Differences were papered over, the Department promised to hire a specialist on Islamic matters, and Mahmoud and I eventually joined hands with the religion professors to sing Aloha 'Oe [Farewell to Thee] and make our departure. Most memorable to me had been Mahmoud's response to a question from a community member who asked whether Muslim women could go to the beach in bathing suits. He replied that as a blind person, he did not care one way or the other, but that the consensus of Muslim scholars was that bathing suits were not appropriate. Cheers from the men in the audience.

Outside the perimeter of the conference proper, I met with the two disciplined professors to hear their side of the story. And then I met separately with one of them, a Pakistani professor of physics, who had a request to make. At that time the American hostages were being held in Tehran, and every effort to negotiate their release had failed. My Pakistani interlocutor asked me to convey to the State Department, upon my return to New York, his willingness to assemble an international delegation of Muslim leaders that would go to Iran and prevail upon Ayatollah Khomeini to release the hostages in the interest of the worldwide Islamic movement.

I asked who these leaders were, and he replied that I would not recognize any of their names because they were not generally known outside the orbits of the movements they led. This did not strike me as particularly promising, but he told me that he himself was well known personally to the American intelligence community because he had been Pakistan's chief spy in Washington in the early 1970s during the presidency of Zulfikar Ali Bhutto, the leader who initiated Pakistan's nuclear weapons program.

As it happened, I knew people in the State Department who were working on the hostage issue. So I made a telephone call and related what the professor had told me. It seemed like a curious coda to an unexpected but enjoyable trip. I thought I would hear no more about it, but several weeks later I received a telephone call from the State Department switchboard asking whether I would be available to take a call later that day about "your plan for the hostage crisis." It was certainly not my plan, but I sat by my phone all afternoon nevertheless. It never rang.

My assumption is that the Pakistani professor did, in fact, command a certain degree of credibility and that a policy option was put forward of contacting him for further information. Then at some level that option was rejected, probably because no one in the US government wanted to be indebted to a shadowy group of Islamists who might well prove more radical than the Ayatollah. If that is what happened, I can't disagree with the decision.

Looking back, I wonder why I even attempted to get involved in a diplomatic issue of such magnitude. But those were strange days. The Iranian Revolution was unlike any other political event, as was the hostage crisis; and very few people, whether diplomats, scholars, or journalists, had a clear, much less incontrovertible, understanding of what was going on. Moreover, the State Department was not averse to seeking help wherever it could get it.

Earlier, on April 24, 1980, for example, I had been invited, along with a group of fellow scholars specializing on Iran, to spend a day with the Iran Working Group exploring the cultural peculiarities of the revolution and of the Iranian clergy. Henry Precht, our host and head of the Iran Working Group, spent the morning bringing us up to speed on the gambits that had already been tried. The afternoon was to be devoted to our responses, none of which struck me as being very helpful. Precht was no longer present, however, because during the break before lunch, his pager had gone off and he had silently departed. The next day we learned that our military had launched an unsuccessful attempt to rescue the hostages. The raid had commenced at about the same time as our colloquium on Iranian culture.

We were the cover story. The figuring must have been that any Iranian spy tracking State Department activities would have been reassured by the arrival of people like me that nothing of import was scheduled for that day. All quiet on the Iran front.

Could we have contributed anything useful? And if so, was the State Department open to new thinking on Iran? My answer to both questions is no. When the crisis began on November 4, 1979, I contacted certain Iranians I knew to ask what was going on. My best informant was a wealthy businessman who had left the country well before the revolution. He made calls to family and friends and reported their consensus that inasmuch as releasing the hostages would cast a political shadow on whoever authorized the move, their release could not be expected until after the constitutional referendum and presidential election scheduled for January, 1980, and probably not before the parliamentary elections the following summer.

I conveyed this view to a friend working in the State Department. He thanked me but said that the release would actually take place before Christmas. Why? Because the White House had directed that it should. Thus began forty years of dealing with Iran according to American preferences rather than Iranian realities.

The Gulf Scenario

IN THE SPRING OF 1981 I was invited to become a terrorist. A former foreign service officer of my acquaintance was helping the Center for Strategic and International Studies (CSIS) in Washington, D.C. produce a crisis simulation game to be televised by the ABC news program *20/20*, and he was seeking to enlist a "white hat" to be a member of the terrorist team. By a "white hat" he meant a Middle East aficionado with a reputation for political neutrality. I was curious about how crisis simulations worked, but I was leery about becoming party to a propaganda event designed to demonize the Palestinians in American eyes. At the time, the PLO was actively involved in the civil war that had been raging in Lebanon since 1975. So I agreed to participate only on condition that the Palestinians would not be involved in the crisis scenario, which was to be kept secret until the real-time exercise began. My acquaintance said that while the details of the fictional crisis were confidential, he had been assured that the perpetrators were not Palestinians.

I arrived in Washington to discover that the terrorist team would consist of me, Michael Ledeen, and a third person, who remained mostly silent and whose name now slips my mind. Michael Ledeen I did not know, but I quickly concluded from various outrageous remarks he made that he had happily been drawn into the game as a "black hat." Indeed, by the time I stormed out in a rage the following day, I had concluded that Ledeen was not only nefarious, but unprincipled and dishonest as well.

The exercise began with the nature of the simulation being explained to all the participants, who included well-known figures with distinguished careers in government and national security affairs. We were told that a group of Turkish radicals had hijacked an oil tanker on the high seas and planned to anchor it in New York harbor. There they would threaten to pump oil out of the tanker if their demands were not met. The crisis was not the pollution of the Hudson River, but rather the explosive power of the natural gas that would come out of solution and accumulate in the hold of the vessel as it was gradually emptied. We were told that it would accumulate enough explosive force to destroy the George Washington Bridge. This scenario was designed to test the ability of the government team, which represented federal, state, and municipal jurisdictions, along with the armed services and various security agencies, to coordinate effective responses to the threat in real time.

Things began to go wrong, from my point of view, almost immediately with the revelation as the ship arrived in New York that the Turkish perpetrators were actually Palestinians. The Control Team, which was in charge of the simulation, had the three of us isolated in a small terrorist office where our discussions were continuously monitored by an ABC camera. Our charge was to decide when and where to begin emptying the tanker, and how to deploy a number of "assets" in different countries around the globe. (Ledeen gleefully insisted that one of those assets was an English professor at Columbia University, namely, Edward Said.) Since the "Palestinian" goal was announced to be recognition of a Palestinian state on the West Bank and a billion dollars in cash, it seemed obvious, to me at least, that wanton loss of life would alienate the United States government rather than opening the door to negotiation. Hence we ordered the kidnapping in London of a prominent American newsman, whom we would try to persuade to be a mouthpiece for our demands. In order to internationalize the crisis, we further ordered, with a naval okay from the Control Team, that the tanker be routed up the East River and anchored beside the United Nations within explosion distance.

In response, the Control Team informed us that our kidnap plan had gone awry and our operatives had machine-gunned a bunch of civilians in a London hotel. And they vetoed our anchorage plan. This proved to be a pattern. Once I was back in my hotel room musing about the day's events, I realized that every "terrorist" action we had dreamed up had been unilaterally converted into a horrific bloodbath by the Control Team. When I arrived for the second day, I discovered that our conspiratorial headquarters in Zurich had been located and our contacts with our assets, including the operatives on the tanker, had been severed. All terrorist actions would now be the prerogative of the Control Team.

Though I am by nature extremely slow to anger, I stormed out of the office in a fury and demanded to know who was running the Control Team, since that individual obviously had a political agenda that included a view of Palestinian terrorism being synonymous with utterly mindless bloodshed perpetrated on civilians. The person who had recruited me for the event reluctantly disclosed that the head of the Control Team was, in fact, an Israeli intelligence colonel. This news greatly magnified my anger, and I demanded to talk to Robert Kupperman, the head of the Center for Strategic and International Studies. Presently he appeared, and I told him that I had been recruited into the simulation on false pretenses and that if my name or image appeared in any form in the broadcast version of the exercise, I would sue the CSIS and ABC. Then, still steaming, I took the train back to New York.

A decade later, Kupperman's recollection of the simulation was recorded in a history of the CSIS:

I was drinking heavily one night at Class Reunion [a Washington after-hours hangout that was popular with the press] with some CIA folks who used to frequent the place. I suggested that what was needed was some elaborate live-actor gaming with real people who might be out of office at the moment, but people who really had experience in making big-time decisions.[1]

When ABC broadcast the simulation as a *20/20* segment, *New York Magazine* began its lengthy review with this scary summary: "What if Palestinian terrorists seized a tanker bearing 65 tons [*sic*] of oil in New York harbor and threatened to dynamite the ship – unless the United States supported an independent Palestine on the West Bank and gave the new state $1 billion?" Note that there had never been an instance of Palestinian terrorism in the United States, nor has any occurred since that time. Threatening Americans has never been a Palestinian political goal. The review went on to talk about the character of the terrorist scheme:

> [Michael Ledeen] commanded terrorist control in Zurich, which dictated to the hijackers on the ship. (In most games, terrorists are merely a part of the control team, but Kupperman had decided to experiment with a roving terrorist organization.) Ledeen was a loose cannon. He instigated the kidnapping of ABC *World News Tonight* anchorman Peter Jennings [– this was my idea –] and had a passenger jet shot down at London's Heathrow airport, just to prove that his side meant business [– this was Ledeen's idea]. Kupperman squelched his attempt to disguise one of the hijackers as a released hostage, who would then announce to the world that these terrorists would never compromise their mission. Ledeen was very unhappy with his communications and complained to control. Kupperman calmed the fanatic terrorist leader down with the following message: "Simulation reflects real life. Compose your soul. Watch incoming messages. Slaughter takes time." Unfortunately, none of these dramatic sideshows survived the final cut. All the terrorist players died on *20/20*'s editing-room floor.[2]

The entire episode, now long forgotten, might be dismissed as CSIS folderol were it not for the fact that it was in that same August of 1981 that Israeli Defense Minister Ariel Sharon, whom Menahem Begin had appointed to the post after the June election, first laid out his plan to invade Lebanon and crush the PLO. The plan, which turned out to be a military and public

1. James Allen Smith, *Strategic Calling: The Center for Strategic and International Studies, 1962–1992* (Washington: CSIS, 1993), p. 112.

2. Philip Nobile, "ABC Plays a Terrorist Game," *New York Magazine*, August 3, 1981, p. 21.

relations catastrophe – remember the Sabra and Shatila massacres – was put on hold until the following summer, but it is not unreasonable to wonder whether the Israeli intelligence colonel who was running the CSIS simulation, if not Kupperman himself, who used the word "slaughter" to characterize the goal of his ersatz terrorist team, had it specifically in mind to persuade the American public, via a respected news organization, that Palestinian terrorism was a direct threat to the United States.

Twenty years later, of course, the George W. Bush administration similarly advanced the threatening image of Saddam Husain's (non-existent) weapons of mass destruction to scare the American people and justify his invasion of Iraq. Secretary of State Condoleeza Rice assured us that "we don't want the smoking gun to be a mushroom cloud."

A few months after the simulation, when my run-in with the CSIS was all but forgotten, a senior colleague from Columbia's Political Science Department, Howard Wriggins, invited me to accompany him on a fact-finding trip to the Persian Gulf and Pakistan. A former US ambassador to Sri Lanka, Wriggins was particularly interested in military and political relations between South Asia and the Gulf; but being without prior experience in the latter region, he invited me along to help him understand the Arab side of things.

Our trip together in 1982, my first to Saudi Arabia and the Arab side of the Gulf, was an eye-opener. I don't think I was able to contribute very much to Wriggins' inquiries, and I was not included in some of the military and political briefings that were arranged for him; but I found the Gulf fascinating and luxuriated in the VIP privileges that as an ex-ambassador Wriggins could call on, indeed stridently demand, from every American embassy.

Everywhere we went, I made inquiries about the Muslim Brotherhood and other religious political movements, but what intrigued me most was the feebleness of the military forces then deployed by the Gulf regimes. In one country after another we found Pakistani military officers playing command roles in the local defense establishment, and virtually no high-level involvement of local Arab citizens. It was my understanding that Saudi Arabia even had some Pakistani units regularly stationed on its soil. As for the American presence, it was vanishingly small and unobtrusive. Its most visible component, aside from air crews bound for the island of Diego Garcia in the Indian Ocean stopping off in Oman for rest and relaxation, was a token naval flotilla operating out of Bahrain. But the exasperated admiral whom we interviewed cited one instance after another of military weakness and lack of training in the armed forces of the oil sheikhdoms. This despite the fact that Saddam Husain had invaded Iran in 1980, and the war between Iraq and Iran was to rage for another six years. (Wriggins and I were sometimes mistaken for American agents of some sort.)

I don't know what Wriggins included in the trip report he wrote on our return, or whom he sent the report to, but my own response was to fantasize about how easy it would be for a determined adversary to take over all of the Gulf sheikhdoms in one fell swoop. The obvious perpetrator of such a scheme would be Iraq, but I had already gotten my fingers burned by making the Iranian religious revolution described in *The Tomb of the Twelfth Imam* too realistic. So I decided to make Pakistan the foe – a very remote possibility – and to use the plot device of a too-realistic crisis simulation game as the core of the narrative. Thus my frustrating experience with the CSIS proved its value in an unexpected fashion.

St. Martin's Press, to which my editor Joan Kahn had moved after leaving Harper & Row, published *The Gulf Scenario* in 1984. Six years later Saddam Husain took over defenseless Kuwait in a single day and was widely believed to have all of the Gulf oil states, including Saudi Arabia, in his sights. Like my first two novels, *The Gulf Scenario* received a number of favorable reviews, but sold rather few copies. It never came out in paperback or stirred any interest in Hollywood. Stylistically, it was better than the fiction I had previously produced, but I was still very much an amateur when it came to writing novels.

One of the most laudatory reviews appeared in the *Wall Street Journal* from the pen of Daniel Pipes.[3] Pipes was already on his way to becoming a no-holds-barred critic of any American Middle East scholar who ventured to criticize Israel or speak well of Islam, but he had started his Middle East career by taking my lecture course in Islamic History as a Harvard undergraduate. I remember going to his graduation party. Coincidentally, at the moment he was writing his review of my novel, I was preparing a much less friendly review of his book *In the Path of God: Islam and Political Power* for the *Middle East Journal*. (After reading his friendly comments, I decided to delete my planned first sentence: "Daniel Pipes is a figment of Edward Said's imagination.") Pipes began his review with a long quotation:

> The countries of the [Persian] Gulf can best be compared to a group of irascible millionaire paraplegics coasting down 116th Street in Harlem in golden wheelchairs at four in the morning. They're wearing guns that they don't know how to use; they're being pushed by poverty-stricken attendants whom they despise; and their main hope of protection lies in the

3. *Wall Street Journal*, March 1, 1984, p. 26.

timely use of a police whistle. Now there's no way in the world that they're going to make it down that street without losing those chairs and ending up in the gutter. The only question is who will do the mugging: the neighborhood bad guys, the attendants, or the police? Since each of these three is uncertain about the plans and capabilities of the other two, however, the millionaires manage to keep going.

He closed by *saying*, "Whatever awakens the Western world to the likelihood of drastic and extreme changes in the Persian Gulf region has an importance that transcends its other purposes." Thank you, Dan. But alas, even though I know that the book found its way into the hands of a number of government leaders in the Gulf region, it was evidently too frivolous to trigger any significant security changes before the 1990 takeover of Kuwait.

Bernard Lewis and Television

In 1985 I NARRATED an educational television series entitled "The Middle East" for TVOntario. In 2012, twenty-seven years later, I was astonished to read the following passage in *The Martyr*, a novel by David Stansfield, who had been the screenwriter for the series. The speaker is a slightly fictionalized version of David:

> "When I was young and idealistic, I swore I would [do something to help the Palestinians]. But I never did. I kept up my Arabic as a hobby because I loved the language so much, but I did nothing to help all those years. Well, that's not quite true, I did try a couple of times, after I'd met Hannah."
>
> "What did you do?"
>
> "Television, actually. Hannah used to be in the educational television business and we put some money into a documentary educational series about the Middle East to be put out by the educational network, TVOntario, in Toronto. You probably heard of them."
>
> "Yes, they do a lot of good stuff."
>
> "What we liked about them in particular was their strict code of journalistic ethics: always striving to be as balanced and even-handed as possible, showing both sides of every question. And then one day Hannah was on a flight back from Montreal after interviewing some possible consultants for the series. She was reading one of the scripts when a man sat down in the empty seat beside her and after a few moments suddenly said that she was working on a television series about the Middle East, wasn't she? She asked him how on earth he knew about that. He replied that they knew everything about it. They also had a list of all our prospective consultants and he reeled them off. He even asked to read the script Hannah had on her lap. Of course she said no and demanded to know who the hell 'they' were. B'nai B'rith, the man said as if that explained everything. The man then stood up and returned to his seat near the back of the plane. I don't know how they found out every detail of what we were doing."
>
> "B'nai B'rith, they're everywhere," said Laila.
>
> "Apparently. A few days later, Hannah and I were summoned by the head of the network – Derek Goddard, his name was – who handed her a list of university professors. 'What's this?' she asked. Goddard said the network had a long and proud tradition of objectivity. We told him we knew that, which was why we'd brought the Middle East project to his network in the first place. And he said – I can remember his exact words, 'It has

come to our attention that the people on this list are not objective.'

"We looked at the list and told Goddard that these were all Arabists, highly respected experts in the language and the culture. 'Exactly,' he said, 'so they're hardly objective.'"

"God!" said Laila.

"We disputed that and said that even if they weren't 100% objective, if we brought any of them on board, we'd balance them with the same number of Jewish and Israeli scholars. Goddard said that wasn't good enough. Then the penny dropped. 'Have the B'nai B'rith been talking to you?' we asked. Goddard handed us a second list: 'These people are also all Arabists.' We looked at the names. They were also all Jewish or Israeli. 'Naturally,' said Goddard, 'so they can give you both sides.' We started to object, but then he cut us short: 'I'm afraid you either go with this new list, or we'll have to cancel the series.' We said he must be joking. He said he had to remind us that TVOntario was a Crown Corporation and most of its funding came from the Canadian government. If we rocked the boat, B'nai B'rith would close the network down.

"Incredible," said Laila. She shook her head. "But typical. So you had to go with the Jewish/Israeli list?"

"Uhuh. But it didn't end there. Goddard said there was one other condition. We had to avoid using the word 'Palestine' at any point in the series, because as we should know perfectly very well, no country called Palestine ever actually existed."

"Ya ... Allah ..." breathed Laila. "Oh, my God ..."

"Palestine," said David, "the last dirty word left in the English language. You can use any four-letter word under the sun on cable TV now, but not that particular nine-letter one."

"Oh," said Laila. "So what did you do?"

David shrugged sadly. "We just had to make the best of it. It was drop the P word, or there'd be no series. So we produced the programs, being as even-handed about the Arabs in general as we could get away with ..."

"And?"

"Well, it was well received – just with a gaping hole where the Palestinians should have been." [pp. 47–49]

What surprised me about the passage was the idea that as the series narrator/consultant I had been vetted for bias against Israel and put on the safe list. I queried David about this, and he replied: "Re the Jewish pressure on us while making the TVO series: that is absolutely true, exactly as both Denise [the Hannah of the quotation] and I remember it. You were indeed considered the 'safest' Arabist on the Zionist list, but that wasn't saying much from their point of view; the numerous other pro-Israel consultants we were forced to use would much rather have had no Arabists involved at all!"

Ever since I first learned about the project in 1982, I had derived a certain amount of malicious pleasure from the knowledge that my role as series narrator had originally been reserved for Bernard Lewis. Stansfield's fiction departs from historical accuracy in saying that he and his wife had dreamed up the series. In fact, the entire series was envisioned as a seven-hour educational television vehicle for Lewis's view of the Middle East, and the million-dollar funding of the effort came from sources that wanted that particular viewpoint.

TVOntario had shot forty hours of film, not videotape, much of it on location: Lewis in front of the pyramids, Lewis at Istanbul's Top Kapi Sarayi. Then they ran out of money before completing a single program. Part of the problem, I was told, was that Lewis refused to read any script that he had not personally written. This remained a problem when TVOntario decided to put in another $250,000 to finish the project. At this point, Lewis bowed out, and David and Denise went looking for a replacement. Lewis ended up on the cutting room floor.

When David first met me in my office, he told me that they had decided to use either a Canadian newsreader or a Middle East scholar who could perform on television, but that in either case, the script would be written by David, who had a background in educational screenwriting. I agreed to read any script that was not out-and-out wrong – there are a lot of "right" ways of looking at the Middle East. I flew to Toronto for a screen test.

I practiced reading from a teleprompter, I learned some of the rigmarole of movie making, and I got to keep the wardrobe the producer and director had bought to make me look professorial. It was all great fun, and the series was quite well received, despite not mentioning Palestine. Fourteen half-hour programs were eventually produced.

Ironically, whoever put my name on the list of "safe" Arabists was unaware that at the time I was being recruited as narrator I was also writing a review of Lewis's book *The Muslim Discovery of Europe* (W. W. Norton, 1982) for the *American Historical Review*. I did not think the book was very good and I said so. Choosing for a title a discovery that the book argued never occurred, unlike the enlightened European discovery of Islam, struck me as gratuitously defamatory.

A few days after the review appeared, J. C. Hurewitz, the Director of the Middle East Institute, called me into his office and said that people were asking him why I was attacking Lewis. I told him: "I calls 'em the way I sees 'em." He responded that I was totally off-base criticizing something written by Lewis. I asked why. He said that if I hoped to become Director of the

Institute someday, I would have to learn to be judicious, by which he meant never criticizing Lewis. Becoming rather heated, I replied sarcastically that if the time ever arrived when I would be considered for the directorship, I could only hope to have gained by then the maturity he found so lacking in me. Then I stormed out of the office.

Daniel Pipes, my former Harvard student turned crusader against academics unsympathetic to Israel, wrote a rejoinder to my *AHR* review lamenting my complicity with the anti-Lewis political claque, and eventually Lewis wrote his own rejoinder. On a personal level, I never had an extended conversation with Lewis during all the years I was at Columbia and he was at Princeton. But I retained a warm feeling in my heart at having displaced Lewis from his television series.

That is, until I read David's novel and discovered that I had been a patsy.

CBS and Censorship

THOMAS WYMAN, THE CHIEF EXECUTIVE OFFICER of CBS in the early 1980s, had the idea of bringing the university into the corporation. He invited different units of the corporation to propose a summer project that would be suitable for a visiting faculty member. The plan got underway in the summer of 1985 with four professors recruited to work with the publishing division, the recording division, the public opinion polling division, and the censorship division known as Program Practices. I became faculty-in-residence at Program Practices, and my project was to think about and involve myself with docudramas, which were known at CBS as DBoFs, for Dramas Based on Fact.

The reason Program Practices wanted someone to consult with was that the CBS broadcast of a docudrama entitled *The Atlanta Child Murders* early in 1985 had deeply riled the entire state of Georgia. The script was taken from the trial and conviction of accused serial killer Wayne Williams, but to many viewers it seemed to select material unfairly in order to cast doubt on Williams' guilt, and thus on Georgia justice. The CBS management wanted to know how so controversial a script could have gotten past the censors. The answer was that Program Practices was skilled in monitoring T&L ("taste and language") and in keeping advertisers from doing outrageous things, like showing a bra on an actual woman, but they had no experience that would enable them to veto a script that could be shown to be based on fact, in this case, the trial record.

I was recruited because I wrote both history and fiction, and I lived in New York City so it was easy to go to the CBS headquarters on Sixth Avenue, known as Black Rock – as opposed to 30 Rock, which was NBC's nickname in Rockefeller Center down the street, or ABC's Hard Rock a block farther uptown. Ten four-day weeks at $1000 per week made it a good summer job. Even before I started, however, they asked me to read Anthony Grey's novel *Saigon* (1982), which they were making into a seven-hour miniseries about the Vietnam War. The story involved the fictional intertwining of an elite American family and an elite Vietnamese family over three generations, but the producers and CBS entertainment executives insisted that it be aired as a DBoF because the war had really taken place. The unquestioned assumption was that any program listed as a DbOF would draw more viewers and earn more advertising dollars than a fictional show.

Grey, a British journalist, sympathized with the antiwar movement, and the scripts made from his story were even more fervently antiwar. Ho Chi Minh was shown as a Jeffersonian democrat and nationalist while the highest-ranking American was a perpetually drunk army intelligence colonel who urged his men not to return home because they had so much innocent Vietnamese blood on their hands. He himself went out into the street as Saigon fell so he could be killed in atonement for his sins.

The semi-factual core of the story centered on the male protagonist, an American journalist who was a composite of several real Americans who had garnered first-hand experience of the Viet Minh movement going back to World War II. He was also the son of a leading senator and thus had access to the highest echelons of American policy making. The message was that the American government was fully aware of the nationalist virtues of the Vietnamese opposition but chose to represent them mendaciously to the American people as dangerous international Communists.

The Program Practices people I worked with – in later years, after network censorship was abolished, no one wanted to admit they had ever worked there – visualized the miniseries polarizing American viewers and generating hatred for CBS among the half of the country that had accepted the government's war rationale. But could political contentiousness be a basis for censoring a script? The immediate answer was that having a composite character in the heart of Washington society striving but failing to get his message of Vietnamese nationalist purity across to the American leadership, was not based on fact. It was a wish fulfillment dream of the antiwar movement.

The Vice President for Program Practices, along with me and two of her New York team, flew to Hollywood to take a meeting with Entertainment. I made the presentation, and the VP concluded by saying that the Saigon project could not continue. Once back in New York, however, we learned that Entertainment was going ahead anyway.

So off we went, back to Hollywood, to take another meeting. This time we took a different tack. Among the standards that Program Practices provided to producers and entertainment executives was one that stipulated that a broadcast version of a published property must be faithful to the main characterization and point of view of the original work. But there was another standard that required producers and writers to offer a balanced treatment of issues that were at the center of public debate. Since Anthony Grey's *Saigon* made no effort to present the American government's rationale for the Vietnam War in an even mildly sympathetic fashion, an even-handed script as stipulated by the second standard would necessarily fall short of the first standard because it would violate authorial viewpoint. Ergo, catch-22: You can't continue the series. This time the message stuck and the series was never finished.

Ironically, all the script would have had to do to make up its deficiency in even-handedness was include a speech by President Nixon or some other policy maker, but Program Practices was prohibited from offering remedies or work-arounds. That would be creative, and Entertainment would absolutely not countenance creative inputs from the censors.

Entertainment's last attempt to win the argument took the form of asking Program Practices to interview Saigon's producer, David Puttnam, the producer of *The Killing Fields* and *Chariots of Fire*. He proved quite a charming man, but utterly unbelievable in his claim that his only interest in Anthony Grey's tale was its clever working out of American-Vietnamese elite family arrangements. We knew, however, that the screenwriter had been paid a bonus for beefing up the story's antiwar message.

On our last day, the four faculty-in-residence had lunch with CEO Thomas Wyman. He brought up the Saigon subject and told us that he had received a phone call from former Secretary of State Cyrus Vance, then a Washington lawyer. Vance asked why CBS was making trouble for his firm's client, David Puttnam. Wyman replied, "Have you read the novel, Cy?" Vance said he had not. Wyman said, "Read it, and if you still have a problem, call me back." Vance never called back. Wyman closed the lunch with the remark that CBS would never make the series. When I returned to the Program Practices offices, my colleagues were flabbergasted to learn that Wyman had been personally following their efforts to deal with the project.

This was the most dramatic instance of a DBoF that was not really based on fact that I was exposed to, but it was not the only one. Another script dealt with a comely psychiatrist's confrontation with teenage elective mutism. She finally got to the core of the problem. The lad had stopped talking after seeing his father throw a frying pan across the kitchen and dashing out his sister's brain. Since this was obviously a case of murder, I ventured to ask whether the father had been prosecuted. The publisher replied that answering the question would breach doctor-patient confidentiality. So we said we had no objection to the script, disgusting as it was, being shot, but without the DBoF label. After that the psychiatrist confessed that the story was typical of the sort of case a person in her position might encounter, but it was not, in fact, based on fact.

Shortly after dipping my toe into the quicksand of Hollywood entertainment, the expansion of cable television, which was not subject to FCC rules on fairness, led the broadcast networks to dissolve their censorship divisions. Questions like whether the word "wuss" was more like "wimp" (permitted) than like "pussy" (not permitted) would henceforward go unexamined, and interns would not be ordered to run onstage before an interview to stuff a bouquet of flowers into the too-revealing décolletage of a late-night interview guest.

In the name of full disclosure regarding the Saigon project, I should mention that in 1970 my first cousin Bob Fassnacht was killed in an antiwar bombing of Sterling Hall on the campus of the University of Wisconsin. He was conducting post-doctoral research on superconductivity and had no connection with war related research.

Claims I heard from antiwar activists that you can't make an omelet without breaking eggs struck me then as grossly immoral, and I have carried with me ever since a deeply negative view of terrorism and state violence promoted by mendacious policy makers.

PART FOUR

Moving On

THE HODGE-PODGE OF ACTIVITIES and publications detailed in the part just finished, which I could have expanded to include chairing Columbia's distressed Anthropology Department for a year and a half and attending myriad conferences and symposia, disguises the sad fact that after twenty years at Columbia, I was losing clarity as to what I was doing and why I was doing it. Becoming director of the Institute in 1985 opened the door to many fun things. Our suite of offices became known for attracting students and researchers interested in non-stop discussions of the Middle East as well as for almost round-the-clock graduate student jollification. We indulged in a lot of computer gaming, and some students inhaled a certain amount of cocaine. All this did not sit well with one or two faculty members. They felt that an academic center should display the sober, businesslike demeanor of a Washington think-tank, with regular hours, fixed appointment times, and no one just hanging out. To this I responded: The more the merrier!

Nevertheless, I had no particular program that I wished the Institute to embark upon because my conviction that Middle East area studies played a valuable role in the university and on the national scene was well on the wane. Nor was I inclined to mold my graduate students in my own image. Since Harvard, Princeton, and UCLA offered more faculty and thus much broader possibilities for historical study than Columbia's Middle East program did, I became accustomed to accepting students who felt drawn by my particular orientation toward historical study. That orientation stressed individuality, diversity, and a little bit of craziness rather than apprenticeship under my lofty guidance. A surprisingly high proportion of my slightly crazy protégés became excellent historians, but few of them became Orientalists.

My own Orientalism was also dwindling. I had published three scholarly books between 1973 and 1979, but after that I had hit a dry spell. I made several starts on sweeping accounts of all of Islamic history, but they quickly went nowhere. When I finally did write a work of synthesis, *Islam: The View from the Edge* (1993), it turned out to be a systematic rejection of the type of history I had been imagining. The Orientalist vision that had been implicit in so many of the classic works I had read in the European tradition no longer seemed persuasive. Instead, I was drifting more and more toward subfields

128

of history that were barely recognized by students of Islam: quantitative history, animal history, history of technology, and world history.

My emerging sense of being an outlier in the history discipline at large, and in Middle Eastern history in particular, dovetailed with what was perhaps a too cavalier attitude toward directing the Middle East Institute. Though I had never warmed myself in the bosom of the History Department, partly because my office was in a different building, I increasingly felt that I wasn't a normal professor. At one extreme, I found myself enticing promising students to study with me by telling them that Hogwarts, Professor Dumbledore's academy of magic, truly existed. It was here at Columbia where despite the vast majority of the students, faculty, and staff being muggles, a few students were capable of learning magic, and a few of us on the faculty were capable of teaching them.

At the other extreme, I warmed to the persona of Professorman, a comic strip I began for my son. In everyday life a university security officer, when danger loomed, he would spin a magical Phi Beta Kappa key and transform into Professorman, who wore a mask with his cap and gown. Professorman would solve the problem by sedating the bad guys with boring lectures and pretentious gobbledygook, or else he would obtusely misperceive the nature of their skullduggery. The pompous Roger Allenby self-parody I had invented for *Kicked to Death by a Camel* had never really disappeared.

Always a voracious reader of non-Middle East related fiction, my list of favorite writers evolved according to what was happening in my life. My favorites after I turned fifty mirrored my growing puzzlement as to what I should be doing with my life.

Before age twenty-five I had been drawn to strong story-telling:

Thomas Hardy (*Jude the Obscure; The Mayor of Casterbridge*)

Thomas Wolfe (*Look Homeward Angel*)

Herman Hesse (*Steppenwolf; Narcissus and Goldmund; Magister Ludi*)

J. R. R. Tolkien (*The Lord of the Rings*)

John Barth (*The Floating Opera; The End of the Road; The Sot-Weed Factor*)

Ford Maddox Ford (*Parade's End*)

Between ages twenty-five and fifty my reading favorites expanded to include experimental fiction:

William Gaddis (*The Recognitions; JR*)

Anthony Powell (*A Dance to the Music of Time*)

Donald Barthelme (*Snow White; The Dead Father*)

John Fowles (*The Magus; The French Lieutenant's Woman; A Maggot*)

Thomas Pynchon (*Gravity's Rainbow; Against the Day*)

William Gibson (*Sprawl Trilogy; Bridge Trilogy; Blue Ant Trilogy*)

J. G. Ballard (*Crash; Concrete Island; Empire of the Sun; The Kindness of Women*)

Harry Crews (*The Hawk is Dying; The Gypsy's Curse*)

But after 1990, graphic novels and fantasies captured my imagination in a way that newly published serious fiction seldom did. My favorites included:

Haruki Murakami (*A Wild Sheep Chase; The Wind-Up Bird Chronicle*)

Neil Gaiman (*The Sandman* [graphic])

George R. R. Martin (*A Song of Ice and Fire*)

Steven Erikson (*The Malazan Book of the Fallen*)

China Miéville (*The City and the City; Railsea; Bas-Lag* series)

Neal Stephenson (*Snowcrash; The Diamond Age; Baroque Cycle; Anathem*)

Alan Moore (*Watchmen* [graphic]; *V for Vendetta* [graphic]; *Voice of the Fire*)

Having reached a pinnacle of sorts through decades of work in the university environment, I gradually realized that more interesting things were transpiring in other arenas.

Comic Books

I N 2005 KAREN GREEN MADE A PITCH to her boss, Columbia's head librarian, that comic books and graphic novels should be added to the university's collection. She was told that this might indeed be done if she could find even one professor who endorsed the project. I turned out to be that professor. Karen's pitch focused on the fact that comic books and graphic novels were becoming the topics of doctoral dissertations and peer-reviewed articles in scholarly journals. My own motivation had more to do with social history and the question of how this despised byway of cultural production came to take over American popular culture from the 1990s onward. The following essay will illuminate this interest:

TV's "Big Bang Theory" geniuses like to hang out at Stuart's comic book shop. Stuart is a sad-sack loser who will never get laid, but beneath his and his customers' geeky caricatures lies the wellspring of American popular culture today. How did comic book readers come to shape our twenty-first century television and motion picture industries?

I warmly remember selecting Golden Age comic books and science fiction paperbacks from rotating wire racks at Nihan & Martin's Drugstore in Rockford, Illinois. The offerings changed regularly as the store's magazine distributor brought in new titles and removed the old unsold issues. The artwork and printing were mediocre in the comic books, but we boys loved Superman and Batman, leaving Archie and Little Lulu to our sisters. Everyone loved Donald Duck.

Adventure comics were also popular with soldiers and reflected the good versus evil ideology of the wartime generation. Blackhawk, a big name in the '40s and '50s, led a band of battling aviators against fascist torturers. His team consisted of stereotyped foreigners: André the pencil-mustached Frenchman says "Sacre bleu" and "oui, oui" (I didn't know what that meant so I pronounced it in my head as "oy, oy"); Olaf, the "dumb" Swede, studs his speech with "Py Yiminy"; and Chop-Chop, the pigtailed, brocade-gowned Chinese cook, plunges into the melée wielding a meat cleaver.

Their radio counterpart was Captain Midnight, who clashed for years with the evil mastermind Ivan Shark, his fanatic daughter Fury, and his henchman Guardo. Stylistically, the action comics of that era owed much to radio. As I lay on the living room rug staring fixedly at the console radio, I heard narration, dialogue, and sound effects, and from these things conjured images in my head. Seeing an actual photograph of voice performers clustered around a microphone was painfully disillusioning. Comic books sacrificed the immediacy of sound and imagined action for visual art that could not be undermined by reality. POW! SCREECH! BAM! replaced the sound effects. Pictures set the scene and the action. Words beneath the pictures replaced voiceover narration. And the characters contributed balloon dialogue that was spare enough to allow the picture to dominate the story and did not challenge a preteen's reading facility.

This halcyon period of comic book innocence collided in 1954 with *Seduction of the Innocent*, a polemic by a New York psychiatrist named Fredric Wertham. Wertham maintained that children must at all costs be spared pictures of blood, gore, and mutilation, no matter how fictitious, lest they copy the violence they saw depicted. An even more subtle danger, according to Wertham, was comic book readers becoming seduced into sexual perversion by reading about Batman and his teenaged ward Robin – obviously, to Wertham, a veiled homosexual relationship – and the crypto-lesbian Wonder Woman.

Unfortunately, Estes Kefauver's Senate Subcommittee on Juvenile Delinquency took Wertham's silliness seriously. Its final report did not directly blame comic books for teen waywardness, but it nevertheless recommended that the comics industry engage in self-censorship. This led to the Comics Magazine Association of America establishing the Comics Code Authority in 1954. Patterned on the Hollywood Production Code of the 1930s, which had focused on suppressing nudity, licentiousness, and sympathy for the bad guys, the Comics Code banned gore, sexual innuendo, and overly buxom babes and stipulated that evil must never go unpunished. Specifically, the Code prohibited depictions of "policemen, judges, government officials, and respected institutions ... in such a way as to create disrespect for established authority."

The wimpishness of the publications that adhered to the Code contributed to the near collapse of the comic book industry over the next fifteen years. But the Code was not entirely to blame. The old distribution system was breaking down. Walgreens, where the malted milkshake had made its soda fountain debut in 1922, became a pharmacy, cosmetics, and sundries chain after 1950 and dropped the soda fountain. Others followed, and as soda fountains disappeared, what remained to entice youngsters to peruse the comic book racks? Parents had always hated to see their kids spend money on comics, but they couldn't deny them a nickel coke at the drugstore. If their kid wheedled them into buying a ten-cent comic book, at least it was a mercifully cheap add-on.

Television also contributed to the comic book decline. Young Americans who had imagined their radio heroes as demigods had to adapt to the corny and dismally produced TV versions of Superman and Batman, just as they had to accept, in the 1960s, the terrible drawing of the Hanna-Barbera animation studio. The art in Golden Age comic books had been of low quality printed on bad paper; but it had nevertheless seemed realer than television's George Reeves with a Superman logo sewn onto his pajama top.

As magazine distributors moved away from peddling the lackluster Code comics and the industry seemed to be on life support, room opened up for a new type of comics establishment: Stuart's comic book store. This new venue created a unique publishing environment whose impact on subsequent decades has not been well recognized. By and large, teenaged boys of my generation weaned themselves of reading comic books in the 1950s and found the television portrayals of action heroes embarrassingly stupid. No one took his collection of comic books to college with him. Direct market distribution changed this and contributed to college students and hippies becoming a significant part of the comic book market.

Phil Seuling, a lifelong Brooklynite, founded Sea Gate Distributors in 1972. By 1978 Sea Gate had captured such a large share of the comic book market that it was sued for maintaining a monopoly. Seuling's direct market system bypassed magazine distributors and sold direct to vendors. The old magazine dealers had stocked the drugstore racks with new issues every week and taken away the unsold stock. Just as in most book publishing today, the leftovers (or their torn off covers) were returned to the publisher for a refund. But with Sea Gate, the vendors could not get refunds on unsold issues. This meant that comic book stores, unlike drugstores or newsstands, rapidly accumulated sequences of titles. The boxes of back issues provided customers with an archive that they could explore to fill out their collections of favorite characters or plug holes in extended series. Not only did this encourage the expansion and interweaving of story lines over weeks, and even months, but boxes of back issues, usually alphabetized by superhero name, filled the entire store.

No one had lingered over the comic book racks in drugstores. Boys looked at what was new, and that was that ... unless they could sneak a moment to look for nudes in the nearby photography magazines. But now the comic book store became a place to linger, schmooze with other buyers, and query the usually well-informed staff about hot new issues. This was not a venue for ten-year-olds, but teenagers, and an increasing number of older aficionados, felt comfortable there. It was nice to have a place to go that no one but other comic book readers ever visited. The customer base was male, literate, imaginative, under thirty, and generally not sportsminded. Nerds, perhaps ... but from the upper end of nerd-dom.

The direct market system gave store-owners a strong incentive to cater to their readers' tastes, and the environment of the comic book store enabled them to keep track of what was popular and what was unpopular. In 1960, a dud issue of Superman would have disappeared unsold and unremembered when the next week's comic arrived at the drugstore. But fifteen years later comic book stores sought to sell not only their new stock, but also their back issues, completing series that increasingly involved complex multi-year plotting, the seed now of our twenty-first-century superhero-based screenplays.

From a reader's perspective, direct market comic book distribution created an essentially exclusive literary domain. Anybody might browse a drugstore newsstand, but scarcely anyone who was not male and between twelve and thirty ever walked into a comic book store. Moreover, the customers could generally rely on their parents, or other self-identified adults, never taking a look at what they were buying, even though their purchases were often categorically dismissed as junk that would rot your mind. Adding to the shape of this new literary arena was the near invisibility of comics advertising outside the covers of the comic books themselves and the premises of the comic book shop. Seldom in the print era had a genre of literature been focused on such a hermetic and narrowly defined readership, while remaining unknown, indeed, despised, by other buyers of books and magazines. How could comic books not have become a vehicle for adolescent male rebellion?

Publishers like Dell and Gold Key, which focused on Disney creations and other feel-good characters, had nothing to apologize for in terms of questionable content and had accordingly opted out of the Comics Code Authority. Their wholesomeness adapted poorly to the new distribution environment, however. Child audiences migrated to television cartoon shows, and Dell and Gold Key products did not appeal to the comic book store clientele, who greatly preferred tragedy to comedy, violence to laughter.

One question faced publishers and store-owners alike: What did their customers want to read? The target audience from the '70s through the '90s ranged from twelve-year-olds growing up in sheltered, middle-class neighborhoods; to hippies and potheads hanging out in crash pads; to literate, if not always well-socialized, college kids who were looking for anything subversive, and entertaining. Publishers responded with head comics for the hippies and, largely from Marvel, superhero comics for younger teens consumed with adolescent anxieties over identity, love, and friendship. Hello, Spiderman.

But a darker and more challenging trend was setting in as well. My personal exposure to adventure comics had ended in the early years of Code era. Instead I read *Mad Magazine*, the brainchild of editor Harvey Kurtzman and publisher William Gaines, the latter notorious for the horror stories in his pre-Code EC Comics. As a magazine, *Mad* was exempt from the Comics Code Authority and thus free to publish whatever it wanted, but it opted for satire and snarky humor instead of story telling.

Then in 1971 I found myself in Tehran with time on my hands while doing research on traces of Buddhism in Iranian history. My host, a friend in US Army intelligence, had installed his family in a spacious house with a nice kitchen for his wife and a whole trunkful of comic books for his four children. I read them all and discovered a new comic book world, one that reflected the mood of the anti-Vietnam War movement and the New Left. Gone was the Code prohibition of stories that "create disrespect for established authority." Superman was still winning battles, but he was clearly losing the war against intergalactic bad guys like Darkseid. The *Daily Planet*, Clark Kent's long-time employer, now belonged to a media conglomerate that was in thrall to this vast web of evil. Also in 1971, Green Arrow's youthful ward and sidekick Speedy became addicted to heroin. This new awareness of social problems and paranoid suspicion of established institutions of government, business, and society gradually bled over into questions as to whether the superheroes themselves were actually sociopaths or ungovernable vigilantes.

The year 1971 also saw the publication of Robert Ludlum's first novel, *The Scarlatti Inheritance*, which ushered in a spate of conspiracy-oriented and paranoia-marinated action novels at the top of the adult bestseller charts. Through the '70s and the '80s the intensity of the attack on the pillars of the establishment grew steadily. One could usefully ask who the comic creators were, particularly once outstanding English writers like Neil Gaiman and Alan Moore got into the game, but the nature of the comic book industry at that time makes it more apt to ask about the buyers. After all, comics had become a demand-driven, single-sex market inhabited by boys and young men who were convinced that no one but they were privy to what was contained in their favorite publications.

If the dark comic books of 1971 had appealed to a closeted clientele of literate, imaginative sixteen-year-old boys, then fifteen years later those buyers were moving on to more sophisticated, better written, and better drawn graphic novels like Alan Moore's *V for Vendetta* (1982–85), *Watchmen* (1986–87), and *Batman: The Killing Joke* (1988); and Frank Miller's *The Dark Knight Returns* (1986), *Daredevil* (1979-present), and *Elektra: Assassin* (1986–87). And some of those buyers had moved beyond fandom to write their own stories, draw their own superheroes, and involve themselves in the industry as publishers and store owners.

The dark graphic novels of the '80s and '90s were still marketed primarily in comic book stores; but over the past two decades many of them, including those already mentioned, were turned into motion pictures and television series. Indeed, comic books, along with computer games, have now become the primary source and inspiration of American action entertainment. And the sixteen-year-olds of 1976, now in their mid-60's, are both making and watching the movie versions of their teen favorites.

I have deliberately left out the story of Stan Lee's *Marvel Comics*, the rebooting of various *DC* storylines, and the struggle of artist-authors to retain ownership of their creations. These would be important chapters in any history of the comic book industry; but to my mind, the key element in the rise of the comic book from Comics Code lethargy to cultural dominance was the shaping of a unique audience of boys reading stories that the so-called adult world dismissed – and still dismisses – out of hand.

Four concluding thoughts:

First, movie reviewers who commonly make comparative reference to a novel or stage play when it is reconceived as a screenplay seem never to have read the original comic book stories that are now being brought to both the big and the small screen. I wonder how many universities with film schools offering Master of Fine Arts degrees have libraries that are stocked with a full range of graphic novels?

Secondly, the male environment of the comic book store retarded the development of female superheroes. Aside from Wonder Woman, a wartime – first issue in the month of Pearl Harbor – demigoddess in WAC's clothing, action comics females are distinguishable from males primarily by their long hair, bustlines, and short skirts. Not until the '80s and later do more estimable female superheroes like Electra and Jessica Jones appear on the scene.

Thirdly, the subject matter of comic book and graphic novel storylines from the '70s onward tends to predict what will show up on television and in the movies fifteen years later. This not only produces surprises, such as a relatively low salience of terrorism and Islamophobia; but it leads one to predict that plots based on Christian religious themes – not evangelical but critical to the point of atheism – will gain greater notice as series like Preacher and Lucifer, that came out as comic books in the late '90s and early '00s, make their way to television.

Fourthly, the academic and serious literary worlds have been, and will probably continue to be, shockingly ignorant of what is happening in American culture. A toplofty recognition that graphic creations like *Maus* and *Persepolis* are "important" enough to be reviewed in the *New York Times* simply underlines the failure of our contemporary intelligentsia to grasp the roots and the significance of what is happening all around them.

Comparative literature professors and influential book reviewers are like the parents of my generation: they don't follow what young people are actually reading, but in their clueless hearts they remain convinced that whatever it is, it is worthless and rots the brain.

Computers and Encyclopedias

I WAS BORN IN 1940. If I had been born fifteen years earlier, I might never have used a computer. If I had been born fifteen years later, I would have taken computers for granted. For most academic humanists in my age cohort, making the transition to computers seemed like nothing more than trading in one variety of electric typewriter for another; but in a broader context it was a once-ever historical moment, on a par with the end of hieroglyphics and cuneiform or the origin of printing. What was the experience like?

My doctoral thesis had involved a quantitative analysis of medieval Arabic biographical dictionaries. But transliterating from Arabic, keypunching the resulting texts on a stack of IBM cards, and getting a mainframe computer to detect significant correlations was beyond my ken. I opted instead for a system I learned from my father. I copied the text of each biographical entry onto a Royal McBee Keysort card, a system that had been around for decades. I coded the data I was interested in by punching the holes around the edges of the card into notches and did an approximate sort for correlations by running a knitting needle through the holes, causing the notched cards to drop out. I then did my final search for correlations by hand. No one would do this today, but there were no personal computers or off-the-shelf applications in 1965. For all of its primitive qualities, however, the process I followed afforded me a database that I can still use almost fifty years later. Most of my contemporaries who made use of early computers lost touch with their data because of subsequent software and hardware changes.

As with so many colleagues, however, my first computer served mostly as a replacement for an electric typewriter. In 1980, my father, a physicist who spent most of his career as an electrical engineer, declared that it was high time I started using a personal computer and bought me the newly available Apple II Plus. It came with 48k of RAM and two 5.25-inch floppy disk drives, one for the program disk and one for information storage.

When we got home from the computer store, my father turned immediately to the manual explaining how to program in Basic. In a matter of days, it became apparent that he wanted the computer much more than I did. So we agreed that when I returned to Columbia, I would procure an identical machine (with his money), and we would correspond with one another by mailing floppy disks. We never did correspond this way, but I never went back to a typewriter, much less to composing in my barely legible longhand. In 1983, I wrote my novel *The Gulf Scenario* on my Apple, causing one unfriendly publisher who looked at the dot matrix printout to remark that it was written "on a word processor by a word processor."

Soon thereafter the director of Columbia University Press, John Moore, invited me to be the chief history consultant for the fifth edition of the *Columbia Encyclopedia*, which after several years of development was published in 1993. This single-volume compendium had been a mainstay of press finances for many years, but its days as a print volume were numbered. For the debut of the fifth edition, speaking events were staged at the Library of Congress and the New York Public Library. Elizabeth Eisenstein, whose masterful study of the impact of the Gutenberg revolution, *The Printing Press as an Agent of Change*, had been published in 1979, spoke about the way printing provided ways of systematizing written communications. Then I talked about the impending demise of the print era.

My speech, "Of Encyclopedias and the End of a World," was published in *Biblion, The Bulletin of The New York Public Library*.[1] Inasmuch as public knowledge of and access to the World Wide Web exactly coincided with the publication of the encyclopedia, and Wikipedia would not be formally launched for another eight years, the views I expressed in the speech offer one historian's glimpse of how the computer era was likely to play out. The text below is unchanged from the original publication

§▲.

From Gutenburg to William Gibson: Of Encyclopedias and the End of a World

In 1951, A. S. Leese published a small, pathetic memoir entitled *Out of Step: Events in the Life of an Anti-Jewish Camel Doctor*. Leese had gained recognition (within an admittedly quite small circle) for his earlier work *A Treatise on the One Humped Camel in Health and Disease*, which was based on his experience as a veterinarian in the British army in India. Returning from India and observing the broader expanse of human affairs, he decided that an international Jewish conspiracy was at the core of all world problems and that English antisemites deserved a more outspoken leader than Oswald Mosely. Accordingly, he founded the Imperial Fascist League and went on to spend the war years in a British internment camp.

From my particular standpoint as a one-time specialist (and, for want

1. *Biblion*, 3/1 [Fall 1994], pp. 49–58.

of competition, still an authority) on the history of camel-saddle design, I have often reflected upon a lesson of Leese's career that I saw borne out, in lesser degree, in the lives of certain other camel specialists I learned about in my research: *do not put too much trust in camel scholars when they stray into areas of important human concern.* The reader is thus forewarned that my ruminations on the future of encyclopedias in an era of worldwide computer networking are but opinions, and as opinions they are affected, perhaps tainted (though not, I hope, rendered dangerously idiotic), by my past experience as a camel specialist, a historian, a novelist, and an encyclopedist.

The recrudescence of an adolescent yen to know everything, the more obscure the better, tempted me into becoming an associate editor of the *Encyclopedia of Asian History,* chief history consultant of *The Columbia Encyclopedia* fifth edition, and co-editor of a forthcoming *Encyclopedia of the Modern Middle East.* The experience has taught me a lot about what encyclopedias are and what they are not, and it has prompted my curiosity as to whether they can or should survive into the age of universal computer networking. My reflections on this subject fall under three headings: continuity, serendipity, and authority.

Twenty-five hundred years ago in Mesopotamia, unremembered scribes pondered among themselves how anyone could prefer making funny-shaped alphabetic scratches on rough parchment or papyrus to delicately poking the tip of a triangular stylus into a well-prepared tablet of clay. A few generations later, the last person who knew the art of cuneiform writing passed away, and the surviving tablets gathered dust, accumulating to many feet in depth, until they were unearthed and laboriously deciphered in the nineteenth century. This drama replays many times in history. Fifteenth-century European scribes may have recognized that the chunk of the printing press was destined to drown out the scritch-scritch of their quills, but they probably could not imagine that printed books would someday so definitively determine what was worth knowing that whole libraries of manuscripts would lie for centuries unread, save by antiquarians looking for something to edit and print.

The twentieth century has witnessed equivalent disjunctions. When the Turkish Republic banned the Arabic alphabet and ordained that henceforward Turkish would be written in Latin characters, it cut its citizens off from those parts of their literary heritage that were not selected for transliteration and republication. One unexpected ramification of this cultural change was the appearance in the late 1930s of an entirely unprecedented array of Turkish personal names. Prior to the alphabet change, Turks bore names that derived, for the most part, from Arabic and Persian. Since the Arabic script has no capital letters, unusual proper nouns are difficult to recognize. Many of today's Turkish names therefore look nonsensical in

Arabic script (for example, Oral, Eren, Ergün) but seem distinctive and euphonius in Latin letters.

Further examples would include the adoption of Cyrillic characters in Central Asia during Soviet rule, and today's imminent transition to Latin characters in the same region, but there's no need to belabor the point. Changes in the code by which language is symbolically and visually rendered cause profound cultural disjunctions and produce unanticipated cultural consequences. Exploring the full implications of this dictum for the transition from typeface to electronic digital coding I will leave to the cyberpunk visionaries. My concern is solely with encyclopedias.

Much, if not most, of what was coded in one way before a symbolic disjunction does not make it across the divide. It took over two millennia for Gilgamesh to make it from cuneiform to alphabetic writing. Manuscript collections in the Islamic world, as well as the Christian, still house tens of thousands of volumes that scholars have not found interesting enough (or easy enough) to edit. Modern Turks have little access to the religious writings of their ancestors because their secular republic has not provided a favorable climate for transliterating and publishing them. By contrast, Arabs and Persians retain much more access to their religious past because of their retention of the Arabic script. As for the citizens of the new Central Asian republics, it is predictable that children schooled only in the new Latin characters will find the ideological writings of the Communist era a closed book. Lenin in Uzbek is unlikely to make it across the divide.

Encyclopedia editors consciously aim at preserving lore that is at risk of being forgotten. They visualize users who somehow run across names like Jaroslav Vrchlicky, or Angkor Thorn, or Lautaro and want to know more. Since print space is always limited, they make choices, prolonging the mortal memory of some while consigning others to oblivion. As edition follows edition, the winnowing proceeds. Old entries tremble like marcescent leaves before the autumnal breeze waiting to see which will fall. Candidates for inclusion – will Johnny Carson make it? will Newt Gingrich? – wait like dormant buds. In general, it's a harmless process. There are always the older editions to go to for things that were dropped. And if something important enough to include was skipped, it can be made good in the next edition.

In a time of symbolic disjunction, however, editorial choice becomes more weighty. Will there be any further print editions of encyclopedias in the twenty-first century? Or will the most recent editions, already entered in computer memory in the editorial process, simply be made available on CD-ROM or on-line? An on-line computer can be updated every month, every week. And there is no reason to delete anything because memory space is limitless. A CD-ROM encyclopedia can similarly be upgraded for licensed users. Tomorrow's ad might read: Buy *the Columbia Encyclopedia, Version 5.0* on disk for $150 and get *the Columbia Encyclopedia, Version 5.1* for $10 by sending in a coupon whenever it is ready. Either option offers ever more information at your fingertips at negligible increment in cost.

But such options also raise the question of how an electronic format can afford a publisher a financial base for undertaking a thorough and retrospective new edition. In print, you can't get the new stuff in the new edition without paying for the old stuff reprinted from the old edition. Old news underwrites new news. New news updates in electronic format are inherently cheaper, which implies that the financial incentive to reappraise the content of the old news may disappear.

People may gradually stop reading printed books altogether. Sounds crazy, but it sounded crazy in ancient Mesopotamia that people would prefer to read flimsy sheets of expensive papyrus instead of cheap, indestructible clay tablets. Students tell me that old books I assign are not in the Columbia University library. When I tell them that the book is too old for the on-line catalog and that they should consult the card catalog, they look as bewildered as if I had told them that the book in question was available only in Tagalog. "Logging on" is already replacing "looking up."

Under these circumstances, the decisions made by the current generation of encyclopedia editors as to what to include, or excise, from the preferred core of human knowledge may never be revisited, except to add bits on. But at the same time, their determinations regarding the content of encyclopedias may become more and more important as bridges across the disjunction represented by the transition from printing press to microchip. For the fifth edition of *the Columbia Encyclopedia* I recommended deletion of all biographical entries of women cited solely for their beauty. If the electronic age had come upon us before the reawakening of feminism, legendary beauty might have made it across the great divide, never to be deleted. *Mais où sont les neiges d'antan.*

I turn now to serendipity, the handmaiden of historiography. Computer sophisticates of my acquaintance assure me that individualized programs that will browse the net in search of succulent items of interest are around the corner, much as depicted in David Brin's novel *Earth*. Daunted by the prospect of a *TV Guide* five hundred pages (lets say five megabytes) long? Chilled by the thought of negotiating the infinite-lane traffic on the information superhighway going through your living room? Get a browsing program with artificial intelligence. Tell it you're interested in camels. When it discovers that from the first 2000 camel references it gleaned from networked databases around the globe you chose to peruse only those on saddle design and put a black mark against all those dealing with trypanosomiasis, it learns to fine-tune future selections and under no circumstances subject you to descriptions of nasty fly-borne infections. It will also discern from your behavior which electronic mail you regard as junk and protect you permanently from alumni solicitations.

But will you be able to program your little browser to feed you occasional unexpected nuggets of information, like the congressional voting record of "Pig Iron" Kelly or James Churchward's decipherment of the Greek alphabet as a secret history of the lost continent of Mu? Serendipity will not be served by random recoveries from the great data dump of the future. Serendipity is neither random nor the product of rational reflection. It arises from the interaction between the two. When you browse a shelf of books, you take one down because it is small and curious-looking, another because you think you recognize the author's name, and yet another because it might just have an entry on camels in its index. There's always a glimmer of a reason.

An archaeologist friend, recently deceased, told me that at every point in his career in the field he felt he was six inches away from the find that would make him world famous. But he never found it. He observed, however, that a few archaeologists somehow managed to find it over and over again. Having a mind that is able to make creative connections between disparate bits of data is a prerequisite for serendipitous enlightenment, but another prerequisite is to have the data arrayed in such a way that you can pick and choose as the inkling moves you. A filled bookcase, a cabinet of curios, even an eleven-pound one-volume encyclopedia: can surfing channels or browsing the net really substitute? Can you really believe you are about to find the unfound when the data you are perusing have already been scanned, key worded, catalogued, and broadcast on the net?

Now what of authority? The monkish game players in Hermann Hesse's *Magister Ludi* are the boring forefathers of the laid-back hackers who inhabit the Sprawl in William Gibson's cyberpunk future. Both excel in navigating oceans of information by means of symbolic analogs: glass beads for Hesse, three dimensional virtual reality icons for Gibson. Hesse's data, the compendia of his Age of the Digest (read Encyclopedia), can't protect themselves from manipulation. Gibson's can. The cranially plugged-in hacker who tries to penetrate the ice surrounding the most valuable data caches risks being turned into a vegetable – wetware system crash – by electronic feedback. Bruce Sterling in *Islands in the Net* conjures the image of data so valuable that whole countries subsist on the profits from being data havens, repositories of illegally obtained data.

The common term of such visions of the future is data as value. Yet today's reality is data as trivia. Specialized encyclopedias proliferate. Conceived in a market that increasingly regards real intellectual content as something to be electrostatically copied, faxed, electronically posted, or delivered overnight on interlibrary loan while hewing to the belief that reference books will survive library budget cuts, compilations predicated on every conceivable affinity base are keeping publishers in business, at least for the nonce. In the long run, is it not inevitable that these encyclopedic gleanings from the library of the past, already in electronic database form because that's the best way to do things now, will be uploaded onto one of the trucks-only lanes of the information superhighway?

I contemplate watching a movie on the tube. Won't I be able to check out electronically how many nude scenes it has, what erotic part is exposed, and how many stars the exposure rates? Won't I be able to call up the biography and credits of each of the actors? Of the director? Of the stunt performers? Of the dolly grip? Of the caterer? I read on the hourly news précis that the Sultan of Brunei has bought General Motors. Won't I be able to call up his biography and photograph? A sample of gamelan music from his homeland? The name of his country's public relations firm and registered lobbyists? The lobbyists' previous tenure of public office? Other holders of that office back to the establishment of the republic? Distinguishing value from trivia will be a colossal challenge in the infinite data dump of the future – less a question of zeroing in on the shimmering, menacing ice protecting megacorporate secrets (or corporate megasecrets) from intrusion than of tediously sifting near-barren sands for the glister of gold.

But this is not so different from what happens in the academic world today. Hundreds of thousands of biographical notices of Muslim scholars and local dignitaries are preserved in hundreds of edited and unedited manuscripts compiled over the past dozen centuries of Islamic history. As one of a handful of specialists on this type of historical source (as well, of course, as on camel saddles), I plow through big chunks of this material trying to extract information or construct generalizations worth conveying to a broader audience. If I did this work on computer instead of on pre-electronic Royal McBee Keysort cards, I might upload my raw data onto a forum bulletin board on the Internet. There it might be accessed by a handful of Arabic-reading medievalists around the world, or by anyone else in a fit of whimsy or masochism. Without my, or someone else's, interpretation, however, its presence on the net would have the same value as a styrofoam cup in a sanitary landfill.

General encyclopedias, and to a diminishing degree more specialized encyclopedias, are distillations of authority. Over 120 carefully chosen scholars selected topics and reviewed articles for the fifth edition of *the Columbia Encyclopedia*. Their charge was to determine which articles from the previous edition needed replacement or updating, which should be deleted altogether, and what new articles had to be written. People consulting the volume can find this out by reading the front matter, but they probably won't bother. They will more likely accept on faith and reputation that what they find within it is authoritative: if it's there, it's important; if 150 words are devoted to it, they include the most important things that are sayable in 150 words.

Will this presumption of authority survive the transition to electronic form? For a while, yes. The mantle of authority will not slip easily from the shoulders of a word as time-honored and venerable as "encyclopedia." But if the reconfiguration of the information market precludes future print editions, and on-line and CD versions are simply updated rather than periodically purged and reconceived, authority will surely diminish. Users initially will be drawn to searching larger data sources rather than numerous data sources. Why check to see if Madonna is in *the Columbia Encyclopedia* (yes, there she is, between Madoera and Madonna Lily), or call up a specialized encyclopedia of rock stars, if there's a mega-encyclopedia on-line that contains 50,000,000 entries instead of 50,000? This user preference for more will eventually erode the notion of authority, however.

As more data get amalgamated into vaster on-line databases, of course, they can be arranged in hierarchies according to importance. But underwriting the imposition of a hierarchical, as opposed to an inclusional, authority structure may not be as feasible financially in an electronic culture as it has been in a print culture. Who will undertake to assemble 120 scholars and pay them to review an entire encyclopedia if the expense cannot be defrayed by sales of a new edition that entirely supersedes the old? Per use fees from an enormous number of users might conceivably generate sufficient revenue, but with constant updating of the existing on-line version, how would the new edition conceive and manifest its claims to superiority and thus attract users from its still extant previous edition?

Perhaps questions like these can be easily answered, but logical solutions do not always work out in practice. The edict on prices of the Roman emperor Diocletian issued in 301 CE showed a cost savings of twenty percent for people who loaded their goods on camels instead of transporting them in oxcarts. This economy was presumably the impetus for the near total replacement of wheeled vehicles by pack animals in the empire's camel breeding provinces. In time, recollections of what wheeled vehicles had looked like disappeared, to be replaced in art by entirely fanciful contraptions, and vocabulary relating to vehicle building and harnessing passed from common use. Except in Tunisia. There people simply harnessed camels to carts and married the efficiency of a stronger, cheaper animal to the mechanical efficiency of the wheel. Why didn't the efficient Tunisian technology spread? Economic logic is persuasive when it works, but it is not always a reliable predictor.

I am inclined to think, as a practical matter, that books and encyclopedias will both survive the next century and that people will look back on ruminations like mine and wonder how at the end of the twentieth century the future could be misread so completely, just as we now look back on would-be prophets who foresaw mass use of private helicopters and wonder how they could have failed to consider the insurmountable problems of air traffic control and landing space. I hope I'm wrong, however. As much as I like to browse through shelves of books and serendipitously uncover rarities and oddities, and as much as I dread the thought of transiting an infinite data dump with no more authoritative guide than an on-line help program, the cataclysmic cultural discontinuity that would surely accompany a universal shift from print-shop to cyberspace exerts a sort of invigorating attraction.

To make reference to one of today's most creative cultural arenas – regrettably known only to frequenters of comic book stores – Neil Gaiman and Dave McKean's graphic novella *Signal to Noise* hinges on a conception of death as a transition from ordered information – signal – to randomness – noise. It tells and illustrates the story of a movie director with terminal cancer rehearsing in his head the final screenplay he will never film. A group of villagers at the turn of the first Christian millennium trek to a snowy mountaintop to await the coming of the Lord. He doesn't come. They leave. But their anticipation of the end of time and assumption into eternal life, like the director's anticipation of death and the merging of his signal with the noise of the universe, charges their lives with meaning, irrespective of ultimate consequences. In William Gibson's *Virtual Light,* a mid twenty-first century character takes a half-dozen odds and ends of twentieth-century detritus to a flea market to raise a little cash. One is a book, the *Columbia Literary History of the United States.* It's the only one that doesn't sell. Exciting, or what?

Iran 4: Khatami's Dialogue of Civilizations

IN 1988 AN IRANIAN ACADEMIC gained permission from Ayatollah Khomeini to convene an International Conference on Aggression and Defense to help spread his country's interpretation of the war with Iraq, which was then in its seventh year. A number of American Iran specialists were invited, but after vetoes by Iranian security agencies, only a half dozen or so received visas and air tickets. I was one of the lucky winners, but I was decidedly uneasy as an American to be heading to Tehran for the first time since the revolution. In the event, I learned a great deal and encountered no friction with my hosts, even though a large banner saying, in Persian, DOWN WITH AMERICA decorated the hotel lobby.

My engagement with the government of the Islamic Republic grew in the following years. I went to a second conference in 1989, and as director of the Middle East Institute I took advantage of a US government ruling requiring United Nations personnel from "unfriendly" countries to seek permission to accept engagements outside a 25-mile radius of UN headquarters. This made Columbia, which was inside that radius, a prime venue for dealings with Iran. I got to know a series of Iranian UN ambassadors and issued the first invitation for an IRI official to make a public address on an American campus.

These contacts eventually led to roundtable talks between the United States and the IRI via the Geneva-based Centre for Applied Studies in International Negotiations (CASIN), headed by Jean Freymond. Co-sponsored by my institute, Freymond's Center, and the Iranian Ministry of Foreign Affairs, the talks provided a venue for discussing outstanding issues between Iran and the West, and for making personal contacts that might contribute to better communication. Our first meeting took place in Geneva in May, 1998, and others followed in Paris, Stockholm, and London. Though nothing specific came of the meetings, I came away from them with a sense that there were contributions I still might make to public debates over Middle Eastern problems despite my reservations about US government policies.

In 1999, President Mohammad Khatami of the Islamic Republic of Iran advanced the notion that the United Nations should adopt the idea of a dialogue of civilizations, partly as a counter to the popularity of Professor Samuel Huntington's idea of a clash of civilizations. At the time, I had good relations with the Iranian ambassador to the United Nations, Javad Zarif, and he asked me how I thought President Khatami's idea might best be followed up. Eventually he commissioned me to write a think piece on the topic.

After the General Assembly of the United Nations voted to designate the year 2001 the Year of Dialogue Among Civilizations, I played a minor role in efforts to flesh out the concept. The brief remarks I delivered on the subject at a UNESCO round table held on September 5, 2000, may be accessed at www.unesco.org/dialogue/en/bulliet.htm. What audience the paper I wrote for the Iranian UN mission may have gained in Iran I do not know. But here are some excerpts from the text:

Dialogue of Civilizations:
Setting the Agenda

Even though the continuous evolution of societies through civilizational dialogue has been the historical norm, civilizational monologues have also appeared at various times in various parts of the world. If civilizational dialogue denotes fruitful interchange among cultures, civilizational monologue is the proper term for historical situations in which one civilization consciously or unconsciously seeks to impose its culture upon whichever societies it contacts and to monopolize cultural discourse....

Though myriad European and American scholars and thinkers [have striven] to understand and appreciate the cultures of the parts of the world that came under Western imperial domination, the fruits of their effort served more often as instruments for enhancing political control than as gateways for a true cross-fertilization of civilizations.

As the twenty-first century begins, no one can say that all elements of Western imperialism have passed away. But the voice of imperialism no longer speaks alone and can no longer maintain that it offers the sole, or necessarily the best, interpretation of human society and values consonant with the economic and technological conditions of the modern world. While some analysts doubt that constructive dialogue is possible and warn of an impending clash of civilizations – the ultimate outcome of an intransigent civilizational monologue – it is undeniable that dialogue has succeeded monologue and that the world's civilizations today interpenetrate and influence one another more than they ever have before....

In visualizing a process of civilizational dialogue suited to today's world, therefore, historical examples are of limited value. Today's problems are of an altogether new kind. They are more often multicivilizational than bi-civilizational. The pace of technological change requires that they be addressed quickly and comprehensively rather than haphazardly according to the occasional needs felt in one or another society. And some of the most important fall outside the parameters of thought that led so fruitfully to the two great covenants of international understanding crafted in the middle of the twentieth century and in response to its conditions: the Charter of the United Nations and the Universal Declaration of Human Rights.

An Agenda for Civilizational Dialogue

[H]ow should the items on the agenda of civilizational dialogue be chosen? ... [T]he task of compiling a list of topics and explaining their rationale should be undertaken by a small, select international body composed of individuals of the highest intellectual and moral reputation. Such a list should be open-ended, since civilizational dialogue in an increasingly integrated global community should be on-going. But the list should also state priorities so that efforts do not become too diffuse.

As a step toward compiling that list, a number of topics will be suggested here and their rationale briefly described. The chief criterion for inclusion, as will be seen, is that each area of conversation focus on a problem or issue that is of significant international concern but that has not already been satisfactorily addressed in the fundamental international covenants referred to earlier. What this criterion means, in practical terms, is that the proposed civilizational dialogue should deal chiefly with matters that are not easily addressed within the global international framework of sovereign nation-states existing within fixed and inviolable boundaries. The nation-state assumption that underlies the United Nations Charter and the Universal Declaration of Human Rights has been of great value in structuring relations among governments and establishing norms for each government's behavior toward its citizenry. But significant issues, including the following, fall substantially outside the parameters set by this assumption:

1 Constitution

Without presuming eventual consensus, a civilizational dialogue on the question of the constitution of states could be of great value. How have different civilizations conceived of political society and of the nature of government? Can or should there be, in the twenty-first century, broad (if not universal) understandings as to the appropriateness of certain constitutional forms to life in an interdependent globe, parallel, perhaps, to the consensus achieved in the nineteenth century as to the inappropriateness of slavery in the modern world?

2   Citizenship

In the second half of the twentieth century, many organizations have
come into existence dedicated to seeking redress of severe state violations
of human rights. In addition, a debate has arisen over the propriety of international intervention to protect citizens against maltreatment by their
governments.

How do intellectual, religious, and political leaders in different parts
of the world value, on the basis of their particular traditions, the role of
international human rights bodies? Is consensus possible regarding the
nature of citizenship and the circumstances in which international action
to protect citizens from their governments is tolerable.

A second issue for discussion under this heading derives from the
increasing numbers of refugees, guest workers, and stateless persons in
different parts of the world. In light of the fact that formal citizenship is
a comparatively recent historical development, is there philosophically a
domain of shared international concern for the status of people who do
not fall into conventional nation-state citizenship categories?

3   Law and Legal Process

With increased personal mobility and access to news about different parts
of the world has come a heightened visibility of and concern for legal
proceedings. Though specialists in international law, or in the law of specific foreign nations, often know in detail how different systems work, a
dialogue on the subject of law designed to broaden world awareness of the
philosophical differences among different cultural traditions could be of
substantial value.

4   Religion and Personal Status

How is religion defined in different cultures? How do different religions
conceive of their roles vis-à-vis the state? How does each religion interact
with other religions? How does each religion view individuals who assert
that they have no religious belief? How can multi-religious national societies function in peace, harmony, and fairness?

5   Sovereignty and Boundaries

How do the absolute limits of state sovereignty and national boundaries
as understood since the Peace of Westphalia in the seventeenth century
function in today's world? What should be the status of transnational
communities within the international system? What should be the status
of infranational communities? Do nations have moral obligations that
reach beyond state boundaries? What limits should exist on actions taken
because of such moral obligations?

6   Education and Dissemination of Information

[R]ecent advances in the electronic dissemination of information raise the likelihood of new educational venues coming into being capable of over-stepping any national or cultural boundary.

Does the commitment to freedom of speech within a national commu-nity imply that any expression of views should be made equally available worldwide, limited only by the technical and financial capacity of a group to exploit new technologies? What is education and how should it be in-stitutionalized in today's world? Should access to information be limited; and if so, by what agency? How can education foster harmony among world civilizations? How can different educational traditions take advan-tage of the content and values of other traditions?

7   The Economic Order

The future is clouded by intimations of growing income disparity between rich and poor nations irrespective of their forms of investment or eco-nomic planning. What do different cultures have to say about the role of equity in a world economic order? What is the relation of wealth accumu-lation to social and moral teachings? Should the increasing utilization of economic sanctions as a weapon be subject to international scrutiny?

8   Social Welfare

Though the Universal Declaration of Human Rights deals in several articles with social welfare, the question of how and by what agency human needs are best provided for brings different responses according to cultural background. What can different societies learn from each other's social welfare policies and institutions?

9   Status and Protection of Children and the Elderly

As the common future of humankind, children warrant special under-standing. Where does the locus of responsibility for the education, wel-fare, and moral upbringing of children lie? By the same token, with the proportion of elderly people growing in many countries, how do different cultures understand and address their special needs?

10 Status of Women

Though concern for the status of women has already been demonstrated in many ways around the world, there is a need for a fuller understanding of cultural differences in this critical area. Where can the world's civiliza-tions find common ground on this difficult subject? How can diversity be honored without destroying equity?

11 The Environmental Heritage

International efforts to address environmental problems focus strongly on technical aspects of various problems. A broader dimension could usefully be addressed in the context of civilizational dialogue. How do different civilizations understand the Earth as the common heritage of humanity? How should conflicts between economic and environmental interests be resolved? How should conflicts between private and public interests be resolved?

12 Medical and Biological Technologies

The second half of the twentieth century saw phenomenal advances in medical and biological technology. What issues of human values arise from such new developments as organ transplants, cloning, and biological engineering of new forms of life? How are questions of equity to be addressed when crucial medical processes are extremely expensive, or of limited availability?[1]

1. Originally drafted June 27, 1999 on commission by the Foreign Ministry of the Islamic Republic of Iran.

From Orientalist to Historian

GEORGE MAKDISI, a Harvard professor of Arabic who subsequently had a distinguished career at the University of Pennsylvania, oversaw my doctoral dissertation after a stroke cut short H. A. R. Gibb's Harvard career. Modeling a hands-off supervisory technique on that of his mentor, Louis Massignon, a giant in the French Orientalist tradition, Makdisi maintained that one should shun secondary historical literature and work only from primary texts. He also frowned on giving too much professorial guidance. Mine was one of the first two history dissertations Makdisi directed, and he paid very little attention to what I was doing. I saw him for about fifteen minutes every two weeks.

This was fine with me. I had my own ideas about history and busied myself developing a coding technique for analyzing the information in three Arabic manuscripts relating to the city of Nishapur in the tenth through twelfth centuries. Richard N. Frye had made the manuscripts available to me, but I'm not sure that Makdisi had access to them beyond helping me decipher the occasional obscure passage. I did not develop a close relationship with Makdisi, and we disagreed strenuously on the origin of the *madrasa*, he maintaining that it began in Baghdad under the Seljuqs and I that it was already more than half a century old in Khurasan before the Seljuqs seized the Abbasid capital. I do not recall consulting him on the conversion of my very sketchy dissertation into a book, *The Patricians of Nishapur* (1972); and I'm fairly sure I never sought his assistance on my second research project, which culminated in *The Camel and the Wheel* (1975).

In the absence of a mentor, my development as a historian was serendipitous and autodidactic. I vividly remember wondering, after completing my PhD, whether I could or should list my profession as "Historian." Being out of step with both the Orientalistic and the historiographic approaches in vogue in American academia in the 1970s probably made it easier to make out the tap-tap-tapping of different drummers in the 1990s. World history, with sub-interests in animal history and the history of technology, became my new passion. As for being either an Orientalist in the European tradition or an American Middle East area studies specialist, neither option seemed as congenial as they had in 1960.

Plumbing the depths of the Saidian critique of Orientalism provided an avenue for some colleagues in the 1990s, but Said seemed more intent on critiquing the past than on constructing new knowledge in the present. Dying in 2004, shortly after President George W. Bush's proclamation of "Mission Accomplished!" in Iraq, Said did not live to extend his critique past that vainglorious pronouncement, which today reads less like a moment of triumph than a starting point for problems and military adventures that would soon cascade out of control. The events of 9/11 fundamentally altered American attitudes and policies relating to Islam and the Middle East, but whether Said's insights continue to illuminate current events, as opposed to theory debates, is an open question that I will return to in the last chapter of this book.

My new passion for world history took me away from current events and baffling theory (post-colonial, deconstructive, post-modern) debates. Unlike *Orientalism*, which, by any definition, was rooted in Europe with only a weak reflection in the United States, the new wave of world history was an American phenomenon that still has not reverberated much in Europe or elsewhere. The reason for this is that it percolated upward from precollege American school systems rather than reaching downward from historians working at elite universities. Here, for example, are some "recommendations for action" aimed mostly at high schools by the Council of Chief State School Officers (CCSSO) in 1985, in which year scarcely a handful of the country's universities, and none of its elite institutions, offered courses in world history:

> The international dimensions of education are fourfold: (1) the capacity to communicate in languages other than English; (2) understanding of other nations, cultures, and people; (3) the capacity to compare educational systems across national boundaries; and (4) the exchange of educational practices.... The CCSSO should provide leadership in improving the quality of second language study and the teaching of international education; federal agencies should strengthen the international education capacities in the U.S. Department of Education programs ... ; state education agencies should work with state boards of education to establish policy statements improving and expanding the international dimensions of education; local education agencies should support programs designed to strengthen second language study and international education; college and universities should establish second language requirements for admission.[1]

Notable here is the educational level being targeted. Area studies programs had come into being on elite campus in the 1950s for the purpose

---

1. Council of Chief State School Officers (CCSSO), Washington, DC. (1985). *International Dimensions of Education. Position Paper and Recommendations for Action*, November 1985. Council of Chief State School Officers, 400 North Capitol, N.W., Washington, DC 20001.

of training handfuls of specialists like me. But now, a generation later, international awareness was being looked upon as a general priority at the lower levels of the school system. The reasons for this expanding concern for international studies are not fully apparent, especially in consideration of the declining reputation of area studies. One likely reason, however, was the spread of the concept of "globalization," which after decades of sporadic usage gained widespread currency through a 1983 *Harvard Business Review* article by the economist Theodore Levitt entitled "Globalization of Markets." With the Vietnam era behind it, America was looking to reconnect with the world. Another reason might be a broader willingness among American educators who had internalized the counter-culture debates of the previous decade to teach multicultural content to students in multicultural classrooms.

State boards wondered who should teach the international studies curriculum. The existing cadres of social studies teachers and high school level historians both lacked specialized training in international affairs; but over a period of years, high school courses on World History emerged as the favored vehicle for introducing students to the world. Yet who would teach those high school teachers? As a focus of graduate study, World History barely existed in 1980, and elite history departments were often disdainful of the entire concept.

Thousands of high school teachers across the country were assigned to teach a course that they themselves had never taken, namely, World History. At the same time, leading historians at the most eminent universities maintained that world history could not be taught, except possibly by a team of high-level specialists. This proved a boon to textbook companies that rushed to publish works on world history. One project involved my Columbia colleague Jack Garraty, a very successful writer of American history textbooks, who in 1972 had joined with Yale historian Peter Gay in co-editing a multiauthored *Columbia History of the World*. Garraty invited me and our colleague Isser Woloch to each write half of a world history textbook that he would then rewrite in his inimitable and highly salable textbook style. My assignment was pre-Renaissance Europe and everything non-European. A generous advance from Harcourt Brace Jovanovich made the project appealing, but it was killed after classroom teachers declared the text we produced unteachable. My autopsy of the book was that Garraty's dictum that we should pitch without winding up, by which he meant that every sentence should be a substantive statement about the past, but none should instruct teachers on what was important or why, worked only for American history, which most teachers knew reasonably well. However, it did not meet the needs of teachers who didn't have a clue as to how to assess the Mayan calendar,

Bantu linguistics, the spread of Buddhism, or trade along the Silk Road. They needed a lot more help.

With that project as my introduction to the challenge of writing world history, I eagerly participated in two subsequent efforts devised by the national educational establishment to come up with models of how high school world history should be taught. One was the "Pathfinder" project of The College Board (1991–93) and the other the "National Standards in World History" project of the National Center for the Study of History (1992–93). Having gained from these activities a much better understanding of the pedagogical challenge inherent in the field, I then joined five other historians in writing a world history textbook being developed by Houghton Mifflin. This time the book was published: *The Earth and Its Peoples: A Global History* (1st ed. 1997; 7th ed. 2017).

In the meantime, history departments at second- and third-tier universities were gradually realizing that those thousands of high school teachers assigned to teach world history deserved to learn about the subject in college or in graduate school. This opened an employment niche for new PhDs who had either the training or the chutzpah to undertake a world history course, and that niche steadily widened. In 2014, almost a quarter of a million high school students took the Advanced Placement test in World History, a number that was exceeded only by those taking psychology, elementary calculus, and specifically American subjects (English language and literature, American history and government).

The graduate history programs at elite universities came belatedly to the field of world history. Where the last big change in historiographical outlook, the adoption of "the new social history," had resulted from the cultural and intellectual enterprise of liberal public intellectuals and social activists, the new world history agenda came from the bottom up. It started in pre-college education, slowly gained a foothold in non-elite universities, and only belatedly gained a place in elite graduate education. Part of the reason for the slow uptake of the new paradigm was the poor fit of class, race, and gender, the triad of interests associated with "the new social history," with the emerging field of world history. To be sure, one could compare the ways in which women, or groups thought of as "the other," have suffered over and over again from discrimination or hardship in different parts of the world at different eras. But the 1960s "consciousness raising" that fueled the spread of these historical topics was rooted in the narrative of modern Western civilization and was only weakly paralleled in narratives proper to other world regions. Historians could contrast the "progress" made in these areas in the West with the slower pace of change elsewhere, of course, but this had the effect of emphasizing an implicit model of European and American exceptionalism, which is precisely the model that the world history movement was trying to escape.

Material history, on the other hand, offered both ideological neutrality and vividly contrasting narratives. How do different and changing suites of plants and animals lead different world areas in different directions? How do different societies react to climate change and intentional or unintentional environmental manipulation? What technologies govern economic and societal differences? How do changes in the material realm characterize key moments in world history? These questions and hundreds more invite historians to explore topics that offer striking contrasts and comparisons across time and space without presuming a world historical narrative defined by the political, religious, or moral rise and fall of one global region or another.

Responses to 9/11 aside, most of the books and articles I authored from 1997 onward were informed by ideas rooted in the material aspects of world history. In addition to *The Earth and Its Peoples*, which adopted "environment and technology" as one of its two central themes, these include *The Columbia History of the Twentieth Century* (1998), a thematically organized work that downplayed political narratives; *Hunters, Herders, and Hamburgers* (2005), a study of how human societies evolved a variety of relations to domestic animals; *Cotton, Climate, and Camels in Early Islamic Iran: A Moment in World History* (2009); and *The Wheel: Inventions and Reinventions* (2016).

Y2K: The Old Millennium Ends

NEW YEAR'S EVE, December 31, 1999, marked the end of a century that no one thought could be surpassed for war, revolution, and wanton bloodshed. The jury is still out on that, but the clouds on the horizon were faint and far away as the clock ticked down in Times Square. I wrote a facetious play for my guests to perform at a combination New Year's Eve party and play reading. Its theme was the origin of the phrase Y2K, the rumored computer catastrophe that was predicted to take place when 1999 ticked over into 2000.

By the next New Year's Eve, all thought of whimsy had vanished for me, though the dolefulness of the new millennium for the country as a whole did not begin until 9/11/01. In March of 2000 two faculty colleagues declared that they did not consider me a legitimate director of Columbia's Middle East Institute because, like all institute directors, I had been appointed to the post on the nomination of the Dean of International and Public Affairs rather than elected like a department chairman. I kicked their questioning of my status upstairs to the dean in question, and after a couple of months of deliberation, she decided, secretly, to relieve me of my post and appoint a committee to deliberate on the proper constitutional structure of Columbia's area studies institutes.

I heard a rumor of my impending dismissal a day before it happened via the academic liaison specialist at the Israeli mission to the United Nations, and I had the details confirmed by a faculty colleague. So when I met with the dean the next day and she began to tell me what she had in mind, I told her that I already knew and that I considered it the height of unprofessional behavior that the Israeli UN mission knew about my dismissal before I did. Being quite angry, I did not solicit an explanation for the dean's action but informed her that I would no longer teach about the modern Middle East or participate in the activities of the School of International and Public Affairs. She gave me a month to vacate my office.

Being summarily fired after serving as director for twelve of the previous fifteen years was the worst experience of my life since the chair of the Harvard History Department informed that I would not be reviewed for tenure twenty-eight years earlier. Over the following summer of the year 2000, the occasional attacks of angina I had been experiencing for several years worsened severely. I was barely functioning at a conference in Jakarta, and I thought I would expire climbing the hill between the guests' residence and the magnificent villa of the Rockefeller Foundation's conference center in Bellagio, Italy. I felt so bad that I even applied for a position in the Columbia administration.

On Groundhog Day, February 2, 2001, the third anniversary of my father's death, I went into the hospital with severe chest pain. By good fortune, a stent was placed in a blocked coronary artery before I experienced a full-fledged heart attack. I immediately felt restored, and I told the committee that interviewed me for the post I had applied for that I now felt too good to devote myself to administration. (This is probably a good example of the sort of impolitic behavior that has convinced so many people that I should never be appointed or elected to administrative or executive posts.)

Recuperating with strong dosages of blood pressure medication, I spent a lackadaisical spring not getting excited about anything. I particularly regret putting on an uninspired performance in delivering the Anne K. S. Lambton Lecture at the University of Durham in England. I was not even aware of how off my game I was. Then in August, the most debilitating medicine was discontinued. Just in time for the World Trade Center and Pentagon attacks of 9/11.

I immediately decided that thinking and teaching about the modern Middle East was more important than my spat with the dean, and over the next five months, while teaching my normal load of three courses, I participated in ninety-nine extracurricular and off-campus events relating to the attacks: lectures, television and radio interviews, op-ed pieces, conferences, etc. Then I went to England for a breather.

A dismal start to the new millennium, but some pun-inspired speeches from my very silly play about Y2K remind me of the lightness of being we enjoyed before terrorism and war consumed our national consciousness.

Now as to Y2K, its roots are buried in the reign of the Sun King Louis XIV. For the millennial anniversary of the discovery of garlic, Louis ordered that a magnificent feast be prepared, every dish to be prepared with the best garlic in his domain. And he sent out a royal decree promising a dukedom to the person who discovered the best garlic. His command, needless to say, caused a stir throughout France; and soon mountains of white and purple garlic bulbs were being carted to Versailles from the farthest reaches of the realm. But what of the little garlic girl, the large-eyed urchin who every day along the banks of the Seine tried to sell her sad little collection of garlic bulbs to haughty passers-by? Is this her story? Yes, it is. For on the night before the grand celebration, as she huddled forlorn in the cold rain on the quay that was her only home, her basket fell into the stagnant, fetid shallows of the river, and all of the garlics but one were swept downstream. When she awoke, she wept at the misfortune that had befallen her, but then joy filled her heart when she saw that she still had one sodden garlic to offer the king. So later that day she joined the throng heading for Versailles and soon found herself on the spacious grounds of the grand palace. There she waited as the royal procession wended its way from garlic-bearer to garlic-bearer, and the royal nose sampled each proffered root. Closer and closer His Royal Highness approached, a look of near despair on his swollen royal face. Then his equerry was before the little garlic girl, telling her to move aside because the king had no time for pathetic urchins from the gutter. Frightened, but not despairing, she held up her basket with its one forlorn garlic. And just then the king turned, his nose twitching, his eyes brightening. He bent his corpulent royal body over the little girl's basket and smelled the lonely garlic marinated in the waste-water of the Seine. "*C'est magnifique!*" he declared. And he led the little garlic girl into the palace and enthroned her as the Duchess of Picardy. Then for all of the world to note, he issued a most royal decree declaring that for all time to come, "*Ail du quay!*" would be the symbol of millennial festivity.

My story begins two months ago when I was on my way to sunny Sardinia to scout out a place for my retirement. I had to change planes at Heathrow, and as it was a longish wait, I settled myself in the TV lounge. Now it happened that a football match was on the telly – Manchester United versus Les Grenouilles de Paris as I recall. Makes no difference. The point is that international football matches have a way of bringing out the worst in the Brits. The match was scarcely underway when louts began throwing furniture about the lounge and threatening passengers with knives and lead pipes. Fortunately, I had a knife and lead pipe with me and I melded easily with the louts and thus escaped injury. Afterwards, I went with the louts to a nearby pub for a celebratory pint, and it was there that I learned of their plans for the millennium. My blood ran cold as they chanted the horrifying words they intended to make a worldwide racist slogan: White UK! White UK! White UK!

The truth is that the phrase originated with Franz Kafka. In 1986 a lost page of *The Trial* was discovered buried in a cemetery in Prague. It was in the grave of Kafka's publisher, who had long sworn that he would take his famous author's secrets to the grave with him. An erudite graverobber, whose name must remain secret, decided to investigate this oath. He opened the coffin and removed a silver amulet case from around the skeleton's neck. When he opened the case, he found in it two slips of paper: Kafka's secrets. One of them said, "Cockroach is a misprint for Ladybug." The other contains an alternative, and probably preferred ending for *The Trial*. As the killers prepare to execute the protagonist, one of them says suddenly, "Why do K?" After a moment's puzzlement, they decide not kill him and ask K to join them for wurst and lager at a nearby inn. Now how these words became a worldwide symbol of hope and fear, I don't know. But that's how it is with Kafka. Things just work out for him.

9/11: The New Millennium Begins

THE 9/11 ATTACKS were more momentous than Pearl Harbor. In 1941 the US government and most of its citizens were already convinced that we would sooner or later be drawn into World War II. But in 2001, no one took seriously the notion that the handfuls of terrorists who had from time to time perpetrated outrages abroad could carry out a devastating mission on American soil. Counterintuitively, just as the American military response to Pearl Harbor had taken Germany rather than Japan to be our foremost enemy, so in 2001 policy makers in both parties envisioned Iraq and Iran as more formidable enemies than the al-Qaeda gang holed up in the mountains of Afghanistan.

The ensuing concatenation of poorly prepared invasions, guerrilla ripostes, refugee floods, and intermittent terrorist assaults appalled the community of Middle East scholars as much as it did anyone else. Despite their knowledge of the region, however, they lacked the means – theoretical, organizational, and practical – of contributing significantly to their country's response to never-ending crisis. Journalists and soldiers soon knew more than Arabic professors and historians, and senior policy-makers in the Bush administration – Dick Cheney, Donald Rumsfeld, and others – relied more on the modernization theories they had learned as graduate students in the 1960s than on area expertise. Democratic nation building, the Holy Grail of the sacred modernization process, became a watchword ... and then a quagmire ... and then a dashed hope when the thrills of the Arab Spring gave way to military backlash and anarchy.

Soon after 9/11, CNN asked me if I would take a look at an al-Qaeda recruiting video that had come their way and offer them some guidance as to its contents. I asked whether I could make the video available to other parties. CNN was eager to disclaim ownership, and I had no fear of al-Qaeda's media committee suing me for unlawful distribution. So I gave the video to CBS, NBC, and ABC and then collaborated with Fawaz Gerges in making it available online, along with appropriate commentary. I felt that it was important for Americans to see and hear how their enemies were thinking.

In 2002 two British police departments asked me to analyze troves of videotapes, audiotapes, and written materials they had seized in raids on suspected terrorist locations. I became very familiar with the baited hooks the terrorist groups were casting out to troll for recruits. For a while, this made me one of those terrorism guys (certainly not an expert). Yes indeed, complete with appearances on Fox and Friends ... until I used too highfalutin a word – "dendritic" – to describe al-Qaeda's organizational structure. What I deduced from my survey of the materials made available to me was that terrorist recruiting had less to do with Islamic religious teachings or guarantees of a place in a hedonistic paradise than with feelings of aimlessness among angry young Muslim men living under unresponsive dictatorships. They yearned for solidarity and brotherhood, and to take action against their enemies. At a small *Time* magazine editorial get together to talk about Islam with leading Muslims (and me, for some reason), one Muslim leader from London responded to a question about where authority lies in Islam by saying: "Authority lies with whoever the *shabab* (young men) recognize as their leader."

My preoccupation with terrorism soon ebbed. The political contest over who would define the topic and dominate America's responses to it, which is still going on, was too partisan and too poisonous. Martin Kramer, an erstwhile scholar who, along with Daniel Pipes, was making a career of defaming the entire field of Middle East studies, ridiculed me in print for asserting that terrorist attacks on the United States were not unforeseeable.[1] Goaded into responding, I wrote a lengthy defense – Kramer refused to publish it – in which I quoted the second edition of my world history textbook published in January, 2001:

> The simultaneous bombing of US embassies in Kenya and Tanzania in 1998 demonstrated the frustration and vulnerability of even the most powerful governments. Osama bin Laden, a Saudi veteran of the Afghan war against the USSR, was named by the United States as the mastermind of the bombings. Yet despite a token retaliatory air attack on his base in Afghanistan, a country with which the United States had no diplomatic relations, he remained untouchable and seemingly continued his terrorist plotting against the United States.

During my stay in England in February, 2002, I decided that combatting the rising tide of Islamophobia was a more important mission than focusing narrowly on terrorism. I dreamed up the phrase "Islamo-Christian Civilization" for a lecture I was invited to give at Cambridge University. It had never occurred to me before, but I liked the sound of it, and it made sense to me historically. So when I returned home I put together a new lecture course on Islam and America and set to writing a book entitled *The Case for Islamo-Christian Civilization*. I conceived of both the course and the book

1. "Jihad 101," *Middle East Quarterly*, Spring 2002.

as responses to the "clash of civilizations" mantra of Samuel Huntington and the "What went wrong?" query of Bernard Lewis. When the book was published in 2004, it received only one or two mainstream reviews in the United States – no *New York Times*, no *Washington Post*, no *New York Review of Books* – but it was quite well received elsewhere. So far it has been translated into Italian, French, Arabic (twice), Persian (twice), Turkish, and Greek.

I also collaborated with the Tunisian novelist and diplomat Mustafa Tlili, Director of Dialogues: Islamic World-US-The West, in setting the agendas for international conferences designed to bring Muslim and non-Muslim political figures into dialogue. The first conference was held in Granada, Spain in 2003. During an intermission between sessions, I met with English police investigators who had flown to Spain to retrieve the terrorism evidence they had sent me and discuss my analysis. A more ambitious conference on "Islam and Elections" took place in Amman, Jordan in 2004. I was the only non-Muslim conferee in the room, and I came away favorably impressed by the seemingly genuine interest the Muslim Brotherhood leaders from Egypt displayed in the prospect of free elections. (I played a lesser role in later Dialogues conferences in Kuala Lumpur, Malaysia and, on the arts of the Muslim world, at the Brooklyn Academy of Music in New York City.)

Iran 5: Ahmadinejad at Columbia

B EING GENERALLY APOLITICAL and averse to public controversy, my involvement in inviting Iran's much reviled President Ahmadinejad to speak at Columbia in 2007 ran counter to my inclinations. But I had my reasons.

In September, 2006, Iranian President Mahmoud Ahmadinejad came to New York to attend the General Assembly meeting of the United Nations. On a Wednesday morning, his UN mission arranged a breakfast meeting for him to meet with some news people and professors. I attended and was standing in the departure line behind Lisa Anderson, then the Dean of Columbia's School of International and Public Affairs. Dean Anderson asked whether Ahmadinejad would be available to speak at Columbia, and through his UN ambassador, Javad Zarif, he said he would be happy to speak on Friday. As we shared a taxi to Columbia, Dean Anderson and I felt excited by this positive and unexpected outcome.

By evening, the invitation had been quashed by the Columbia administration on the grounds that two days was insufficient time to arrange a visit by such a controversial public figure. When news of this leaked out, along with the information that Dean Anderson was stepping down from her post – a decision actually made known to faculty several months earlier – many people connected the two events and unfairly concluded that she was being punished for proposing Ahmadinejad's visit.

For my part, I set forth my feelings about Ahmadinejad in an op-ed essay that no one chose to publish. What I wrote reflects some of my motivation in urging a renewal of the speaking invitation eleven months later.

Ahmadinejad's Win-Win Strategy

Is Iran's president, Mahmoud Ahmadinejad, trying to goad the United States into staging a military attack? The question could not be avoided after his two-hour breakfast meeting with academics and journalists last week in New York.

He didn't bluster. He didn't boast. He never mentioned Islam. In most people's opinion, he came across as a skilled debater with a cheerful and informal manner. Yet he stated several times that the United States would not attack Iran. No elaboration. It just flat out wasn't going to happen.

When an attendee observed that in a month's travel throughout Iran over the summer he never met an Iranian who expressed concern about an American attack, Ahmadinejad concurred. No Iranian, he said, feels that an attack is in the offing. And rumors of American military preparations don't appear in the Iranian press.

Americans, however, think differently. Sooner or later, with the smart money betting on sooner, they believe the United States is going to make a move to take out Iran's nuclear facilities. Many are horrified at the prospect of launching another war, and are praying that the common sense of a Pentagon that already has one war too many on its hands will keep it from happening. Many others are convinced that there is no other way to stop a Holocaust-denying madman.

So what is going on? The underdog players bask in blissful denial while the team with the monster linemen bang one another's shoulder pads and shout anti-Iran slogans to get their war juices flowing. Shouldn't it be the other way around? America cool, confident, and a bit disdainful while the mullahs quake in their sandals and fanatically scream defiance?

No one with an ounce of sense, of course, believes that Iran's military brass are as insouciant as their president. Armchair strategists in the United States make lists of the cards Iran might play in response to an attack. Iran's generals can scope out a dozen ways to fight back just by reading American newsmagazines. But nothing of this comes through in the smooth talk of their president.

Is denial, then, a political strategy? Let's look at a comparison.

Ever since 9/11, President Bush has been preparing his fellow Americans for another big terrorist attack here at home. The resulting fear has worked for him politically and has damped down America's weariness with the quagmire in Iraq. Now, with another election coming up, the terrorism talk is back, and no one is surprised. If al-Qaeda attacks, it proves Bush right in the War on Terror. If it doesn't, it's because the War on Terror is so successful. Win-win.

President Ahmadinejad is taking the opposite tack but aiming at the same result. He deliberately tweaks the lion's tail by stalling on nuclear negotiations and infuriatingly calling for "more research" on the Holocaust, as if it were not already the most thoroughly researched event in history. Yet he declares that neither he nor his countrymen have the slightest worry about an American attack.

Politically this is a win-win tactic. If the sabers are never drawn from their scabbards, he wins because he kept his cool – he is a very cool customer – and faced down Bush's bluff.

But if someday soon the cruise missiles do home in on Natanz and Bushire, he wins the 9/11 way. A country of 70 million people pull their heads out of the sand in tears, horror, and outrage at what they will surely see as totally unprovoked aggression by the world's super-thug. In response they rally around their "blameless" president the way Americans rallied around President Bush in the aftermath of the World Trade Center, or rallied around President Roosevelt, another "war president," after Pearl Harbor.

Quenching the Bush/Cheney war fever at this point is probably beyond Iran's capacity. True, Ahmadinejad could abruptly terminate his nuclear program, profess eternal love for Israel, and deliver Hezbollah's Sheikh Nasrallah to Tel Aviv to stand trial. But that would probably not be enough. Today's Iran-bashers want "regime change" the way yesterday's Saddam-haters – pretty much the same people – would accept nothing less than his head on a platter.

So acting naïve while poking a sharp rhetorical stick in the collective American-Israeli behind might be a sensible strategy. Iran is big enough, and daunting enough as a war target, to make it all but certain that President Ahmadinejad will still be president after his labs and atomic reactor are blown to bits. And he will then enjoy not just the full-throated support of the Iranian people, but also international political support in countries that don't believe it's right for the United States to initiate wars without solid justification.

My fear that the hawks in the Bush administration would press for a war with Iran before time ran out on his administration was still haunting me in July, 2007, when I wrote another op-ed on the subject.

Warning Iran or Stalling Israel

Who listens to Bush administration threats against Iran? Not the Iranians, certainly. President Ahmadinejad openly scoffs, and the American people enjoy greater popularity in Iran than anywhere else in the Middle East.

Not the American public. A current poll finds that "a majority of Americans are ready to accept a deal allowing Iran to engage in limited [uranium] enrichment if it also agrees to give UN inspectors full access to ensure Iran is not developing nuclear weapons." (World Public Opinion.org July 22).

It's possible that the only serious listeners are the Israelis.

According to recent reports, Vice President Cheney's pit bulls have rescued the Iran attack scenarios from the shredder bin where Secretary of State Rice tossed them more than a year ago. Word is that the military option is back on the table. Thus the tired saber clanks from its scabbard one more time.

High school drama clubs have revived "Oklahoma" less often than Bush spokesmen and leakers and revived the "Axis of Evil" act. But no American analyst – Air Force brass excepted – believes that "shock and awe" will be more decisive over Tehran than it was over Baghdad. Or make America any safer.

The view from Tel Aviv is different. Politicians of a certain ilk declare portentously that if nobody has the guts to defang Iran, a second Holocaust is just around the corner. The question for them is whether to go it alone – militarily a tough and uncertain job – or to rely on American protection.

Here's the problem. When asked recently how Iran would regard an Israeli attack, a high-ranking Iranian official answered unequivocally, if not for attribution: No Israeli attack is conceivable without American permission and support. Hence, an attack by Israel would be an attack by the United States.

Israel going it alone is a worst-case scenario for the Bush administration. While Hezbollah and Hamas might heat up Israel's borders in retaliation, Iraq geographically buffers Israel against direct counterattack. But the plausible Iranian assumption that Israeli bombers and missiles cannot penetrate Iranian airspace without American knowledge, approval, and back-up would lay the American forces in Iraq open to all manner of counterstrikes.

Supposing Israel really did take both Iran and the United States by surprise. American soldiers would suffer the consequences. And the American public would ask why our ally did not warn us in advance. On the other hand, if Israel did give advance warning, then the Iranians would be justified in retaliating against the United States. In either case, Israel would have a shot at achieving its goal, but the United States would end up paying the price.

Alternatively, the United States, as per Cheney's war talk, could preempt the Israelis by launching its own strike on Iranian nuclear facilities. Once again, the American forces in Iraq would pay the price. Israelis might feel relieved, but Bush's dream of "victory" in Iraq would recede even farther into Never-Never Land.

The better alternative, or at least the one that lends a glimmer of rationality to Cheney's bluster, is to warn that Bush will not leave office without grievously harming Iran first. And hope that the threats are convincing enough to persuade the Israelis to hold their fire until the next administration.

Even by Israeli estimates, the lead-time for a first Iranian bomb is way more than the seventeen months remaining in Bush's presidential term. Bush can do nothing and still be certain that Iran won't go nuclear on his watch the way North Korea did. Yet still the threats, even though every day that passes makes them more improbable.

Not even Bush would begin a war between the time of his successor's November election and January inauguration. That narrows the attack window to fifteen months. Nor could anything short of a major Iranian provocation justify attacking during the party conventions or the ensuing presidential campaign. So that makes it thirteen months. How about the primaries? A Bush attack during primary season would turn every vote into a war referendum, with the Republican Party painfully trying to explain the aggression. That moves the calendar back to the Iowa caucuses in January, leaving the administration only five more months to pull the trigger.

But this assumes that the administration will bypass Congress. In 2002 it took weeks and the delusional specter of mushroom clouds over American cities to get authorization. With Iran's mushroom-makers still a glimmer in Ahmadinejad's eye, war will be a harder sell. A Congress whose majority party understood the 2006 election as a popular plea to bring the troops home will not sanction a new war based on a hypothetical future danger. So that pretty much closes the president's window of opportunity.

So why another round of threats? The peril to the United States today lies not in Iran, but in the possibility of a solo Israeli strike on Iranian nuclear sites. So if Cheney's beating of the war drum can keep the Israeli tail from setting the American dog awaggle, his neocon zealotry may for once serve a useful purpose.

A month later I received a telephone call inviting me to come to midtown and meet the new Iranian ambassador to the United Nations. I was expecting to be part of a meet-and-greet session for New York's Iran watchers. Instead it was just me, and the matter on the ambassador's mind was the possibility that I might make a discreet inquiry at Columbia about the possibility of renewing the invitation to speak that had been quashed the year before.

As I explained to the ambassador that Columbia's president, Lee Bollinger, had stated at a meeting of the University Senate that the previous invitation had been canceled solely because of time constraints, not because of any bar on President Ahmadinejad coming to campus, and that he might indeed by reinvited if provisions were made to challenge his provocative and offensive policies regarding Israel, it occurred to me that a public speech might show Americans what kind of man Ahmadinejad was and thereby help prevent a war that still seemed within the realm of possibility for the lame-duck Bush administration.

Though the decision to reauthorize the invitation was taken by President Bollinger and by John Coatsworth, who had replaced Lisa Anderson as dean, the event would not have come about if I had followed my usual practice of staying aloof from politics (except for writing op-ed pieces).

In the event, Ahmadinejad did speak at Columbia in the most publicized and politicized campus speaking event since Fidel Castro's visit to Harvard in 1959. His bland performance (as opposed to some of his earlier public statements) showed him to be more of a pipsqueak than the Hitler that many Americans had imagined. At the same time, President Bollinger's harsh attack on him before he had a chance to speak set a world record for lack of courtesy toward an invited guest. I thought that both men missed an opportunity to communicate. And I worried that one or the other party would blame me, the midwife, for the debacle.

In the event, neither party criticized my participation. The Bush years came to an end without another war, and I felt that in some small way I had a hand in that outcome.

PART FIVE

Conclusions

THOUGH TRAUMATIZED BY BEING DISMISSED from the Harvard faculty, my coming to Columbia afforded greater freedom to follow my intellectual bent than I would ever have experienced in Cambridge. One door closed in my face; a better one opened as I was at the point of despair.

Being dismissed from directing Columbia's Middle East Institute twenty-seven years later was similarly distressing at an emotional level. But it gave me the opportunity to wean myself from day-to-day preoccupation with how post-9/11 Middle Eastern affairs should relate to academia. I could write op-ed essays without worrying about blowback on the university. And I could write other things as well: five scholarly books and two novels since 2001. Again, one door closed in my face, but another opened.

The traumas of my personal life intertwine with those of the country at large, whether the Arab-Israel war of 1967, the Iranian Revolution of 1979, or the attacks of 9/11. With the latter touching off a crisis of previously unimaginable magnitude, how was a scholar with fifty years of contemplation of Islamic history under his belt to comport himself?

Should I have decided that the Eurocentric distortions of past and present Orientalists make it imperative to withhold public expression of my scholarly opinions lest I contribute to fresh imperialist evils? I have heard well-informed colleagues refuse to respond to questions inspired by governmental policy dilemmas for just this reason. They did not want to be tarred with the stigma of collaboration. But this option leaves an open field for the growing army of Islamophobes.

Should I have put my opinions forward provisionally but emphasize that scholars working within, or with at least DNA connection to, the Middle Eastern and/or Muslim cultural traditions should be considered a priori to have superior knowledge and insight deriving from their status as post-colonial beings? If so, should I have felt free to suggest which post-colonial voices are the most persuasive? And which the most idiotic?

Or perhaps I should have acted and spoken from a counter-Orientalist position that assumes that all acts of United States governments, past, present, and future, deserve denunciation as imperialist endeavors. To have done so would again cede the function of assessing and recommending government policy options to the Islamophobes.

Finding a tenable position under national conditions that changed so profoundly once Americans became convinced, not implausibly, as it turned out, that they were engaged in a violent struggle with forces that regarded them as a mortal enemy, required yet another reconsideration of what Orientalism was, is, and might become in the future. One door surely closed on 9/11. But did another open?

Methodism and Islam

I BEGAN THIS BOOK with some thoughts about how my Methodist upbringing in the Middle West unconsciously skewed my historical reconstruction of social life in an eleventh-century Iranian city. The implication underlying those thoughts was that American Methodism serendipitously overlapped with Islam in my imagination. A more historical approach to the overlap suggests the possibility of deeper connections relating to my being culturally an American instead of a European.

At the beginning of the eighteenth century, the interior of Arabia was the wild and sparsely settled hinterland of a sophisticated Islamic cultural tradition centered on cosmopolitan urban centers like Istanbul, Cairo, Damascus, and Isfahan. The hardship, starkness, and simplicity of life in the heart of the peninsula contrasted sharply with the comforts available in those imperial centers.

At the same time, the interior of what would become, by century's end, the United States of America was similarly wild and unsettled in the experience of European colonists. Most Europeans lived in the small cities on the Atlantic coast and looked to London and Paris for culture and sophistication. European faces were seldom seen west of the Appalachian Mountains. The most sophisticated Bostonians and Philadelphians felt like bumpkins when they traveled to Europe, and the people of the frontier lived lives no less stark and simple than those of the bedouin of Arabia.

In 1703 two men were born whose teachings would find fertile ground in these remote and scantily populated lands: Muhammad ibn Abd al-Wahhab and John Wesley.

After an early upbringing in Najd, in central Arabia, Muhammad ibn Abd al-Wahhab traveled to the bustling commercial city of Basra to acquire an education in Islamic law and theology. When he returned to Arabia, he called for a purification of Islamic religious practice and a return to the simple ideals and lifestyle of the early Muslim community (*salaf*). Opposition to his preaching caused him to seek refuge with Muhammad ibn Saud, the ruler of the town of Dir'iya. Politically, their alliance planted the seed of the Saudi kingdom just as religiously it gave rise to the Wahhabi form of Islam, and more broadly to the current of Salafism that is today so often associated with Muslim militancy around the world.

John Wesley was born near London and educated at Oxford, where he led a revivalist "Holy Club" whose members were taunted as "Methodists." "Wahhabi" similarly originated as a pejorative term for Ibn Abd al-Wahhab's followers, who called themselves "Muwahhidun," that is, those who affirm God's unity (*tawhid*). In 1735 John and his brother Charles traveled to the fledgling colony of Georgia leaving their friend George Whitefield behind to advance their revivalist work in England. Though the Wesleys spent only one year in the New World, George Whitefield followed them abroad, making seven trans-Atlantic voyages and delivering riveting open-air sermons that touched off the tumultuous revivalist movement known as the Great Awakening.

Wesley died in 1791, a year before Muhammad ibn Abd al-Wahhab. The Methodist and like-minded Protestant preachers who inspired later waves of popular revivalism focused on simple living and abstinence from sinful practices like drinking alcohol, gambling, and dancing, always aware that even the most pious person could deviate from the right path. Their message was enormously popular in the frontier lands of the American South and Middle West and remains so today.

The doctrinal differences between Wahhabism and Methodism are immense, but their followers nevertheless shared certain traits. Both groups endured the charges of their enemies that they were preaching fanaticism. Both stressed in their daily lives a constant and active adherence to God's laws, as they understood them, and a similarly energetic avoidance of practices they considered evil. Both believed that you had to continually show your faith in your actions if you were to merit salvation. And both tirelessly spread their beliefs and practices among others of their faith, Muslims or Christians respectively, both at home and in faraway lands.

Historians of the modern Middle East usually remark that the United States played a negligible role in the region prior to World War II. At a political level, leaving aside the influence of Woodrow Wilson's advocacy of national self-determination, this is a sound judgment. At the religious level, however, it overlooks the massive commitment of American Protestants to missionary work throughout the world. Originally inspired by the periodic waves of revival that began with George Whitefield and the Great Awakening, tens of thousands of young Americans, often educated in the best colleges, journeyed abroad to spread their faith and demonstrate to others the virtues of American Protestant life. The Ottoman Empire, Iran, and the Persian Gulf were particular areas of American missionary enterprise.

An analogous Wahhabi zeal for reviving Islam expressed itself in the eighteenth and nineteenth centuries, both in missionary activities in areas like India and in militant action to suppress what Wahhabi preachers deemed idolatrous practices, particularly those connected with Sufism, Shi'ism, and the veneration of saintly tombs. Expanding from these roots, Wahhabi and Protestant missionary activities turned Saudi Arabia and the United States into what they are today, the world's two principal exporters of religious missionaries. The techniques, training, and political involvement of the two sorts of missionaries differ in various ways. But both movements draw strength from almost unlimited private financial donations, and from the reluctance of the American and Saudi governments to put limits on such donations. That many Wahhabi and Protestant missionaries see nothing but evil and political subversion in the actions of their counterparts serves to conceal the fundamental similarity of their social and religious origins.

Comparison with what were once the cultural heartlands of desert Arabia and frontier America makes this similarity clear. Europe today is largely post-Christian, and Europeans are often dismayed by the importance of evangelical Christianity in American social and political life. In return, evangelical Americans see sinful Europe as a land that is in need of religious revival and, in the minds of some, in danger of conversion to Salafism. In the same way, once great Islamic cities like Istanbul, Cairo, Damascus, Tunis, and Fez are seen by Salafi Muslims more as dens of secular iniquity in need of revival than as sites of original religious inspiration.

This shared history of religious revival and puritanism on the peripheries of the old cultural and imperial centers of Europe and the Middle East sometimes serves as an excuse to ignore imperial history. The Middle East area studies curriculum that introduced me to my profession taught me that the United States rightfully rejects any connection with British and French imperialism and thereby acts as though it has nothing to learn from their historical experiences. Saudi Arabia similarly regards the histories under imperialism of other Middle Eastern states as being irrelevant to its own standing in the region. Neither government wastes much time studying history.

Yet their parallel religious pasts pose problems. No one doubts the depth, sincerity, and political influence of the evangelical communities of the American South and Middle West, though many more-or-less secular Americans on the East and West Coasts complain bitterly about them. No American president can make foreign, much less domestic, policy without taking their views and potential opposition into account. Yet as a country constitutionally committed to separating religion from government, the United States government will never formally endorse or condemn the private and church activities of overseas missionaries and their legion of financial backers at home. Despite its constitution, the United States has been and continues to be a religiously enthusiastic country. Just not at the level of government.

The ruling family of Saudi Arabia is unconstrained by any constitution, but its history of identification with Wahhabism exerts similar constraints. No matter how vocal the complaints of outsiders that Wahhabi missionaries and Wahhabi supported institutions coerce fellow Muslims and engage in unsavory political activities, a Saudi king can no more curtail his subjects' private financial support for the propagation of their faith than an American president can stop evangelical radio and television ministers from collecting donations to support missionary activity.

Religiously engaged American Christians generally think badly of Salafi Islam even if they do not show disdain for Muslims categorically. The clamor in Christian circles for state legislation to oppose implementation of Islamic Shari'a law is one manifestation of this. The people advocating for such laws know less than nothing about the Shari'a, but they clearly imagine it to be most reprehensibly enforced in Saudi Arabia, and by groups like ISIS that hold Salafi ideological positions.

For my own part, I find both evangelical Protestantism and Salafi Islam unappealing, but my Methodist upbringing urges me to show respect for the religious outlook embodied in the former, just as my decades of studying Islam give me an appreciative understanding of the latter. Over the course of my career, this mixture of respect for conservative Muslim and Christian views and firm rejection of them at a personal level has led numerous people to ask why I am not a Muslim. The standard response I developed was a cynical prevarication, but it effectively cut off further questioning. I would say that I understood enough about Islam to know that I could not frustrate God's will if it were to dictate that I die a Muslim. So I was simply waiting to see if something would ever occur to make me convert to Islam, or reconvert to Methodism. The one time this sophistry failed was in a discussion with the deputy qadi of Kyrgyzstan in 1993. He looked me in the eye and told me that the Qur'an demands that a person should make a choice.

So what do I think about Islam after half a century of consideration of its history and teachings? At the beginning of this memoir, I raised the question of what constitutes "a good life." Despite being drawn to the notion of living according to a Methodist *sunna,* a code of culturally endorsed values and behaviors, my grandfather C. J.'s apolitical, anti-social, and non-religious individualism, which most closely resembles classical Epicureanism, seems equally appealing. This inconsistency affects how now, toward life's end, I assess what I have gleaned from my study of Muslim social history and the ways those gleanings contribute to my reservations about the Protestant American traditions I grew up with:

Education and Upbringing

Education in medieval Nishapur put very young students in contact with quite old teachers – often unpaid volunteers who in their youth had learned from some other old men – because the fewer the steps in the oral transmission of lore about the Prophet, the greater the likelihood of accuracy. This had the effect of valuing the ends of the age table rather than concentrating education, as we do, on not very old professors teaching students in their teens and twenties. It was also common for adults in Nishapur to attend *hadith* sessions along with children. My own experience with mixed age classrooms, by which I mean "life-long learners" auditing lecture courses, has always been positive, and I think it would be valuable to give students in high school a taste of the college learning environment. On the whole, I think we are much too fixated on age differences – "gen-" this and that.

As for the thorny problem of disciplining males who feel they have outgrown parental supervision but have not yet acquired work or family responsibilities, the medieval Muslim institution of the *futuwwa* (Arabic for "young manhood") provides a model. Young men joined *futuwwa* clubs that engaged in collective athletic activities, but unlike modern sports clubs were imbued with a religiously inflected code of discipline. These clubs might serve as local service groups or militias in times of need, and they were sometimes affiliated with specific trades, but their primary purpose was channeling youthful male rowdiness.

The modern scouting movement is an analogue, but its appeal to boys wanes well before the age of twenty. In its American version, it was also structured around romanticized outdoor life – camping, nature lore, halfbaked notions of native American woodsy nobility – while the actual problem of undisciplined young males is largely urban. College sports come closer to filling the bill, but the rowdiest young males don't make the team.

Political Life

Muslim students from abroad have occasionally told me of their shock at the boastfulness of Americans running for elective office. Why, they have argued, should anyone vote for a politician who has the gall to say that he or she is THE BEST? In some religious circles, serious consideration is given to a *hadith* that declares that one should not seek leadership. Leadership that is gained by campaigning, according to the Prophet, puts the burden of success solely on the person selected; but God will assist the person to whom leadership comes unbidden. Simplistic and naïve as this may be in a democratic system, there is no question but that boastfulness and expensive, non-stop campaigning have diverted American elections from choosing the most capable candidates for office. I sympathize with Muslim thinkers who have tried to limit the campaign period and equalize the resources of contenders for office.

I once had a conversation with former Vice-President Walter Mondale in which I suggested that a measure of humility and modesty might be a welcome quality in a candidate. Despite his own measured political persona, he thought my suggestion bizarre. But the presidency of Donald Trump has shown us how absurd the pursuit of office solely for ego-gratification can become.

Wealth

Teddy Roosevelt inveighed against "malefactors of great wealth," but our economic system considers the accumulation of wealth to be the measure of a person's success, and inheritance of wealth to qualify an heir for high regard. In my view, unconstrained wealth accumulation has encouraged the worst in Western society and is currently doing so to a greater degree than ever before.

Islamic law stipulates that the estate of a decedent must be distributed in fixed shares to his or her blood heirs, though one-third of a person's fortune may be disposed of by specific bequests. As is well known, female relations inherit at half the rate of males. But they do inherit, and they retain control of their assets even after they marry. This resulted in Muslim women, even living in seclusion, being active agents in real estate and other commercial transactions throughout the pre-modern centuries. Disinheriting all but the eldest son, as is done in some European traditions, or heirs who have displeased the decedent, also strikes me as less humane than the Muslim practice.

The institution of *waqf*, a personal trust established either as a socially beneficial (*khairi*) endowment to support a public good, such as building and maintaining a mosque, school, hospital, or fountain, or as a family (*ahli*) endowment to collect the annual income from some sort of property and distribute it in fixed shares to the descendants of the founder, served several valuable functions. First, it funded all manner of public services, the administration of which was thenceforth overseen by the Islamic courts. Secondly, it allowed a person to favor specific family members as legatees.

Family trusts, for example, frequently stipulated that payments to female descendants should equal those to males.

What the *waqf* did not do was allow a fortune acquired through commercial enterprise to be handed over intact to an heir chosen to be its successor CEO. The administrator of a *waqf* was entitled to a modest administrative fee for his or her services, but the property included in the trust had to be specified in the founding document, rather than varying according to acquisitions or business deals made by the founder's successors. This limitation upon the transfer of a business from generation to generation helped spur wealthy individuals to create *khairi* endowments. That way, even if they could not pass on a commercial fortune intact, they could garner for their descendants a family reputation for good works. This tended to elevate family reputation above wealth as an enduring source of honor and social eminence.

It has been argued that this inheritance and trust system stood in the way of capitalist accumulation and the creation of great fortunes, and that is probably true. On the other hand, capitalist accumulation has not been an unalloyed blessing. At our current historical juncture in the United States, I would like very much to see greater efforts to induce billionaires to donate their fortunes for public benefit, that is, to become "benefactors" rather than "malefactors" of great wealth.

Gender and Sexuality

The seemingly universal disparagement of Muslim practices in the area of gender and sexuality conceals a few things that I find laudable. I have already mentioned women's legally stipulated inheritance of property and continued possession of such property in marriage. In addition, it is noteworthy that despite the many disabilities they faced in public life, women were equal to men as transmitters of the *hadith* of the Prophet. True, they seldom held sessions for transmitting *hadith* outside the family circle, but their status in this all-important aspect of the continuance of Muslim social, religious, and legal traditions was that of equality.

One of the greatest Muslim religious thinkers, Abu Hamid al-Ghazali (d. 1111), opined that a legal wife had a right to the fulfillment that comes with motherhood. Hence she could sue her husband for financial damages if, without her consent, he practiced birth limitation by withdrawing before orgasm. This is the only "right" I have read about that does not have a counterpart in the West. It speaks, I think, to the Muslim opposition to celibacy and a conviction that in the normal course of affairs everyone should marry.

It also raises the question of whether our vocabulary of rights is too single-mindedly Western.

Geographic identity

Ethno-linguistic nationalism has been the scourge of Western history since the eighteenth century. Its equivalent was refreshingly absent in medieval Islam. In most regions, nomadic zones excepted, cities with their respective hinterlands provided the core of social identity. The name of one's city of origin often served as what we would call a surname. Your native locale was your *watan*, your homeland. If you settled permanently in another city, the verb *istawtana* could be applied to you. It means, "he has adopted such-and-such a place as his homeland."

In the twentieth century the word *watan* was recoined to mean "nation," but for a long time people felt themselves to be local first and little drawn to a national identity. For example, people would identify as Aleppan or Damascene rather than Syrian; or as Baghdadi, Basran, or Mosuli rather than Iraqi. Folklore, food recipes, jokes, linguistic peculiarities, and clothing styles reinforced this localism. This is not tribalism. It is a healthy attachment to one's home instead of to a multi-million-inhabitant capital city in which one's local roots are lost.

Coming from Rockford, a city that was proudly not Chicago, I approve.

The same thing with language. For many important Muslim historical figures we don't really know what language(s) they spoke under varying circumstances.

Modesty

I have found Muslim traditions particularly appealing in this area, probably because my father drummed into me over and over again that self-promotion was the worst of human behaviors. In the absence of real estate developers dictating that every house in a neighborhood should sit on a quarter-acre lot with a fifty-foot setback from the street, the rich and poor of Nishapur often resided in the same neighborhoods. But prosperity was displayed within one's house or walled courtyard rather in public view. Similarly, both women's and men's outdoor costumes covered pretty much everything and varied little except in the quantity and quality of the fabrics utilized. It was expected, of course, that political grandees and their acolytes would openly display great wealth, but this was not the way of the patrician religious elite.

A favorite genre of light reading dealt with conmen and schemers taking advantage of the pride the patricians took in their piety and learning.

American cons revolving around the hope of making a fortune out of a tiny investment did not figure in this literature. Instead people chuckled at tales of fake Jews who would pretend to convert to Islam in return for financial inducements, and then repeat the act in the next town down the road. Or they would read about a hell-fire preacher – a Muslim Elmer Gantry – who collected fat fees from pious sinners and then moved on to the next gullible assembly.

Among the people I found most appealing in Nishapur were the Malamatis. These were Muslims who had drunk deeply of the doctrine that open manifestations of piety were indistinguishable from acts of pride and vainglory. So they kept their piety to themselves, although stories about who they were leaked out anyhow. Top-lofty detractors who felt that the Malamatis would go so far as to flout the religious law – copulate like dogs in the street! – to conceal their inner piety eventually destroyed their reputation as praiseworthy Muslims, but I find them appealing, just as I do the Malamati sentiments underlying St. Bernard of Clairvaux's *Steps of Humility and Pride*.

My selection of topics in this recitation has been idiosyncratic and in no way represents the full array of my thoughts about Islam and Muslims. I have not presented it here either to praise Islam or in ignorance of other features of Muslim life that do not appeal to me so much.

My purpose has solely been to unburden myself of thoughts I have been having about who I am and what I have done with my life. That this has amounted, in the end, to the suggestion that Rockford and American society could usefully think about, and benefit from, exchanges of views with our Muslim neighbors about our respective traditions has come as a surprise. A happy surprise.

American Orientalism after 9/11

I CHOSE TO LABEL MYSELF AN ORIENTALIST for this book. Why? First, because it is the traditional term for the educational path I set out upon as a Harvard undergraduate and pursued to the doctoral level. Rooted in a desire to read classical texts in languages other than Greek and Latin, Orientalism involves a good deal more discipline and toil than the American pseudo-discipline of Middle East area studies invented in the 1950s. I studied the latter as an inescapable add-on, but my interest in contemporary Middle Eastern and Islamic affairs was quite limited for the first fifteen years of my career.

My combined Orientalist and Middle East area studies education segued into deep involvement with institutions that were created in the aftermath of World War II on the premise that America needed specialists on the Middle East and other world regions to help understand societies that American governments feared were at risk of falling to communism. Those institutions were Harvard's Center for Middle East Studies, Columbia's Middle East Institute, and the Middle East Studies Association of North America.

My second reason: By the time of the 9/11 attacks of 2001, my institutional involvement in Middle East studies had greatly diminished, but I continued trying to contribute useful ideas to the public debates that the attacks engendered. This was precisely the type of activity that had come by then to bear the stigma of Edward Said's redefinition of Orientalism. Through hundreds of radio and television interviews and scores of op-ed essays and public speeches I bought into the notion that my expertise, such as it was, should be made available to the American government and my fellow citizens. That my expert observations excited little or no interest among those audiences did not vitiate my intent.

As Said's reformulation of Orientalism met with increasing acclaim, I reexamined my career trajectory. I was a Protestant from the Middle West who had neither family connections with, nor personal experiences of, the culture I chose to study. Orientalist was a well-established term for describing such people, especially when they concentrated on old written works produced by highly literate societies. The term anthropologist was similar, but was reserved, for the most part – some people would say intrinsically – for researchers who sought out personal experience with non-literate, non-Western cultures, or studied the non-literary evidence of such cultures. Said ascribed to the Orientalists a conscious or subconscious disdain for their subjects and/or a desire or willingness to produce knowledge that could reinforce Western imperialism. Some anthropologists subsequently ascribed the same shortcomings to some of their own early luminaries.

Be that as it may, shunning the study of non-Western cultures with which one does not have biological links in order to escape demeaning or subverting them, either accidentally or otherwise, seems to me preposterous. Equally preposterous, for people of my intellectual bent, is pretending that simply knowing how dreadfully certain bodies of Orientalist knowledge had fed into imperialist thinking in the past could prevent the ideas I put forward as my "expertise" from being used by imperialists in the future. After all, any statement one might make about the culture of a non-Western society is vulnerable to being sucked into the sausage-making machine of government policy. So was it possible to be a "good" Orientalist? And if it was, how was one to know whether one had achieved that status?

Though unable to affirm with certainty that I was a "good" Orientalist, I continued to engage in myriad curricular and off-campus activities that involved offering public opinions about the Middle East and the Muslim world. In time, as I have recounted in earlier chapters, I reoriented myself – if that is the proper term – toward being a world historian focused on social, economic, and technological matters. But being conscious of this evolution, which took place over a period of years, confirmed my sense that what I was evolving away from was Orientalism. Hence I acknowledged that my earlier career was that of an Orientalist.

Thirdly, I affirmed the Orientalist label because it is undeniable that a desire to become informed about non-Western cultures and societies is integral to the concept of Western civilization. It is not a universal characteristic of highly literate cultures. Therefore, it is useful to have a term to describe categorically the intellectual bent of people who devote themselves to that enterprise. Is there a better term than Orientalist? "Middle East specialist," "Arabist," and "Islamist" do serve in limited ways, but they define the individual so designated by area or cultural topic, not categorically. Some maintain that "racist" is a useful synonym, but racism requires and implies no learning. Indeed, it is most often equated with profound ignorance of "the other." Moreover, in their foundational usages, Orientalist and Orientalism stood for learning that crossed chronological as well as cultural divides. Ancient Sumer, Assyria, Israel, and Egypt – though not Greece and Rome – along with ancient and medieval China, Japan, Korea, India, and Islam were at the heart of Oriental studies through most of the nineteenth century.

The variety of Orientalist interests made the collective term Orientalism useful for identifying a particular turn of mind within European culture. Severing the works of an Assyriologist like A. Leo Oppenheim from that of a Sinologist like John King Fairbank or a scholar of Persian literature like E. G. Browne may make topical sense, but in their own minds they were all Orientalists insofar as they chose to devote their life's work to a culture other than their own. The Saidian recoinage of the term both excludes the Sumerologists, Assyriologists, and Hittitologists who considered themselves Orientalists at the time his book was published, and describes the sub-category of people he chose to disparage – expanded beyond the world of scholarship to include artists and travelers – exclusively in terms of their baleful contributions to imperialism and the denigration of non-Europeans.

But explaining a devotion to studying Islam and the Middle East as first and foremost a manifestation of a desire to degrade a cultural "other" is unconvincing. The cultural "others" that Americans have most frequently disparaged are not Arabs and Muslims, but Blacks and Native Americans. There is no questioning, of course, the fact that some Orientalists offered assistance and justification to imperialist regimes; but the vast majority did not. Equally there is no denying the demeaning imagery and negative generalizations contained in some works by some Orientalists. But not in all. Not by a long shot.

In sum, I believe that Orientalist and Orientalism remain useful terms. I shall come back to how I think they should be understood post-9/11 at the end of this chapter.

In 1997, Seyed Kamal Kharazi completed his tour as Iran's ambassador to the United Nations. I had had a number of cordial and informative meetings with him, and before he departed I had an especially collegial conversation with one of his principal deputies. Iran's war with Iraq had ended a decade earlier, and the revolution itself was almost two decades old. I stressed during the conversation how complicated Iran's situation in the world was bound to become as the generation that carried out the revolution, led mostly by clerics and men who had received their higher education in the West, moved into retirement and the indigenously educated generation that fought Saddam Hossein succeeded to the country's leadership positions. My interlocutor agreed and commented that we would need great skill to get through that transition. "The challenge is greater for you than for me," I replied "Why? Because you are a stakeholder and I, as an American, am not."

Time makes liars of us all. After 9/11, Americans suddenly became stakeholders. However, the stake they acquired differed from that of the British, the French, the Italians, the Spaniards, the Germans, the Dutch, and the Russians. Not only did these Europeans have histories of imperial domination in Muslim lands, but most of them had inherited complex pre-imperialist sentiments about Muslims as contributors to, or violators of, their national identity. Fourteen countries in modern Europe have shared their living space with Muslims for one to four centuries. For the most part, Spain excepted, those centuries have been expunged from their modern national consciousness, or dismissed as tyrannical alien occupations. Yet negative sentiments about Muslims derived from historical periods of cohabitation in Spain, France, Sicily, Russia, Ukraine, and the Balkan peninsula did not, by and large, reach the United States in the baggage of immigrants from those lands.

Americans did develop an interest in the Holy Land as a place of pious visitation and in the condition of Christians living under Muslim rule, and that interest did resonate with the sentiments of some immigrants, notably those from Ottoman Syria and Palestine. But actual colonial engagement with Muslims came about only in the Philippines after the Spanish-American War. Though the American government, like Great Britain in Egypt in 1882, did not initially visualize decades of occupation, it did think in terms of opening the country to economic development, whether the Filipinos wanted it or not.

That first confrontation with Muslims gave rise to paradigms of the best and the worst in American behavior. In 1902, Colonel Frank Baldwin, a crusty two-time medal-of-honor winner (Civil War and fighting the Cheyenne), decided to teach a lesson to some troublesome Maranao-speaking Muslims living around Lake Lanao in the center of the island of Mindanao in the southern Philippines. His unauthorized campaign resulted in the death of 300–400 Maranao warriors at a cost of eleven Americans, and it brought the United States to the brink of war.

The American military governor, General Adna Chaffee, who "prefer[red] lots of talking to shooting," promoted Baldwin and reassigned him to a place where he could do less harm. To replace him in Mindanao he chose Captain John J. Pershing, who would later command the American Expeditionary Force in Europe during World War I. Pershing set about meeting with the Maranao chieftains, who required that he come to the parlays unarmed, learning some of their language and customs, answering their questions about American intentions, and promising to protect freedom of religion while building roads and opening the interior of the island to progress. Though his campaign to "win hearts and minds" did not prevent further violence, it did set an example of how to be a colonial presence in the Muslim world without adopting European excesses.

After 9/11, the memory of Pershing's approach to "nation building" was resurrected in military circles and held up as an example to be imitated in Iraq and Afghanistan. But along with that memory came another, attested to in Pershing's memoirs as the tactic of a colonel named Colonel Frank West. West buried a pig with every fallen Muslim warrior to prevent his soul from entering paradise. Pershing remarked: "It was not pleasant to have to take such measures, but the prospect of going to hell instead of heaven sometimes deterred the would-be assassins."

These military attitudes derived from contacts with cultural "others," in Pershing's case through combatting the Sioux, and later Pancho Villa on the Mexican border, but not from American academic expertise on Muslim affairs, which was negligible at that time. Dealings with Islam after 9/11 similarly differed from Europe's colonial experiences. Instead of Europe's arrogant feeling of superiority over cultural inferiors, the defining trope of Said's Orientalism, the American man on the street became consumed by fear of terrorism and, in a steadily growing stream, by hatred of all things Muslim. Measures designed to ward off attacks on American soil did avert an array of terrorist plots, but homeland security became a (sometimes idiotic) ritual of American life. Handbags, for example, were assiduously inspected at Metropolitan Opera and New York Philharmonic performances, but never at the huge multiplex cinema across the street. "Terrorism expert" became a household term, and books condemning Islam far outsold the more conciliatory works penned by a few Orientalists.

The institutional interest in "modernization" that had engendered Middle East area studies a half-century earlier lost its audience as counterterrorism specialists and military strategists rose to prominence. The dream of nurturing a handful of American Lawrence of Arabias and Gertrude Bells that had contributed to the rise of Middle East area studies paled as thousands of soldiers and CIA operatives set about learning Arabic and Persian. On university campuses, meanwhile, scholars embarking on teaching careers dealing with Islam and the Middle East shifted from people like me, with no deep biographical or cultural roots in the area, to being mostly Muslims and/or Middle Easterners. Few among this new cohort of teachers saw themselves as training students to help formulate and carry out government objectives. Though some of their students entered the world of think tank analysis, a greater number focused on religious, literary, and cultural topics that had little to do with the American agenda in the region.

Thus post-9/11 America saw a robust revival of the classical Orientalist disciplines: editing, translating, and digesting written works emanating from the high culture of Islamic societies. However, most practitioners shared a conviction that Said's critique of Orientalism was valid and saw no irony in fostering ever more detailed studies of exactly the same sorts of things that had enthralled most European Orientalists for the two centuries that preceded the Iranian Revolution.

My concluding judgments, therefore, are three. First, "Orientalism" remains a useful term for the peculiar inclination of Western scholars to study the literary and artistic output of non-Western societies, but with the understanding that most of the people who engage in those activities today follow an intellectual path blazed by Europeans, but are not personally of European ethnicity or heritage.

Secondly, "Orientalist" as a term of disparagement is contingent on a shifting intellectual landscape. In the colonial era, a few prominent scholars, artists, and travelers contributed *nolens volens* to a debased portrayal of the cultures dominated by their political, military, and commercial agents; but most individuals who devoted their efforts to Orientalism as a scholarly quest did not do so. In particular, America's Middle East studies enterprise followed a trajectory that was more closely tied to the triumphalist mentality of post–World War II social scientists, a restatement of nineteenth-century feelings of Manifest Destiny, than it was to the Orientalism brought to the United States by scholarly emigrés from Europe. Blaming modernization theory on Orientalists does the latter a profound disservice.

And thirdly, we are in need of a new term to designate the increasing influence of think-tanks from the 1990s onward. By and large, the tenure code protects university professors from pressure to follow the dictates of university funders. An individual can choose whether to bend his or her efforts to furthering a government objective, such as going to war with a Muslim country, or with Islam itself. But think-tank employees, who have the same academic credentials, are bound to following the policy analyses and prescriptions of their employers at risk of dismissal. While Said's portrayal of some Orientalists as running dogs of imperialism has historical merit, the kennel has migrated from the college campus to the think-tank since 9/11. So to restore the honor of Orientalism, we need a new term of disparagement: Policy dudes? Think-tankers? Islam haters? Take your pick.